The Care Act
2014

Sara Miller McCune founded SAGE Publishing in 1965 to support the dissemination of usable knowledge and educate a global community. SAGE publishes more than 1000 journals and over 800 new books each year, spanning a wide range of subject areas. Our growing selection of library products includes archives, data, case studies and video. SAGE remains majority owned by our founder and after her lifetime will become owned by a charitable trust that secures the company's continued independence.

Los Angeles | London | New Delhi | Singapore | Washington DC | Melbourne

The Care Act 2014

Wellbeing in Practice

Suzy Braye
Michael Preston-Shoot

SAGE | Learning Matters

⑤SAGE | **⑰ LearningMatters**

Learning Matters
An imprint of SAGE Publications Ltd
1 Oliver's Yard
55 City Road
London EC1Y 1SP

SAGE Publications Inc.
2455 Teller Road
Thousand Oaks, California 91320

SAGE Publications India Pvt Ltd
B 1/I 1 Mohan Cooperative Industrial Area
Mathura Road
New Delhi 110 044

SAGE Publications Asia-Pacific Pte Ltd
3 Church Street
#10-04 Samsung Hub
Singapore 049483

Editors: Catriona McMullen and Kate Keers
Development editor: Sarah Turpie
Senior project editor: Chris Marke
Project management: Deer Park Productions
Marketing manager: Samantha Glorioso
Cover design: Wendy Scott
Typeset by: C&M Digitals (P) Ltd, Chennai, India

Library of Congress Control Number: 2019946418

British Library Cataloguing in Publication Data

A catalogue record for this book is available from the British Library

ISBN 978-1-5264-4686-2
ISBN 978-1-5264-4687-9 (pbk)

Contents

Series Editor's Preface

During recent teaching sessions for student social workers I have been struck keenly by the changes permeating our contemporary world. Values and ethics lie at the heart of social work, and social work education, and we address these throughout all the books in the series. The positions that we take in terms of values and ethics are, to an extent, determined by context, time and experience and these are expressed in different ways by students coming into social work education today. Since the turn of this century we have witnessed shifts and challenges as the marketised neoliberal landscape of politics, economy and social life may attract little comment or contest from some. We have observed the political machinery directing much of statutory social work towards a focus on individuals apart from their environment. However, we have also seen a new turn to the social in the #MeToo campaign where unquestioned entitlement to women's bodies and psychology is exposed and resisted. We have seen defiance of those perpetuating social injustices that see long-term migrants alongside today's migrants abused and shunned by society, institutions as well as individuals. It is likely that, as a student of social work, you will lay bare and face many previously unquestioned assumptions, which can be very perplexing and uncover needs for learning, support and understanding. This series of books acts as an aid as you make these steps. Each book stands in a long and international tradition of social work that promotes social justice and human rights, introducing you to the importance of sometimes new and difficult concepts, and inculcating the importance of close questioning of yourself as you make your journey towards becoming part of that tradition.

There are numerous contemporary challenges for the wider world, and for all four countries of the UK. These include political shifts to the 'popular' Right, a growing antipathy to care and support, and dealing with lies and 'alternative truths' in our daily lives. Alongside this is the need to address the impact of an increasingly ageing population with its attendant social care needs and working with the financial implications that such a changing demography brings. At the other end of the lifespan the need for high quality childcare, welfare and safeguarding services has been highlighted as society develops and responds to the changing complexion. As demand rises so do the costs and the unquestioned assumption that austerity measures are necessary continues to create tensions and restrictions in services, policies and expectations.

It is likely that as a social worker you will work with a diverse range of people throughout your career, many of whom have experienced significant, even traumatic, events that require a professional and caring response. As well as working with individuals, however, you may be required to respond to the needs of a particular community disadvantaged by local, national or world events or groups excluded within their local communities because of assumptions made about them.

The importance of high quality social work education remains clear if we are adequately to address the complexities of modern life. We should continually strive for excellence in education as this allows us to focus clearly on what knowledge it is useful to engage with when learning to be a social worker. Questioning everything, especially from a position of knowledge, is central to being a social worker.

The books in this series respond to the agendas driven by changes brought about by professional bodies, governments and disciplinary reviews. They aim to build on and offer introductory texts based on up-to-date knowledge and to help communicate this in an accessible way, so preparing the ground for future study and for encouraging good practice as you develop your social work career. Each book is written or edited by people passionate about social work and social services and aims to instil that passion in others. The current text introduces you to the complex arena of the Care Act 2014; legislation that addresses concerns in England but the substance and arguments translate across borders. This edited work brings together academic, practice and expertise by experience and is written by specialists in their fields. It represents a solid foundation for students and practitioners who wish to further develop practice knowledge in working with adults in contemporary society.

Professor Jonathan Parker
June 2019

About the Editors

Suzy Braye

Suzy Braye is Emerita Professor of Social Work at the University of Sussex, England, and a Fellow of the Academy of Social Sciences. Her professional background is in social work and in local authority social services management, following which she worked in the university sector as a social work educator and researcher. Her specialist interests are law and social work, adult social care, safeguarding and self-neglect. Her research on self-neglect (with David Orr and Michael Preston-Shoot) has been influential on the development of national policy and practice. She now practises as an independent consultant in adult safeguarding, engaging in research, training and practice development, and acting as an independent reviewer in safeguarding adult reviews.

Michael Preston-Shoot

Michael Preston-Shoot is Professor (Emeritus) of Social Work at the University of Bedford-shire, England. He is a Fellow of the Academy of Social Sciences and a Senior Fellow of the Higher Education Academy. His publications, research and training have concentrated on law and social work practice. His latest research has focused on adult safeguarding, completing with Suzy Braye and David Orr major studies for the Department of Health on governance of adult safeguarding and on effective practice with adults who self-neglect. He is currently Independent Chair of Lewisham and of Brent Safeguarding Adults Boards. He has authored safeguarding adult reviews, has researched reviews of self-neglect cases and has completed thematic reviews of safeguarding adult reviews completed by Safeguarding Adults Boards in London and in South West England since implementation of the Care Act 2014.

About the Authors

Simon Abbott is a Senior Lecturer in the department of social work and social care at Kingston University and St George's, University of London. He also practises as a mental health social worker and Approved Mental Health Professional in South London. His practice in mental health has involved work in community mental health teams, including specialist community services for people experiencing psychosis. He has practised as a forensic social worker in London, working with mentally disordered offenders in regional secure services and in the community. His doctorate at the University of Sussex explored how social work Approved Mental Health Professionals use the law in practice. Simon's research, teaching and practice interest involve the relationship between law and social work.

Peter Beresford OBE is Professor of Citizen Participation at the University of Essex, co-chair of Shaping Our Lives, the national disabled people's and service users' organisation, and Emeritus Professor of Social Policy at Brunel University London. He was awarded an Honorary Doctorate by Edge Hill University in July 2017. He is a long-term user of mental health services and has a longstanding background of involvement in issues of participation as a writer, researcher, activist and teacher. He writes regularly in the UK's *Guardian* newspaper. His most recent book is *Social Policy First Hand: An International Introduction to Participatory Social Policy* (jointly edited with Sarah Carr, Policy Press, 2018), and forthcoming is *Madness, Violence And Power: A Critical Collection* (jointly edited with Andrea Daley and Lucy Costa, University of Toronto Press, 2019).

Alison Brammer is Professor of Law at Keele University. She initially qualified as a solicitor and worked at a local authority with a social services caseload. Alison's publications include her textbook *Social Work Law* (4th edition, 2015), and she is series editor of the 'Focus on Social Work Law' series of specialist texts for social workers, which includes her own authored volume *Safeguarding Adults* (2014). Alison is Legal Editor of the *Journal of Adult Protection* and a trustee of BASW. Her research interests focus on the law relating to social work practice and the developing law relating to safeguarding adults. Recent research projects include an ESRC seminar series on the Implications of the Care Act 2014 for Safeguarding Adults in Civil Society.

Nic Brimblecombe is Assistant Professorial Research Fellow at the Personal Social Services Research Unit, London School of Economics and Political Science. Nic is a mixed-methods researcher with research interests in unpaid care, care needs, health and care inequalities, youth mental health and children's and young people's services. She is currently leading a study on young adult unpaid carers, having previously worked on a longitudinal study on unpaid care and carers' employment. Other research includes support for carers following the 2014 Care Act, studies on the long-term economic impacts of childhood mental ill health and of being bullied in childhood, and an economic evaluation of youth mental health services.

Vic Citarella is a social worker registered with the Health and Care Professions Council. His substantive practice background is in residential child care and the management of social services provision and commissioning. A former Director of Social Services, he has, since leaving local government in 2000, built a consultancy business advising and supporting local authorities, NHS bodies and private and voluntary social care providers with improvements in standards and quality. He remains an active member of both the Association of Directors of Adult Social Services and that of Directors of Children's Services. Vic's current work includes serious adult reviews, expert opinion, improvement support to providers and commissioners, mentoring, governance and leadership advice to small businesses and not-for profit providers. He has supervised several safeguarding adult reviews (often young adults who have been in care), co-authored the Winterbourne View report, and is currently working on a whole systems approach to accountability in care homes. Vic is chair of a safeguarding scrutiny committee for a care provider and trustee of the Residential Forum – an influential leadership network and exchange focused on promoting residential care and supported living as a positive choice for all age groups across the UK.

John Crossland DSW is a Senior Lecturer in Adult Social Care at the University of Portsmouth. He teaches adult development and adult social care policy and practice, with a particular focus on older adults, on the BSc and MSc social work programmes, and supervises doctoral students with interests in older adults' health and/or social care. He spent over twenty years in local authority adult social services in London and Brighton, first as a specialist practitioner in sensory impairment services and later as a manager, including several years managing adult social care complaints. His research interests are primarily focused on how policy is enacted in practice, with particular interests in older visually impaired adults and older adults in LGBT communities, and comparative interests in German social care policy. He publishes in both English and German and has longstanding connections with the Catholic University of Applied Sciences Berlin.

José Luis Fernandéz is Deputy Director and Associate Professorial Research Fellow at the Personal Social Services Research Unit, London School of Economics and Political Science. A health and social care economist, he specialises in ageing-related policies, the interaction between health and social care, and the economic evaluation of health and social care services and systems. In 2010, he co-founded the International Long-term care Policy Network (ILPN) linking academics and policy makers on the analysis of long-term care. He is director of the National Institute for Health Research (NIHR) Adult Social Care Policy Research Unit and deputy director of the NIHR Economics of Social and Health Care Research Unit, both funded by the NIHR on behalf of the Department of Health and Social Care. He has advised bodies such as the Department of Health and Social Care, the UK Treasury and the World Health Organisation.

Margaret Flynn is the Chair of the National Independent Safeguarding Board for Wales and the joint editor of the *Journal of Adult Protection*. Since the Welsh Government published her report 'In Search of Accountability: A review of the neglect of older people living in care homes investigated as Operation Jasmine', Margaret has led work in England and Northern Ireland concerning the harms endured by people with learning disabilities and older people in service settings,- most recently at Muckamore Abbey Hospital. Such work prioritises the importance of people with learning disabilities and their families telling their stories of injustices and injuries, and setting these in the context of the compromised practice of service commissioners place-hunting for people whose support needs cannot be met locally. Margaret's personal experience of life-long family advocacy has confirmed her faith in the extraordinary and compassionate supports required to deliver people's aspiration for 'ordinary lives'.

Mark Holloway began working with brain-injured people in 1991, qualified as a social worker in 1995, and has been a brain injury case manager at Head First since 2001. He is an advanced member of the British Association of Brain Injury Case Managers and a trustee of the Brain Injury Social Work Group. Mark has experience in providing expert witness reports for the courts and has given evidence in civil, criminal and criminal injury compensation cases, in the Court of Protection, and provided written evidence to the House of Commons Select Committee on Head Injury. He is an Honorary Assistant Professor in the School of Sociology & Social Policy (University of Nottingham), and his research interests include mental capacity in the context of executive impairment and poor insight and the family experience of acquired brain injury. He is a regular speaker at conferences and training events relating to acquired brain injury, nationally and internationally.

Cath Holmström is currently Head of Social Work and Social Policy at the University of Brighton. Her practice background was largely in working with young people including care leavers and young offenders, in a variety of roles including court-mandated interventions and post-release work with young people. Cath retained her interest in law for social work practice when lecturing on social work courses in her first university post at the University of Sussex, and also studied law, completing the law conversion diploma whilst also working full-time. Cath has been able to draw upon this work with students and also in her current funded research project that is focused upon models of engaging and working with vulnerable young men. In addition, she has spent some time shadowing social workers and managers to observe legal decision making in action in recent months in order to maintain a link with practice.

Martin Knapp is Professor of Social Policy and Director of the Personal Social Services Research Unit at the London School of Economics and Political Science (LSE). He is also Director of the School for Social Care Research, a position he has held since the School was established by the National Institute for Health Research (NIHR) in 2008. His main research interests are in the areas of social care, child and adult mental health, dementia and autism, with much of his work using economic arguments and evidence to inform policy discussion and influence practice development.

Jill Manthorpe is Professor of Social Work at King's College London. She is Director of the NIHR Health and Social Care Workforce Research Unit and an Associate Director of the NIHR

School for Social Care Research. Jill has undertaken many research studies related to social care and health services, commissioning, law and policies, with special interests in workforce roles and activities, dementia, risk and safeguarding. She is a trustee of three charities and the SR Nathan Visiting Professor at the National University of Singapore and at Melbourne University. She contributes to continuing professional development activities for social workers through Making Research Count and regular advisory work for local authorities and government agencies.

Jo Moriarty is Senior Research Fellow at the NIHR Health and Social Care Workforce Research Unit at King's College London and a Senior Fellow of the NIHR School for Social Care Research. Her research activities span a number of areas; these include leading research studies on workforce leadership, education and training, especially social work education, support for family carers, dementia, service user involvement, ethnicity and ageing. Jo is particularly committed to the translation of research into practice. As well as authoring resources aimed at summarising research findings for practitioners, Jo blogs regularly, aiming to critically appraise recent social care findings in an accessible way. She is currently playing a major role on a variety of Unit projects that draw on her expertise, including studies of hospital social work, new nursing roles, personal budgets, and a continued evaluation of the MTM Signs of Safety approach.

Laura Pritchard-Jones is a Lecturer in Law at Keele University where she is currently Course Director for the MA Safeguarding Adults: Law, Policy, and Practice. Prior to joining Keele University she completed her PhD in bioethics and medical jurisprudence at the University of Manchester. Her research interests lie in both the doctrinal and theoretical aspects to social welfare and social work law as they apply to adults, adult safeguarding, and mental disability and mental health law. She has a particular interest in how these areas of law operate in relation to older adults.

Forough Ramezankhah PhD is a Teaching Fellow at Keele University. She is a socio-legal researcher with principal interests in International Refugee Law, sociological theory and qualitative methodology. Her primary research concern lies in the field of asylum law and process and their interplay with the lived experience of refugees. In the course of her research, she utilises aspects of disciplines as diverse as international relations, sociology and psychology. She employs a free association narrative interview method inspired by psychoanalysis as the mode of data collection and analysis. She is also skilled in immigration and asylum practice, with many years' experience acting as a legal adviser in different capacities, including work with asylum seekers and refugees on a voluntary basis.

Colin Slasberg qualified as a social worker in the 1970s and then followed a career as a practitioner, supervisor, operational manager and strategic manager, working in children's, adults' and mental health services. Since 2008, he has worked independently with a sole focus on exploring what it will take to transform the social care system to one that is person-centred. He has produced a number of academic articles, both jointly with others and singly, that have explored evidence of and reasons for the failures of current and past policies that have transformational aspirations. He has also worked as a consultant with a number of councils. The most significant was a two-year intensive project with a council to explore how it could authentically personalise its mainstream assessment and support planning system. This enabled the development of a 'blue-print' that addresses the practice, policy, financial, legal and political implications. He has campaigned in this period to influence sector leaders.

Tom Snell is a Research Officer at PSSRU at the London School of Economics and Political Science. His research interests include social care targeting and financing, the impact of central and local government targeting policies, and the economic evaluation of preventative care services. Much of Tom's work focuses on measuring relative levels of social care need and variations in targeting behaviours at the local authority level. Recent research has included the derivation of Relative Needs Formulae (RNFs) – allocation formulae used to allocate central budgets between local authorities – and a series of studies estimating the impact of Care Act reforms.

Tim Spencer-Lane is a lawyer specialising in mental health, mental capacity and social care law. He is currently on secondment to the Department of Health & Social Care, where he is working on the Mental Capacity (Amendment) Bill. He has previously led three high-profile social care law reform projects for the Law Commission: the review of adult social care law, the final report for which (2011) formed the basis of the Care Act 2014 and the Social Services and Well-being (Wales) Act 2014; the review of the regulation of health and social care professionals (2014); and the review of the Deprivation of Liberty Safeguards under the Mental Capacity Act 2005 (2017). He has wide academic experience teaching on social work law and has written extensively on this. Among his publications is the *Care Act Manual* (2nd edition, Sweet & Maxwell, 2015).

Imogen Taylor is Emerita Professor of Social Work, University of Sussex. On qualifying in social work (University of Toronto, 1976), she became a family therapist in mental health. Appointed to the university, she developed two research streams that continued following her return to the UK in 1989. Best known is her work on the pedagogy of education for social work and related disciplines, which was also her PhD topic (University of Bristol). She published extensively and was invited to undertake reviews of social work education and research nationally and internationally. She was elected as Fellow of the UK Academy of Social Sciences in 2014. Her other research interest initially explored women's caring in the context of intimate family violence, and then shifted in the UK to caring in rural communities. In her chapter for this book, she integrates practice and research knowledges to inform an intensely personal reflection on caring for her very elderly parents in a rural area.

Colin Whittington is Visiting Professor, Department of Psychology, Social Work and Counselling, at the University of Greenwich and a registered social worker. His career began in adult services and his work on the Care Act reconnects with that time and its underlying family, political and ethical sentiments. Experience as a practitioner and team manager ignited his interest in the organisational and interprofessional contexts of practice and the importance of sociological perspectives, influences which shaped his career and wide publishing record. They formed the basis of research fellowships at Keele University and King's College London where, respectively, he gained his Master's and PhD. University lectureships were followed by positions as education adviser and research director and then as London regional head of the UK's social work education council. He was later Principal, R&D, for England's first national social care training organisation. These experiences and subsequent postgraduate study provided the foundations for the consultancy that he has run since with Margaret Whittington.

Achieving a Social Work Degree and Continuing Professional Development

Achieving a social work degree and post-qualification continuing professional development

This book helps develop capabilities from the Professional Capabilities Framework (BASW, 2018a, b), which sets out the values, knowledge and skills to be expected of social workers at different levels of experience and role: social work students, newly qualified social workers, social workers, experienced social workers, advanced social workers and strategic social workers. Knowledge and use of law is referenced at all levels of the PCF, with expectations becoming more complex through the career journey. Regardless of level, this book supports the need for legal literacy that enables practitioners and managers to understand relevant legal rules and to connect them with the professional priorities and objectives of ethical practice. The PCF domains particularly supported are:

1. Professionalism
2. Values and ethics
3. Rights, justice and economic wellbeing
4. Knowledge
5. Critical reflection and analysis
6. Skills and interventions
7. Contexts and organisations

For social work degree students, the book also supports development of the following knowledge, understanding and skills as set out in the Quality Assurance Agency's *Social Work Subject Benchmark Statement for graduates in social work (QAA, 2016)*:

5.2 Social work theory, particularly (viii)
5.3 Values and ethics, particularly (ii) (v) (vi) (ix) (xi)
5.4 Service users and carers, particularly (i)
5.5 The nature of social work practice, particularly (iii) (iv) (v)
5.6 The leadership, organisation and delivery of social work services, particularly (v) (vi) (xii)
5.11 Managing problem-solving activities
5.12 Gathering information
5.13 Analysis and synthesis
5.14 Intervention and evaluation
5.17 Skills in personal and professional development

For qualified practitioners, the book will support development of the knowledge and skills expected following the first year of qualified practice, as set out in the Department of Health's (2015d) Knowledge and Skills Statement for Social Workers in Adult Services. In particular:

2. The role of social workers with adults
3. Person-centred practice
4. Safeguarding
5. Mental capacity
6. Effective assessments and outcome-based support planning
9. Organisational context
10. Professional ethics and leadership

Additionally for qualified practitioners, the book assists in meeting HCPC (2017) Standards of Proficiency, particularly:

2. Practise within the legal and ethical boundaries of the profession
4. Practise as an autonomous professional, exercising their own professional judgement
10. Maintain records appropriately
13. Understand key concepts of the knowledge base relevant to their profession

Table of Cases

Local Government Ombudsman Cases

Case Law

Foreword

England's 2014 Care Act promised great transformation in social care and much of that promise remains. But the Act was born into contradiction and prompted serious questions as to whether its key aims and functions could, or would, be realised. Analysis of the Act has been urgently awaited, as implementation proceeds. Now, Suzy Braye and Michael Preston-Shoot have used their great depth of experience and expertise to assemble a powerful set of evidence-based accounts of the Act in practice.

The Act's bold central purpose was to establish a person-centred approach to social care, the essence of which is the promotion of the wellbeing of people in need of care and support. Enactment swept away layers of earlier legislation that connected contemporary social care to the seminal 1948 National Assistance Act, which had played such a formative part in the foundation of Britain's Welfare State. Announcements about the new Act, however, came without tributes to the Welfare State from the presiding Conservative-Liberal Democrat government. On the contrary, since coming to office in 2010, the government had pursued a campaign connecting 'welfare' with 'waste' and promising to reform an 'out of control' welfare state 'that our country can no longer afford' (Osborne, 2010). Three years later, this aim was consolidated into an explicit policy to permanently shrink the state (Cameron, 2013). The hallmark of the policy was austerity. Its target was most visibly the system of working age benefits, or 'welfare', as ministers and allies in the tabloid press labelled them in a calculatedly stigmatising use of the term. But the cuts that austerity embodied were spread widely across the public realm and were continued by successive Conservative governments beyond the Care Act's implementation in 2015. Those cuts have been inflicted especially deeply into local government, the very heart of the social care services (IFS, 2019).

This is the first paradox of the 2014 Care Act. A law created in cross-party cooperation and wide consultation, and embodying clearly humanitarian and progressive values, had delivered a raft of new statutory duties and procedures to be enacted by local authority social care services in cooperation with others. The aims clearly necessitated investment in staff and infrastructure of local services yet, during the first year of implementation, the services were already reported to be reaching breaking point (Whittington, 2016a).

A second paradox is that such an intendedly far-reaching Act should have slipped into law so quietly (Brindle, 2014) and that its commitment to base a service on a very widely-defined idea of wellbeing provoked so little public comment. Despite predictions that social care services will eventually touch the lives of most of us, social care, in contrast to its counterpart the NHS, has tended mostly to occupy the margins of public consciousness, except among those in immediate need of its care and support. Only controversy about social care funding appeared to enliven media attention in 2014 (BBC, 2014). Otherwise, the avowedly momentous Care Act failed to break through.

The Act had nothing like this low public profile across the sectors urgently preparing for implementation in 2015. If the demands of this huge programme added to the burdens of an already pressured set of services, the Act nevertheless generated real optimism (Carers Trust, 2016a) and it is important to acknowledge the efforts of all involved since then to meet expectations. Hopes were also high in some quarters of England's social work 'establishment' (Whittington, 2016a). During the Act's consultation stages, the former College of Social Work had urged government to free social workers from the mechanistic care management practice model that had come to dominate adult social work practice under the NHS&CC Act 1990. With the Care Act came encouragement that social work would at last be liberated to contribute the skills and values of its contemporary practice models: they would serve the Act's commitment to individual wellbeing, a community orientation, preventative intervention, safeguarding and holistic, strengths-based approaches. The Act thereby promised a renaissance of adult social work, a vision supported by successive Ministers (Whittington, 2016a; 2016b). At last, perhaps, social work was 'coming home'.

Around these ambitions, however, a further paradox has materialised. It relates to the adoption of strengths-based approaches promoted in the Act's Statutory Guidance from the start (Whittington, 2016a; 2016b). These approaches have since been actively encouraged and converge closely with social work's liberal professional aspirations. Yet in an environment of deep funding cuts, there is a risk of their being misapplied to rationalise inaction. The Association of Directors of Adult Social Services has described them as important sources of savings (ADASS, 2018a, legitimately implying a rational calculus of 'health economics'. But the ADASS also worries that as budgets continue to reduce, councils unable to afford interventions to build on people's strengths are pressed towards a fine line between promoting independence and abandoning people.

A related issue concerns the assumption that local communities exist as a bedrock of expandable social capital, to which commissioned and purchased services act as supplements (DHSC, 2018a). It is important to value and build on the strengths of local people and organisations, but social capital – civic engagement, supportive relationships, volunteering, and access to local networks, education and work – is not a simple potentiality, stable and unvarying over time and locality. Simply put, some localities are much poorer than others in their stock of social as well as economic capital. What is more, social capital is harmed by the long-term effects of recession and austerity. In short, austerity's legacy can damage the very community to which the Care Act turns for support and self-help. Austerity has arguably brought not a Big Society but a smaller one, at least in poorer communities where council cuts have been greatest (IFS, 2019) and the enduring effects of hard times may have hardened into enduring social scars (Alston, 2019; Clark and Heath, 2014).

While the context of austerity proves inescapable in any evaluation of the Care Act, as Braye and Preston-Shoot's collection demonstrates, implementation issues are not all rooted in funding. Some, as the volume shows, are to do with the tasks of conceptualising and operationalising an ambitious law through complex systems and alongside existing law, using multiple human services. Other issues, like the reliance on an increasingly unstable provision of outsourced and privatised care, are embedded in the too rarely-questioned acceptance of the normality of markets in care. This has brought us the chillingly neutral coinage of 'hand backs' and 'ceased trading', which describe home and residential care providers who fail or hand back contracts to the local council and, with them, responsibility for people with care and support needs. In 2018, 66% of English councils and many thousands of individuals were affected, with a significant impact on their wellbeing (ADASS, 2018b).

If the effects of market ideology and almost ten years of austerity policies were not test enough of attempts to realise the aims of the Care Act, the services of social care, along with almost every other element of the system formerly known as the welfare state, have struggled for attention, funding and desperately needed improvement in the face of Brexit disputes and seeming domestic policy paralysis. At the time of writing, unresolved Brexit conflict has been given as the latest ministerial excuse for the continued delay in publishing the urgently needed Social Care Green Paper (Haynes, 2019). The Green Paper will address the controversial 'funding of care' question but is expected to encompass other significant issues entailed in the Care Act but not settled by it (Jarrett, 2019).

Two imperatives arise here. First, the cause of improved social care must be kept firmly on the agenda, promoted with evidence, and championed alongside the claims of other policies competing for public and government attention; and second, the consultations and policy proposals that flow from the publication of the Green Paper must not be dominated solely by the important funding question, that is, there must be informed, research-based analysis *across Care Act functions*. Those twin missions receive a major and timely contribution from Suzy Braye and Michael Preston-Shoot's collection, and the expertise and experience of contributors. The volume does this by dissecting key dimensions of the Care Act and advancing findings on statute, structure, organisation, learning and practice. The wide scope of the chapter topics provides both a rich review and a critical comparator, against which the content of the promised Green Paper and future proposals may be assessed. But if the book offers policy-makers a rare evaluation of the Care Act to date, it also provides a platform upon which future social care research may be formulated. There are findings for service user and carer organisations and guidance for managers, educators and the social work practitioners whose role it is to implement key parts of the Act. The book clearly shares the aim in Statutory Guidance, of social work excellence. More broadly, and above all, this edited collection seeks to provide the kinds of substantive evidence on which the eventual realisation in practice of the Care Act's humanitarian 'wellbeing principle' will depend.

Colin Whittington MA, PhD
Visiting Professor, Department of Psychology, Social Work and Counselling,
The University of Greenwich, UK

1 Introduction

The Care Act 2014 – outcomes in context

Suzy Braye and Michael Preston-Shoot

Setting out

When the Care Act 2014 received royal assent, the government's care and support minister hailed it as *'the most significant reform of care and support in more than 60 years, putting people and their carers in control of their care and support'* (Lamb, 2014). The Act was the opportunity to consolidate and modernise the law relating to adult social care in England, which had developed incrementally since 1948. But was it an opportunity grasped or missed? Looking back over the four years since its (partial) implementation on 1 April 2015 provides an opportunity to evaluate its impact and outcomes, and to reflect on how far the Act has transformed adult social care. There is much interest in the mapping of these early directions of travel, as demonstrated by levels of participation in a series of national seminars[1] to *'explore how the new law emerged through a policy process, the challenges of interpretation that emerge and how practitioners and their organisations can be supported to deliver the intentions and requirements of the Care Act 2014 and to keep people safe from abuse and harm'* (Penhale et al., 2017:172).

The Act emerged through a complex policy process, and the next chapter in this collection, written by Tim Spencer-Lane who was closely involved in the Law Commission's work to prepare for the Act, outlines the drivers for and aspirations behind the reform. It sets the scene for exploring what has been achieved and the barriers or challenges that have confronted practitioners and managers as they have sought to realise the ambitions embodied in the Act's focus on wellbeing, prevention, integration, collaboration, market shaping, meeting needs and safeguarding.

Drawing variously on evidence from research and Safeguarding Adult Reviews (SARs), case law, Ombudsman judgements, and service user and carer testimonies, each of the subsequent chapters in this edited collection evaluates how far the ambitions for this legislative reform have been realised in practice, some exploring also its interface with other legal rules that have a significant impact upon adult social care.

Contradictory contexts

Any journey from the law in theory to the law in practice (Jenness and Grattet, 2005) has to negotiate difficult terrain. The Care Act 2014 reforms are no different. Policy aspirations to prevent or delay the development of social care needs, to increase people's choice and control over the types of care and support they receive, and to maximise their wellbeing, have been planted in a financial context that has created significant challenges for implementation.

Prior to implementation of the Act, researchers were warning that budget reductions were undermining the policy objectives of personalisation and early intervention (Beresford, 2014; Lymbery, 2014). Since implementation, the cascade of concern and criticism has increased. Phillips and Simpson (2017) have analysed the wide variations in spend across local authorities and observed that financial austerity has hit councils hardest in the poorest and most deprived communities. The National Audit Office (2018a) has commented that rising demand for adult social care has coincided with a 49% reduction in government funding for local authorities since 2010/11. Concern has been expressed that local authorities may be unable to fulfil their statutory duties (Communities and Local Government Committee, 2017), fuelled by evidence that the number of people with complex needs who are accessing services is falling sharply and the number of older people with unmet needs is rising; that the care market is often not providing high quality care; that the number of delayed discharges is rising; that there are shortages of mental health and nursing home beds, and increasing numbers of home care providers have ceased trading (Communities and Local Government Committee, 2017; CQC, 2018a; 2018b; 2018c). The Local Government Association, issuing its own green paper for adult social care and wellbeing while awaiting that from government (LGA, 2018a), identifies that despite a deep commitment to the legislation, councils are struggling to meet even the letter of the law; in a 2018 survey, only 34% of directors were fully confident of meeting all their statutory duties in 2018/19, only 10% were confident of meeting them in 2019/20, and no director anticipated 2020/21 with any confidence at all. With regard to social work, it notes the profession has one of the highest vacancy rates in local government (10.8%) with a staff turnover rate of 15.6%. In a later report (LGA, 2018b: 8), consultation responses to its green paper described a system that is failing across the board as a clear consequence of under-funding: '*People's needs are not being met, services are being withdrawn, quality is deteriorating, improvement is stalling and in some cases is in reverse, the ability to prevent the need for social care in the first place is rapidly being lost, providers are unable to stay afloat and unpaid carers and the care workforce are being put under impossible and unbearable pressure*'.

Financial constraints and the emphasis on eligible needs within the statutory guidance (DHSC, 2018a) stand accused of undermining the aims of personalisation, person-centred practice and wellbeing, compromising the spirit and intent of the legislation (Slasberg and Beresford, 2016a; 2017a; Wydall et al., 2018), and of exacerbating unmet need and risking lower quality services (Stevens et al., 2018a). Indeed, notwithstanding the Act's opening emphasis on promoting wellbeing, establishing this as a fundamental duty of the local authority in undertaking its care and support functions (s.1(1)) and regarded as the Act's most radical innovation (TCSW, 2014), case law continues to uphold the local authority's discretion when allocating scarce resources, providing the provision made has a reasonable chance of meeting identified needs (Preston-Shoot, 2019). Comparing cases either side of the Act's implementation, user choice, control, dignity and wellbeing are ultimately relegated in favour of a council's determination of how to respond to eligible needs (*R (McDonald) v Royal Borough of Kensington and Chelsea* [2011]; *R (Davey) v Oxfordshire County Council* [2017]). Reduced care packages are scrutinised for the lawfulness by which they have been achieved (for example, contrast *R (JF) v Merton LBC* [2017] and *R (MG) v Brent LBC* [2018]), namely the degree to which the requirements in statute, policy guidance (DHSC, 2018a) and administrative law have been adhered to. Reference to aforementioned policy ambitions, rights and ethics appears only if illegality (including irrationality and unreasonableness) is found, as illustrated in an Ombudsman decision (*LGO and Hammersmith and Fulham LBC* (2016)) in which maladministration was found in the local authority's failure to give reasons for reducing the care package (administrative law) and to complete a thorough assessment (statutory duty), meaning that it had also failed to recognise the importance of dignity. Tellingly, the PAC (2016), in the summary of its report on personal budgets in social care, observes 'we are not assured that local authorities can fully personalise care while seeking to save money and are concerned that users' outcomes will be adversely affected'.

The impact of financial austerity is a theme that permeates this entire book but is most explicit in the chapters by Margaret Flynn and Vic Citarella, who draw on SARs to pinpoint concerns about market shaping and the quality of commissioning and service provision, and by Peter Beresford and Colin Slasberg, who explore the contradictions inherent in the Act and its statutory guidance regarding wellbeing, choice, assessment and eligibility.

The financial context is just one component of a challenging working environment for adult social care staff. Their lived experience of work continues to be characterised by high caseloads, irregular supervision, lack of support in response to threatening behaviour, poor quality IT systems, staff vacancies and reliance on agency staff in a context of recruitment and retention challenges, lack of training opportunities, and hot-desking that undermines peer support (Baginsky and Manthorpe, 2016; Ravalier, 2017). The evidence-based endorsement of devoting time to complex cases frequently collides with organisational systems that (have to) prioritise management of workload demand (Braye et al., 2014; Lonbay, 2018). The chapter by Suzy Braye and Michael Preston-Shoot in this volume, drawing on previous evidence (Preston-Shoot, 2016), argues that SARs have devoted too little attention to the impact of this working environment on decision-making.

A mosaic?

To what degree is the Care Act 2014 a recognisable, coherent image when pictured from its constituent elements? Every aspect of adult social care practice should promote an individual's wellbeing as set out in section 1 of the Act. Unsurprisingly therefore, wellbeing is a theme that permeates the entire volume, with chapter writers variously concluding their analysis of outcomes in practice. Research too has criticised the ambiguity of some elements within the Act's definition of wellbeing in section 1, for example the meaning of an individual's contribution to society (Diaper and Yeomans, 2016).

Section 5 of the Act deals with promoting diversity and quality in service provision, an essential element of providing personalised care and support. Research into the implementation of local authorities' market-shaping responsibilities, commissioned by the Department of Health & Social Care's Policy Research Programme (www.birmingham.ac.uk/schools/social-policy/departments/health-services-management-centre/research/projects/2017/shaping-care-markets.aspx), has not yet been reported, but it is clear that a number of factors may combine to place the health of the social care market under threat, particularly in the context of austerity. Stevens et al. (2019), for example, identify the potential for changing patterns of commissioning and contracting to have challenging implications for the stability of care markets. Section 48 of the Act seeks to address responses to provider failure. Whilst many people receive good quality care, the picture is inconsistent, with one in six adult social care services and one in five mental health services needing to improve, and one-third of Directors of Adult Social Care reporting that home care providers have ceased trading (CQC, 2018c). An apparently never-ending sequence of SARs and reports has exposed failures in the quality of provision in care settings and in oversight by commissioners and regulators (Braye and Preston-Shoot, 2017a; Flynn, 2015; 2017; Flynn and Citarella, 2012; Preston-Shoot, 2017a). Central government has also had to recognise the challenges involved in reconfiguring the type and quality of care provided following findings relating to the care of people with learning disabilities, complex needs and challenging behaviour at Winterbourne View (DoH, 2015a). Safeguards and meaningful standards appear elusive, in practice if not in theory. Vic Citarella and Margaret Flynn consider the evidence anew in this volume.

The Act sought to remove the postcode lottery with respect to assessment by setting a low threshold (section 9). Section 13 and the Care and Support (Eligibility Criteria) Regulations 2015 (DoH, 2015b), described in detail in statutory guidance (DHSC, 2018a), outline where local authorities have a duty, following assessment, to arrange the provision of care and support. Sections 18 and 19 make provision for meeting people's needs, followed by requirements for care and support plans (sections 24 and 25) and personal budgets (section 26). John Crossland's chapter in this volume evaluates the outcomes of these provisions. Mark Holloway's chapter reviews the evidence relating to planning for care and support in the context of acquired brain injury, identifying the particular challenges of a model of assessment and support provision that can run contrary to the underlying impairments and needs that are present.

Peter Beresford and Colin Slasberg offer perspectives informed by service users' experiences and draw on evidence to suggest that the transformational ambitions of the Act are not being delivered. Personal budgets are a central element of the legal framework, intended to embed personalisation within the care system and enable people to exercise choice and control over their support. Their chapter demonstrates the shifts that have taken place between ambition and delivery, and the widening gap that only significant changes to national policy can bridge. Research findings on personal budgets are indeed mixed. Needham et al. (2018), reviewing the literature relating to market shaping and personalisation, report that it is direct payments rather than personal budgets *per se* that provide the strongest evidence of positive outcomes for service users. The state of the provider market potentially compromises personalisation, with choice and control contingent upon the availability of a diverse range of provision and thus upon proactive market-shaping initiatives. Yet the evidence suggests that commissioning and contracting patterns arising from the introduction of personal budgets have destabilised social care markets. As Stevens et al. (2019: 43) note: '*Without a pluralistic and vibrant social care market, it is much harder to increase consumer choice of services from a range of possible providers and therefore fulfil the government's purposes for personalisation, particularly in a context of falling revenues from LAs*'.

Here as elsewhere the spectre of resources is never far away. The Act's focus on wellbeing is compromised by the operationalisation of eligibility criteria as well as by the latitude available to local authorities to provide care and support that has a reasonable (as opposed to the best) chance of meeting the needs identified. There are no specific time limits within which decisions must be made, the administrative law principle being that planning must be concluded in a timely way and consider all relevant options (*R (D) v Brent LBC* [2015]).

The Act provides similar rules of assessment and support planning with respect to carers. The chapter by Jill Manthorpe and colleagues reviews the evidence from research, case law and Ombudsman judgements on outcomes for carers. Imogen Taylor provides a personal perspective on the experience of being a carer. Research evidence (for example Milne et al., 2013; Woolham et al., 2018) routinely reports that carers feel unsupported, with entitlements to assessment being overlooked. SARs also uncover shortcomings with respect to the availability of carer assessments and the involvement of carers in care and support planning (Braye and Preston-Shoot, 2017a; Preston-Shoot, 2017a).

For both service users and carers, the Act introduced new provisions (sections 37 and 38) regarding the portability of care and support. Here too the research evidence points to the challenges faced by individuals who wish to relocate (White et al., 2016), with experiences of poor transitional arrangements, delays in reassessment and variations in eligibility not uncommon. Similarly, for both service users and carers, the Act requires that care and support plans are reviewed (section 27). Here too practice appears variable. In *OH v Bexley LBC* [2015] for example, the local authority failed to review the case and supply a revised support plan, to give reasons for a reduction in care, and to take reasonable steps to reach agreement, all contrary to statutory guidance (DHSC, 2018a). In a further innovation, the Act gave local authorities responsibility for identifying, assessing and meeting adult prisoners' social care needs; the local authority in whose area prison is located must identify and assess prisoners with social care needs, regardless of their geographical origin or likely destination on release. Drawing on national surveys, Tucker et al. (2018) found that 1,835 prisoners were identified in the first year of implementation, with 1,593 assessments taking place, which resulted in 790 deemed eligible for social care. Most local authorities had a process in place for identifying prisoners with social care needs, and assessments were for the most part being done by social care staff, with either prison healthcare staff or external domiciliary agencies used as providers. Further research was needed to explore the different options, to include also further exploration of the tools used to identify prisoners, of the extent of training to prepare staff for this specialist context, and of arrangements that were sometimes noted for other prisoners to support inmates with aspects of social care that do not relate to personal care. Nonetheless, the authors conclude that the findings represent a substantial step forward in the care and support of prisoners.

Primary legislation and statutory guidance cannot guarantee good practice but rather just codify the framework to support it. The Act's provision for appeals (section 72) has not yet been implemented, meaning that service users and carers must first use the local authority's complaints procedures before either applying for judicial review or requesting an Ombudsman investigation. Councils, however, do not always follow their complaints procedures (for example, *LGO and Central Bedfordshire Council* (2016)). Moreover, perhaps reflective of a care system under intense pressure, it is noteworthy that complaints to the Ombudsman about adult social care have risen by 169% since 2011, and in 2017/18 formed the second highest number of complaints received (LGSCO, 2018a) (with the highest number relating to education and children's services: see LGSCO, 2018b).

The Act also made arrangements for the provision of advocacy (sections 67–68) and legislated on adult safeguarding for the first time. Outcomes with respect to advocacy are evaluated in several chapters in this volume. Research has identified that advocates can represent effectively an individual's wishes to those with statutory powers, promote their rights and improve decision-making, but concerns remain about patchy availability and low numbers of referrals (Newbigging et al., 2015; CQC, 2018a; Lonbay, 2018). The different legislative schemes for advocacy (which include the Mental Health Act 1983 (amended 2007) and the Mental Capacity Act 2005 as well as the Care Act) have given rise to some confusion about potential overlap and discrepancies, with a lack of legislative clarity about when a supporter from within the person's own network might be deemed inappropriate, thus triggering the statutory advocacy duty (Dixon et al., 2018). SARs (Braye and Preston-Shoot, 2017a; Preston-Shoot, 2017a), Ombudsman judgements (for example, *LGSCO and Salford City Council* (2018)) and case law (*R (SG) v London Borough of Haringey* [2015]) also highlight failures to involve advocates in assessment and care planning.

The chapter by Suzy Braye and Michael Preston-Shoot evaluates the new provisions (sections 42-45) on adult safeguarding. What is significant here is what is not included in the new framework. The Act does not include a power of entry for social workers, unlike in Scotland (Adult Support and Protection (Scotland) Act 2007) and Wales (Social Services and Well-being (Wales) Act 2014). Research (Stevens et al., 2017a) and SARs (for example, Newcastle SAB, 2014; City & Hackney SAB, 2016; Kent and Medway SAB, 2018) have identified cases where carers have hindered social workers and other professionals from speaking directly with an adult at risk. Despite the evidence from Scotland that assessment, removal and banning orders strike a careful balance between an individual's human rights and protection (Preston-Shoot and Cornish, 2014), no such orders have been included in the Act, raising the question of whether the Act really provides a comprehensive adult safeguarding system (Pritchard-Jones, 2016a).

Woven throughout the Act's provisions is the requirement on all agencies with a contribution to make towards meeting people's care and support needs to collaborate (sections 6 and 7), and for adult social care and NHS commissioners and providers to integrate care and support provision with health provision (section 3). Yet SARs continue to provide evidence of poor interagency communication and collaboration (Braye and Preston-Shoot, 2017a; Preston-Shoot, 2017a), calling into question the degree of leverage that can be exercised through the statutory duties of cooperation. Equally, the integration agenda, despite being driven by a series of initiatives dating back many years, has had limited success. Exworthy et al. (2017) note ongoing challenges from fragmentation of commissioning responsibilities and widely dispersed budgets, debates about the role of Health and Wellbeing Boards and concerns that Sustainability and Transformation Plans,[2] intended as a key vehicle for integration, have been developed with little public involvement or external scrutiny. They express pessimism as to whether the outcomes to which integration policy aspires can be achieved. As Glasby (2018) points out, there are fundamental differences between health services that are national, universal, and largely free at the point of delivery and social care services that are local, targeted, and means tested. He argues that national, not local, action is needed to resolve fundamental structural and systemic barriers.

An unanswered question

Section 15 of the Act sought to resolve the longstanding question about care costs by imposing a cap. Implementation, however, has been deferred and proposals are awaited (at the time of writing) from government about this aspect of social care reform. Meanwhile, case law and Ombudsman decisions continue to highlight the challenges facing commissioners and care home providers regarding the setting of fees and the difficulties facing councils and individuals with respect to care costs. For example, individuals cannot be ordered to pay a top-up towards their care home accommodation because of market inadequacies; councils must ensure that people have genuine choice with regard to accommodation (*LGO and Solihull MBC* (2016)). Councils must give explanations to service users about charging structures for care homes, including top-up payments (*LGSCO and North Yorkshire CC* (2018). Councils must pay a reasonable price for placements in care homes (*Abbeyfield Newcastle upon Tyne Society Ltd v Newcastle CC* [2014]), calculated on the actual cost of care rather than simply benchmarked against what other local authorities are paying (*R (Members of the Committee of Care North East Northumberland) v Northumberland CC* [2014]; *R (Redcar and Cleveland Independent Providers Association) v Redcar and Cleveland BC* [2013]).

A jigsaw of meeting needs?

Whilst the Care Act consolidated the law relating to adult social care, it largely left untouched provisions in other legislative mandates that can contribute to meeting people's social care needs. Thus social workers and other practitioners, with their managers, have to manage the interface between this Act and other legislative mandates, notably the Mental Capacity Act 2005, Mental Health Acts 1983 and 2007, legislation relating to housing, public and environmental health, trading standards, immigration, powers of entry and anti-social behaviour, as well as the key underpinnings of the Human Rights Act 1998 and the Equality Act 2010. There are international conventions to be observed, particularly the United Nations Convention on the Rights of Persons with Disabilities 2006 and the European Convention on Human Rights and Fundamental Freedoms. Court processes can take practitioners into the criminal courts as well as to the Court of Protection and the High Court.

The degree to which these different legal mandates converge or diverge, that is how far they form a coherent picture for practice when their various pieces are assembled, is the focus of several chapters and represents a unique contribution to debate about the outcomes of the Care Act 2014. Discussion of human rights and equality permeates the volume. Laura Pritchard-Jones considers the interface with the Mental Capacity Act 2005, whilst Simon Abbott does the same for the Mental Health Acts 1983 and 2007. Alison Brammer and Forough Ramezankhah focus on asylum seekers and refugees, whilst Cath Holmström considers the interface of the Act (sections 58-66) with the Children and Families Act 2014 in her discussion of transition, namely arrangements for care and support for disabled young people and young people leaving care as they enter adulthood.

The picture that emerges is one of complexity, with practitioners and managers needing to draw on their legal literacy to find the synergies between different legal mandates in order to promote people's wellbeing, to meet their health and social care needs, and to safeguard them from abuse and neglect. The analysis in these chapters chimes with other evidence. SARs have routinely highlighted shortcomings in understanding and implementing the provisions of the Mental Capacity Act 2005 and have sometimes pinpointed learning with respect to mental health provision, such as the use of after-care (section 117, Mental Health Act 1983) (Braye and Preston-Shoot, 2017a; Preston-Shoot, 2017a). Ombudsman decisions have found fault in how some councils have managed the process of transition, for example for disabled young people, characterised by assessment delays, decisions not supported by proper reasoning, inadequate involvement of parent carers and gaps in care and support (for example, *LGSCO and Bromley LBC* (2017)). Research too has highlighted challenges. For example, Lonbay (2018) found that the principles of the Mental Capacity Act 2005 were not necessarily adhered to in work with older people, where ageism was also present, for instance in failing to ask older people what they wanted the outcomes of an adult safeguarding process to be.

Whither social work?

The Chief Social Worker for Adults, at the point of the Act's implementation, gave strong endorsement to the role of social work in achieving its goals: *'Social workers have a vital role in delivering the kind of personalised and integrated care and support, centred on prevention and wellbeing, which is at the heart of the Care Act (2014), making a real difference to people's lives'* (Romeo, 2015: 206). She has since (Romeo, 2018) expressed an upbeat evaluation of social work's achievements in preventing and delaying need and promoting relationship-based and person-centred practice. She does, however, highlight concerns about a lack of funding and concedes that there is more to do to embed the reforms envisaged by the Act. Less positively, the Local Government Association's green paper and consultation response (LGA, 2018b) make little mention of social work, prompting the British Association of Social Workers to publish an open letter calling on the LGA to recognise the fundamental role of social workers in delivering the statutory responsibilities contained within the Care Act 2014 (BASW, 2019).

Colin Whittington's forensic analysis (2016a; b) of the statutory guidance for how it portrays social work (DHSC, 2018a) questions whether social work has been liberated in order to deliver the aspirations within the Act or whether the political, financial and organisational context within which it is predominantly located will constrain it as well as compromise the Act's focus on wellbeing and personalisation. While he notes that the statutory guidance, in making it a requirement for each local authority to appoint a Principal Social Worker, has significant convergence with social work's aspirations for its role in implementing the Care Act (TCSW, 2014), he also issues the caveat that true transformation in the context of deep social injustices requires a different order of economic and political action.

Each chapter within this volume considers the evidence and the prospects for ongoing implementation of the Act to achieve its goals and for social work's contribution within the overall context of adult social care, with Jill Manthorpe's concluding chapter pulling the threads together. All of the chapters end with suggestions for further reading; these key texts have been selected by each chapter author to expand on the issues explored in their chapter. Many of the chapters also close with a short case study that illustrates how the particular aspect of the Care Act that is the focus of the chapter might be applied in circumstances typical of those encountered in practice.

The subtitle of this book, 'Wellbeing in Practice', was deliberately chosen to reflect social work's commitments to maximising people's human rights, promoting their dignity and autonomy, and enhancing social justice by recognising diversity, counteracting discrimination and challenging unequal citizenship. Such practice requires practitioners to demonstrate confidence, courage and resilience in their use of knowledge, values and skills. It needs legal literacy as well as understanding of the contribution that other literacies, not least research, can make when assessing and addressing people's care and support needs. It also requires a favourable legal, policy, organisational and financial context.

Is the Act the difference that will make a difference? This edited volume provides some preliminary answers to that question.

Notes

1. Funded by the Economic and Social Research Council: https://safeguardingadults.wordpress.com/

2. Sustainability and Transformation Plans are collaborative, 'place-based', 5-year plans (made in 2016) designed to set out the future of health and care services in a local area. They cover all aspects of NHS spending and must focus on better integration with social care and other local authority services. www.kingsfund.org.uk/topics/integrated-care/sustainability-transformation-plans-explained

2 Overview of the Care Act 2014

Tim Spencer-Lane

Introduction

The Care Act 2014 introduced long-awaited and fundamental reform to the adult social care system. It came into force following five years of what the government described as, 'one of the most collaborative processes ever used to develop legislation' (Hansard HC, 2014a). The Care Act represented the biggest change in the law governing adult social care in England since the National Assistance Act 1948 and the abolition of the poor law. It not only consolidated and streamlined into a single statute over sixty years of piecemeal legislation, but also placed personalisation and adult safeguarding on a statutory footing.

The drivers for reform

The following factors can be said to have driven the process that culminated in the passing of the Care Act: the inadequacy of the previous legislative framework, the Law Commission's review, demographic trends, the funding crisis, the Commission on Funding Care and Support's review, and safeguarding failings.

The previous legislative framework

The previous legislative framework for adult social care (known as 'community care law') had long been criticised for being complex, outdated and often incomprehensible. It consisted of over 30 Acts of Parliament, dating back to the National Assistance Act 1948. The Law Commission (2008, para. 2.1) summarised this framework in the following terms:

> *Adult social care law remains a confusing patchwork of conflicting statutes enacted over a period of 60 years. Some of these statutes reflect the disparate and shifting philosophical,*

political and socio-economic concerns of various post-war governments. Other statutes were originally Private Member's Bills and represent an altogether different agenda of civil rights for disabled people and their carers. The law has also developed with an inconsistent regard for previous legislation: some statutes amend or repeal previous legislation; others repeat or seek to augment previous law; and others can be categorised as stand-alone or parallel Acts of Parliament.

The widespread confusion was compounded by the vast array of regulations, directions, circulars and guidance regularly churned out by central government. The sheer volume of law made it virtually impossible for service users, social workers or lawyers to understand the law, particularly rights to services, or keep updated of legal changes.

The government policy of personalisation, and how it was developed, epitomised many of these failings. Some of the elements of personalisation had been introduced via statute law; for example, direct payments were provided for in the Community Care (Direct Payments) Act 1996, and later the Health and Social Care Act 2001. However, the growth of personalisation – including the provision of personal budgets and self-assessments – was achieved largely through guidance, circulars and policy statements rather than any reforms to the underlying statutory framework. This led to friction and uncertainty when personalisation came up against this framework.

The Law Commission's review

In response to the criticisms of the legal framework, the Law Commission[1] announced a three-year review of adult social care. This began with a scoping report (Law Commision, 2008), which was followed by a consultation paper and full public consultation (Law Commission, 2010) and a final report in 2011 (Law Commission, 2011). The Commission's final report concluded the framework urgently needed to be consolidated and simplified through the introduction of a single unified adult social care statute. It recommended that the new statute, setting out the core functions of local authorities, should form the first level of a new three-level structure (Law Commission, 2011: paras. 3.1–3.34). The second level would be regulations made by government to provide more detail where necessary and to allow for developments of policy in the future. The third level would consist of a code of practice.

Demographic trends

The need for new adult social care legislation was also driven by fundamental demographic change, described as 'change in human society on a Darwinian scale; for the first time in history the human race will be living substantially longer than ever before' (Hansard HL, 2013a). Population projections have long indicated that the UK population is ageing rapidly, with numbers in the oldest age groups increasing the fastest. For example, in 2010 there were 1.4 million people in the UK aged 85 and over, and this number is projected to more than double by 2035 (ONS, 2011). Clearly, an ageing population presents economic and social opportunities, and will mean that many people will lead longer and fitter lives. But it also presents challenges for the public sector, since as people get older, they are more likely to need health and care services.

Moreover, advances in medicine are enabling more young disabled people to reach adulthood, and more adults to live longer with multiple and complex needs. Between 2002 and 2041, the number of disabled people is expected to double (Hancock et al., 2006) Once again, this is presents exciting opportunities for individuals and society. There will also be challenges due to the increased demand for health and social care.

Funding crisis

The impact of demographic trends has led to rising concern about the future affordability of adult social care. In England around 1.1% of GDP is spent on adult care and support, which is expected to rise to 1.25% by 2025–26 (Department of Health, 2013a: para.12). To meet the demographic pressures, it is estimated that an additional £400 million a year of public expenditure is required to maintain existing expenditure levels (Hansard (HC), 2013a; Hansard (HC), 2014b). The government predicts that by 2028 there will be a funding gap of over £6 billion in adult social care (HM Government, 2008).

Concerns about the future affordability of care and support also need to be set in the context of the post-2007 economic downturn and cuts to public services. In 2012–13, 26% fewer people aged over 65 were receiving publicly-funded social care, along with 24% fewer disabled people, compared to 2008–09, the year in which the global financial crisis struck. The decline has been sharpest (30% cent) amongst those receiving care and support at home (Commission on the Future of Health and Social Care in England, 2014).

Commission on Funding Care and Support

The combined effect of the demographic trends and funding crisis on adult social care pointed towards an urgent need to establish a new funding system, as well as a more effective legal structure. In July 2010, the Commission on Funding Care and Support, chaired by the economist Sir Andrew Dilnot, was tasked by the government with making recommendations on how to achieve an affordable and sustainable funding system for adult social care. In particular, it was asked to examine how best to meet the costs of care and support as a partnership between individuals and the state, and how people could choose to protect their assets, especially their homes, against the costs. Following a public consultation, the Commission reported in July 2011 (Commission on Funding of Care and Support, 2011). It put forward a limited liability model whereby, in addition to the current means-tested assistance system, the state would pick up the cost of care for people who met a maximum financial contribution (this was called 'the cap on care costs'). The Commission also recommended an increase in the upper means test threshold for state support, free state support for those who enter adulthood with care and support needs, and the development of financial products to support people in making their individual contributions.

Safeguarding failings

The years leading up to the Care Act also saw a number of adult safeguarding scandals which reinforced the need for a new statutory framework. This began in May 2011 when a BBC *Panorama* broadcast, 'Undercover Care: the Abuse Exposed', showed staff at Winterbourne View Hospital in South Gloucestershire mistreating and assaulting adults with learning disabilities and autism. The abuse included water-based punishment, the use of illegal and dangerous methods of restraint, needless suffering of patients and the transgression of professional boundaries. Moreover, whistleblowing concerns had been ignored by the managers of Winterbourne View, and by the Care Quality Commission. The Serious Case Review (Flynn and Citarella, 2012) detailed a litany of failings by the hospital, its owners, NHS commissioners, the local authority, police and regulators.

In Wales, an investigation by Gwent police started in 2005, known as Operation Jasmine, uncovered instances of historic neglect and abuse in care homes. This was the biggest investigation into care home abuse ever undertaken in the UK, with 103 alleged victims of abuse and neglect. However, only three convictions were secured for wilful neglect by staff. Moreover, charges brought against the care home owner did not directly relate to poor care for residents in his homes, but instead to breaches of health and safety legislation and false accounting. In 2013, the Welsh Government announced a review of Operation Jasmine (see Action on Elder Abuse, 2013; Hansard (HL) (2013b); Hansard (HC) (2013b).

The period leading up to the Care Act also saw one of the worst hospital care scandals of recent times. An estimated 400–1,200 patients are believed to have died between January 2005 and March 2009 as a result of poor care at Stafford hospital. The standard of care provided by the Mid Staffordshire NHS Foundation Trust was the subject of several investigations and reports, culminating in a public inquiry. The final report of the public inquiry, known as the Francis Report, was published on 6 February 2013 (Francis, 2013).

Towards the Care Act

In July 2012 the government published a White Paper *Caring for our Future*, a draft Care and Support Bill, its formal response to the Law Commission's report, and a progress report on the reform of the funding of adult social care (HM Government, 2012; Department of Health, 2012a, b, c). The government accepted the vast majority of the Law Commission's recommendations.

The draft Bill was subject to public consultation, and it was also decided that the draft Bill should receive pre-legislative scrutiny by a joint committee of both Houses of Parliament. The Joint

Committee was set up in November 2012, and chaired by the former Minister for Care Services Paul Burstow MP. It held a total of 16 meetings. In response to its call for written evidence, it received 143 submissions. It also held 17 evidence sessions during which it took oral evidence from 61 persons, including the relevant government Ministers. The Joint Committee was also able to consider the views given in response to the government's consultation on the draft Bill, in addition to those replying to the Committee's call for evidence. The Joint Committee's report (House of Lords House of Commons Joint Committee on the Draft Care and Support Bill, 2013) was published in March 2013 and made 107 recommendations.

On 9 May 2013 Earl Howe (Parliamentary Under Secretary of State at the Department of Health) introduced the Care Bill in the House of Lords. As well as the Law Commission's recommendations, the Bill gave effect to a new funding system based on the model recommended by the Commission on the Funding of Care and Support, and many of the recommendations made by the Joint Scrutiny Committee. A significant number of government amendments were made to the Bill during its passage through Parliament, including new rights to independent advocacy and the power to introduce an appeals process to challenge local authority decisions. The Bill received Royal Assent on 14 May 2014. Most of the reforms contained in the Care Act came into force on 1 April 2015.

Overview of the Care Act

The Care Act is divided into five parts and eight schedules. The legislative framework for care and support is contained in Part 1 (sections 1 to 80) and Schedules 1 to 4. Part 1 applies to local authorities in England only (with a small number of exceptions such as cross-border placements (section 39(8) and Schedule 1)). This is because social care is a devolved matter for Scotland, Wales and Northern Ireland.

The Care Act is supported by statutory guidance (DHSC, 2018a) issued under section 78 and available online.[2] Local authorities must follow this guidance unless they have good reason not to, but without the freedom to take a substantially different course.[3]

The following provides a brief summary of the Care Act's key provisions.

The general duties

Sections 1 to 7 place a number of general duties (also known as target duties) on local authorities. These are not expressed as being owed to any specific individual but rather towards the relevant population as a whole. Local authorities have considerable discretion in determining how to implement these duties and they can therefore be difficult to enforce.

Section 1 is a general duty on local authorities to promote the wellbeing of the adult when carrying out functions under the Act. This applies to every decision under the Act which relates to an individual. The Act does not precisely define wellbeing, but sets out a list of outcomes and a list of matters that must be considered before a decision is made.

Section 2 requires local authorities to provide or arrange prevention services, facilities or resources, or take other steps aimed at prevention. This includes services which are intended to prevent, reduce or delay needs for care and support for all local people (for example, exercise classes, befriending schemes and information centres).

Section 3 places a general duty on local authorities to carry out their responsibilities with the aim of integrating services with those provided by the NHS and other health services. Integration can mean many things including joint commissioning, single assessments, sharing information, and the delivery of care and treatment through generic teams and single locations.

Section 4 requires local authorities to establish and maintain a service for providing people in its area with information and advice relating to care and support. The service should be available to all people in the local authority's area regardless of whether they have needs for care and support.

Section 5 places a general duty on local authorities to promote the efficient and effective operation of the market of care and support providers. This is known as 'market shaping'. In particular, local authorities must aim to ensure that there is a range of different and high-quality services and providers to choose from.

Section 6 requires local authorities and their 'relevant partners' (such as the NHS and the police) to co-operate with each other in the exercise of their respective care and support functions. In addition, section 7 enables a local authority to request co-operation from a relevant partner, and a relevant partner to request co-operation from a local authority.

The needs assessment

Section 9 contains the duty to carry out a needs assessment. The duty is triggered where it appears to a local authority that an adult may have care and support needs. This sets a low threshold; the duty is triggered irrespective of the level of the adult's needs or financial resources. The adult in question is given a right to refuse the assessment (section 10). However, this does not apply if the adult lacks the capacity to do so, and the assessment would be in their best interests, or if there are safeguarding concerns. In such cases the local authority must persist with the assessment.

The assessment must involve the adult, their carer, and anyone else named by the adult. Regulations issued under the Care Act make provision for supported self-assessment, where the individual and the local authority carry out the assessment jointly. They also require that assessments must be 'appropriate and proportionate' and that assessments concerning an individual who is deafblind must be carried out by a specialist.[4]

The carer's assessment

Section 10 contains a duty on local authorities to carry out an assessment when it appears that a carer may have support needs. Like the needs assessment duty, this sets a low threshold. In carrying out the assessment the local authority must also have regard to whether a carer works or wishes to work, or participates in, or would like to participate in, education, training or recreation. Under section 11, the refusal by a carer of their carer's assessment would, in all cases, discharge the local authority's duty to assess.

The eligibility criteria

Following an assessment, local authorities must decide whether a person's needs are sufficient to meet the eligibility criteria. The national eligibility criteria for adults with care and support needs and carers are set out in the Care and Support (Eligibility Criteria) Regulations 2015 (DoH, 2015b).[5] In order for an adult to meet the eligibility criteria, the following must apply:

- the adult's needs must arise from or be related to a physical or mental impairment or illness,

- as a result the adult must be unable to achieve two or more specified outcomes (the list includes, for instance, managing toileting needs, and developing or maintaining relationships), and

- consequently, there is (or is likely to be) a significant impact on the adult's wellbeing.

The regulations also include separate eligibility criteria for carers, which are similar to the above, but have been adapted to reflect the different situation of carers.

Charging and the funding system

Unlike the NHS, social care is not (and has never been) a free, universal service. Section 14 gives local authorities the power to charge for meeting needs (subject to the financial assessment). The detail is contained in regulations.[6]

The Care Act also includes provisions which would introduce a cap on care costs and other reforms recommended by the Commission on Funding Care and Support (see above). However, these reforms have not been implemented.

Duty to meet needs

Section 18 places a duty on local authorities to meet an adult's needs for care and support, if the needs meet the eligibility criteria, and the adult is ordinarily resident in the local authority area (or has no settled residence in any area, but is living in the local authority). There is a complicated interaction between this duty and the charging regulations, but in broad terms the duty will arise if:

- the local authority does not charge for the type of care and support, or regulations provide that it is to be provided for free, or
- the local authority does charge for the type of care and support, and
  - the adult's financial resources are assessed as being at or below the financial limit,
  - the adult's financial resources are assessed as being above the financial limit, and the adult requests that the local authority meets their needs,[7] or
  - the adult lacks the mental capacity to arrange care and support, and there is no other in a position to arrange that care and support on their behalf.

Section 19 gives local authorities the powers to meet needs, for example if the adult's needs fall below the eligibility criteria or in urgent cases in lieu of an assessment being completed.

Section 20 provides a duty and powers to meet a carer's needs for support, which are very similar to those which apply to adults with needs.

Care planning

If a local authority is required or decides to meet the needs of an adult or carer, it is required under section 24 to provide a care plan. The key components include a list of the needs that the local authority is going to meet and how it will meet them, and information and advice on reducing and preventing needs. The plan must also include the person's personal budget – which is the amount of the money the local authority has decided is sufficient to meet the person's needs. In some cases, direct payments will be available to allow the adult to arrange services for themselves (sections 31 to 33).

Continuity of care

Sections 37 and 38 aim to assist existing service users who are moving from one local authority area to another. They require that if a service user intends to move, the new authority must carry out a needs assessment. If the authority does not carry out the assessment before the adult arrives in the new area, it must provide care and support based on the care and support plan of the original authority until it is able to carry out its own assessment.

Advocacy

Sections 67 and 68 place duties on local authorities to arrange for independent advocates to represent and support the adult. These apply to individuals who experience substantial difficulty in understanding, retaining, or using or weighing relevant information, or communicating their views, wishes and feelings, and if there is no other appropriate person to represent and support the individual.

Safeguarding adults from abuse and neglect

Section 42 requires local authorities to make necessary safeguarding enquiries, or cause such enquiries to take place, in individual cases. This duty is triggered if the person has care and support needs (irrespective of whether or not those needs are being met by services), is at risk of or experiencing abuse and neglect, and is unable to safeguard themselves.

Section 43 requires a local authority to establish a Safeguarding Adults Board, which is a strategic body that aims to help and protect adults at risk of abuse and neglect. One of its key functions is to arrange Adult Safeguarding Reviews in certain cases when an adult with care and support needs has died as a result of abuse or neglect, or is still alive and has experienced 'serious abuse or neglect'. The duty to arrange such reviews is contained in section 44. The aim of the review is to identify the lessons to be learnt, and apply those lessons to future cases. Access to information is crucial to how an Adult Safeguarding Board exercises its functions. Section 45 places a duty on a person to share information when requested by the Safeguarding Adults Board if certain criteria apply.

Early messages from case law

At the time of writing the implementation of the Care Act has not generated the tsunami of case law that was predicted by some. Instead, there has been a steady trickle of reported cases, and no major decisions on matters of legal principle. There are many possible reasons for this, such as the lack of availability of legal aid to fund such cases. In addition, local authority decisions can only be judicially reviewed on the basis of unlawfulness and irrationality, which are challenging to prove when much of the Act gives local authorities flexibility and discretion.

The courts have been willing to order local authorities to quash flawed assessments and order them to be redone. For example, in *R (SG) v Haringey Council* [2015], the failure of the local authority to provide an advocate to an asylum seeker who suffered from mental health problems (including PTSD, insomnia, depression and anxiety) meant that the needs assessment had to be carried out again.[8] In *R (JF) v Merton* [2017] the court decided to quash an assessment which had failed to explain why the person no longer needed a residential college placement which included support from an onsite multidisciplinary team and appeared to have been carried out on the assumption that this placement would no longer be available.

The courts have also confirmed that the wishes and feelings of disabled people can be a primary influence but do not amount to an overriding consideration for local authorities making care and support decisions. In *Davey v Oxfordshire* [2017], a disabled man argued that the cuts in his personal budget had failed to take into account sufficiently his wishes and feelings and his rights to independent living under the UN Convention on the Rights of Persons with Disabilities. However, the court found that the section 1 wellbeing duty of the Care Act sets a balance between the wishes and feelings of the person and the assessment of the local authority, and that ultimately decisions are taken by the local authority.[9]

The care planning process under the Care Act has received some consideration by the courts. For example, in *CP v North East Lincolnshire Council* [2018] the court emphasised that local authorities need to ensure personal budgets clearly set out what services they are intended to fund and how the budget is calculated, to ensure it is sufficient to fund all of the proposed services.

Few cases have considered the general duties of local authorities. A notable exemption was *R (Care England) v Essex County Council* [2017], where it was held that the local authority had not breached its section 5 marketing shaping duty when making a limited increase to the fees it paid to care home providers. The court accepted that one aspect of promoting market efficiency can be by ensuring that fees are not set too high and that benefiting care providers was not the purpose of section 5.

Outside of the court system, the Local Government and Social Care Ombudsman investigates complaints against local authority decisions under the Care Act. Their 'landmark cases', which are those which give authorities an opportunity to learn and check their own practice, have included the following:

- Problems in commissioning suitable homecare which meant that a married couple had to spend 10 months apart because the woman couldn't return home after a routine operation. In this case the local authority agreed to identify which other families may have suffered an injustice and act accordingly (LGSCO and Lincolnshire County Council (2017)).

- Delays in providing a specialist chair which meant that a man spent the last month of his life in bed. In this case, the local authority agreed to a number of steps to improve services, including looking at how it resourced occupational therapy services (LGSCO and Lancashire County Council (2017)).

On a few occasions, local authorities have resisted the Ombudsman's recommendations. Ultimately such cases may end up in court. One such case involved a disabled woman who had approached her local authority for support, and was told that her personal injury award would be taken into account for the purpose of the financial assessment and charging for services. Following a successful complaint by the woman, the authority disputed the Ombudsman's view that personal injury awards should be disregarded. The case went to court which dismissed the authority's case as being 'totally without merit' (LGSCO, 2018b: 7).

Some general observations

The Care Act is an unusual hybrid of different legislative approaches. In some places it is designed to be non-prescriptive and encourage innovation. Section 1, for example, sets out the core purpose of promoting individual wellbeing, which intentionally covers a broad range of general outcomes and matters. This duty is something that guides social workers to ask the right questions and sets a pathway to be followed, rather than providing the answer. But it would be a mistake to think that the Care Act lacks specificity. In many places the Care Act is prescriptive and process-driven, for example detailing what assessments must cover, how an assessment should be carried out and the contents of a care plan. The Care Act also maintains strong legal duties which are owed to service users; most notably the enforceable duties to carry out an assessment and to meet needs. Social workers and other decision-makers will therefore need to be clear about which provisions they are acting under, and the implications for the legal rights of service users.

The Care Act was intended to deliver a more personalised approach. The key elements of personalisation are now codified in legislation, such as self-assessments, personal budgets and direct payments. There has been a move away from a deficit-based assessment towards greater focus on the outcomes that people want to achieve, and recognition that the individual is best-placed to judge their own wellbeing. Delivering personalisation remains challenging in the current economic climate with financial cuts being made to local authority budgets. The use of self-assessments, personal budgets, and direct payments can be empowering for many people, but also brings challenges (especially where safeguarding issues or the needs of carers go undetected) and has been criticised by some as a cost-cutting exercise. Social workers will need to be alive to the opportunities that personalisation offers for many service users, as well as the dangers.

Integration and co-operation between social services and other organisations (particularly the NHS) is rightly seen as essential for effective service delivery. Numerous high-profile cases have also provided vivid reminders of the potential tragic consequences when service users fall between services. The Care Act nudges local authorities towards integration and co-operation through its general duties. However, barriers remain such as cultural differences, a lack of trust between organisations, and a lack of resources to explore new approaches. It is also vital to recognise that as a matter of law, health and social care are separate entities. Health care is governed primarily by the NHS Act 2006 and in broad terms is a universal service delivered free at the point of use. In contrast, social care is often targeted toward those with high needs and means tested. The divide between health and social care continues to be highly contested, and the Care Act does little to change this situation.

The introduction of a national eligibility threshold was intended to provide greater certainty and consistency on who is entitled to services. Local authorities are no longer permitted to vary the upper threshold for services (which had previously led to accusations of a 'postcode lottery' for service provision). Sections 18 and 20 of the Care Act require local authorities to meet a person's needs, and these duties apply irrespective of local authority resources. However, concerns remain that in practice individual social workers and local authorities interpret the criteria in different ways, and the provision and quality of services in different local authority areas varies.

Self-funders were intended to be major beneficiaries of the Care Act. For example, the duty to assess was carefully drafted to apply to self-funders, information and advice (including how to access) is available to self-funders, there is a duty on local authorities to offer a deferred payment scheme, and in certain circumstances local authorities are required to arrange the care of self-funders. Yet many benefits of the Care Act have not been fully realised for self-funders. For example, the duty to meet the needs of self-funders has only been implemented for those who need domiciliary care, and not those who require residential care. Furthermore, plans to introduce a cap on care costs and an increase in the upper means test threshold for state support have not been taken forward.

Adult safeguarding was for the first time in England given statutory recognition in the Care Act. Yet, for some, the framework – which primarily consists of an investigation duty and statutory boards – is viewed as minimalistic. This is not the case across the UK. For example, the Adult Support and Protection (Scotland) Act 2007 includes various compulsory powers intended to protect adults who are unable to safeguard their own interests, such as compulsory removal and banning orders. The Social Services and Well-being (Wales) Act 2014 also provides for orders to authorise entry to premises (if necessary by force) in safeguarding cases. Consequently there is no consistent UK-wide approach to adult safeguarding powers.

Conclusion

It is vital that the Care Act can provide an effective framework governing adult social care. At some point, most of us will need care and support, either for ourselves or for a friend or family member. The overall numbers are likely to continue to grow. The Act has laudable aims. It places the wellbeing, needs and goals of people at the centre of the legislation to create care and support which fits around the individual and works for them. It provides a focus on preventing and reducing needs, and putting people in control of their care and support. It brings carers into the heart of the law, on a par with those for whom they care. The ongoing challenge for social work practice is to ensure that these aims become a reality.

Further Reading

Commission on Funding of Care and Support (2011) *Fairer Care Funding: The Report of the Commission on Funding of Care and Support: Volume 1*.

Law Commission (2011) *Adult Social Care, Law Com No 326*. London: Law Commission.

Spencer-Lane, T. (2015) *Care Act Manual* (2nd edn) London: Sweet & Maxwell.

R (Davey) v Oxfordshire CC [2017] EWCA Civ 1308.

Notes

1. The Law Commission is a non-political independent body, set up by Parliament in 1965, to keep all of the law of England and Wales under review, and to recommend reform where it is needed.

2. www.gov.uk/government/publications/care-act-statutory-guidance

3. See para 472 of the explanatory notes, and *R. v Islington LBC, Ex p Rixon* (1998) 1 CCLR 119.

4. SI 2014/2827.

5. SI 2015/313

6. SI 2014/2672.

7. However, this only applies to needs that are not being met by a care home placement.

8. Other aspects of the local authority's care planning were upheld in *R(SG) v Haringey LBC* [2017].

9. The local authority's decision was upheld in *R (Davey) v Oxfordshire CC* [2017].

3 Implementing the Care Act: assessing need and providing care and support

John Crossland

Introduction

This chapter focuses primarily on assessment and care planning for adults with care and support needs. Where appropriate it touches on the interface between assessment and other themes in this book, including carers, safeguarding adults at risk, and the interface with the Mental Capacity Act. The chapter proceeds from the assumption that assessment is a professional practice (or set of practices) that is undertaken in the context of the framework introduced by the Care Act 2014 (and not that the Care Act itself defines assessment practice). Therefore it begins by outlining a fundamental tension between the legislative promise of the Care Act and the financial climate within which it is being interpreted and applied, a key background theme that will be returned to throughout the chapter. It then explores what is understood by 'assessment' in social work more generally, before setting out and unpicking key aspects of the legislation in relation to different ways in which assessment and care planning can be undertaken. It also presents relevant findings from a small-scale unpublished study conducted by the author between 2016 and 2018 in collaboration with a single local authority, which explored how social workers and other assessment staff were making sense of the Care Act in practice.

Context

It is important to acknowledge a core tension framing the Care Act's continuing implementation. The new legislation, which was subject to detailed and lengthy public consultation (Law Commission, 2011) and developed with support across the political spectrum (including a Parliamentary joint select committee), has many widely recognised positive features (Cooper and Bruin, 2017; Crossland, 2016; Feldon, 2017a; Romeo, 2018; Whittington, 2016b). These include the embedding of safeguarding in primary legislation and a focus on social networks, community assets and strengths-based approaches that embraces modern social work more explicitly than the previous legislative framework.

However, its implementation in the increasingly difficult financial climate of austerity, which has impacted especially on local government (*The Economist*, 2017), clearly constrains its potential. This tension is highlighted in Whittington's (2016b) early analysis of the statutory guidance (DHSC, 2018a). This not only finds positive evidence of social work orientated, person-centred and socially-contextualised practice, but also highlights the political and economic environment that threatens to compromise those positive elements. Similar concerns emerged in a hard-hitting joint report from the King's Fund and the Nuffield Trust (Humphries et al., 2016), which quantified the problem in relation to social care for older people and warned of a serious risk that local authorities will struggle to meet their statutory duties within a five-year timeframe. It is not an exaggeration to speak of a crisis in social care funding (ADASS, 2018a).

However, the challenges inherent in identifying needs in contexts of limited resources is neither new (Ellis, 2011) nor unique to England (see for example Dunér, 2017, who investigates this issue in the context of older people's services in Sweden). There is a longstanding tension between social workers' roles as gatekeepers of resources and as advocates of socially excluded citizens (Symonds et al., 2018). However, it is also important to recognise local variation in the circumstances of (and approaches to) the implementation of the Care Act across 150 English councils with adult social services responsibilities and to acknowledge that, even within the most constrained circumstances, there is always space for discretion (and therefore professional judgement) at the micro level. The degree to which discretion in social work is curtailed by policy, procedures and/or management has long been contested (Ellis, 2011; Evans and Harris, 2004; Howe, 1991; Lymbery, 1998) but, as Evans and Harris argue, the existence of rules does not preclude discretion; their existence in fact creates the conditions for discretion. The question always remains of which rules apply in which circumstances, creating space for an element of 'street-level bureaucracy' (Lipsky, 1980) that, in this context of assessment and care planning under a new piece of legislation that has barely been tested in the courts, points to the crucial role of how social workers interpret the legislation in their day-to-day practice (Feldon, 2017a). Indeed, Preston-Shoot (2000) highlights the multiple accountabilities of professional social workers and the role legal literacy can play in challenging or resisting agency pressures to interpret legislation in ways that may be so restrictive as to be unlawful.

The wider policy tension at the macro level clearly needs to be addressed and the anticipated (but significantly delayed) Green Paper on social care for older people (Jarrett, 2019), with its core focus on funding, needs to be seen as a response to this, however well or badly it addresses the depth of crisis in the sector. For the present, however, this tension must be taken as read in relation to the remaining sections of this chapter.

Assessment

Milner et al. (2015) note the wide-ranging legislative reforms in the early 1990s that clarified the distinction between assessment and intervention. Of these, the 1990 NHS and Community Care Act (NHSCCA) and its associated statutory guidance set out in most detail how assessment was to be understood and enacted as a key but separate component of a process of 'care management', the variant of case management prescribed at the time (Department of Health, 1991). This distinction has since become commonplace. Summarising a range of definitions of assessment, Milner et al. define 'assessment' as a five-stage process of exploring a situation, which includes: preparing for the task; collecting data, including from service users and other agencies; applying professional knowledge for analysis, understanding or interpretation; making judgements based on that analysis; and deciding and/or recommending what is to be done.

In this definition *analysis* refers to sense-making activities that include synthesising events and statements to come to an overall picture of a situation and what is currently happening, with some conceptualisation of how the situation has come about, using one or more of a range of theoretical frameworks. *Judgement* concerns what is (and is not) good enough, what is dangerous and what is safe. *Deciding* is about future action and inaction, review and accountability. Milner et al. note the differing levels of guidance found in policy that often focuses on the data-gathering phase and less often on data analysis, which as we shall see is also a factor in the Care Act. They also highlight Smale and Tuson's (1993, cited in Milner et al., 2015: 48) identification of three models of assessment linked to social workers' ostensible focus on risk, resources or needs. In the *questioning* model, the social worker acts as an expert following a format of questions shaped by the social worker's (often risk-focused) agenda, combined with listening to and processing answers according to the practitioner's preferred theories of human functioning. In the *procedural* model, the social worker acts on behalf of the agency to determine whether the criteria for the provision of services (resources) are met, and in the *exchange* model people are viewed as experts on their own problems and social workers 'exchange' information by tracking (rather than interpreting) what people say (to identify needs, strengths and goals) and consider how best to help service users to engage both internal and external resources to reach the goals they have set for themselves.

Aspects of all three models can be identified in the Care Act and associated guidance (DHSC, 2018a). Nosowska (2014) in turn highlights two central values, autonomy and fairness, that must be balanced in the practice of assessment in statutory settings, which then link to two key roles of assessors as both empowering helpers and agents of the state. Autonomy underpins actions to support people in making their own decisions and pursuing their individual wellbeing. Fairness ensures that resources are distributed according to need. It is in the balancing of these two roles that the increasing tensions between the ambitions of the legislation and the current financial climate are played out.

Assessment and eligibility under the Care Act

Assessment is a core legal right for all adults who may have needs for care and support (section 9(1)) and has been a central feature of adult social care legislation since the NHSCCA (Law Commission, 2011). The threshold for the duty to assess was confirmed in the case of *R v Bristol City Council ex parte Penfold* (1998) as 'very low', specifically that local authorities must assess where there is an appearance of needs for care and support or if an adult is disabled. In this section, key aspects of the current legislative framework for assessment are set out and considered in relation to the wider professional task of assessment.

There is an enormous volume of legal information on assessment and eligibility for support that practitioners need to take into account, spread across the Act, its regulations and the related statutory guidance (DHSC, 2018a). The latter component alone contains over 35 pages of detailed guidance on assessment. In addition, there is considerable supplementary guidance from other sources such as the Social Care Institute for Excellence (SCIE, 2015a), which produced an early guide to eligibility determination, and more recently, Feldon's (2017a) comprehensive guide to the legislation for social workers. It is important to keep in mind the challenging circumstances in which practitioners are expected to absorb new knowledge too (Bee, 2015; Diaper and Yeomans, 2016), an issue raised by senior practitioners in my study, who spoke of the tensions associated with learning 'on the hoof'.

Neither the Care Act nor the statutory guidance tell social care professionals specifically how to conduct an assessment; rather they give advice on certain aspects and set out principles that must be incorporated into the encounter, in particular that it must be person-centred, appropriate and proportionate. Indeed, there is now a duty to have regard to the wishes and preferences of the individual (section 1(3)b). The Local Government Ombudsman's decision in *LGO and Barking and Dagenham LBC* (2016), for example, found fault in the Council's failure to show how Mr Z's needs and wishes had been taken into account in a reassessment and subsequent care plan.

The Care Act, then, presents a framework for a person-centred[1] system, which acknowledges people's strengths and capabilities as well as their needs, and places the concept of 'individual wellbeing' at its heart. It introduces a duty to provide independent advocacy support (section 67) where it is clear that, without such support, the individual would experience substantial difficulties in engaging with both assessment and care planning processes (confirmed in a judicial review, *R(SG) v London Borough of Haringey* [2015]). It creates a general legal duty for a local authority to promote individual wellbeing in the exercise of its care and support functions, which include assessment and care or support planning. It outlines nine different dimensions of wellbeing, all of which are to be regarded as equal to each other. There is no hierarchy, for example, that suggests 'protection from abuse and neglect' is more important than 'participation in work, education, training or recreation'.

The Act also outlines a number of additional principles the authority must have regard to, which include assuming the individual is best placed to judge their own wellbeing (section 1(3)a), emphasising the importance of prevention (the focus of section 2 of the Act), and incorporating the principle of the 'least restrictive option' (section 1(3)h), all of which are central to assessment. Section 18 details the local authority's duty to meet eligible needs for care and support, as long as specific conditions regarding ordinary residence and financial assessment are met.

However, a key difference in the new legal framework lies in the fact that local authorities no longer have a duty to provide particular *services* or to determine whether adults are in need of those services (Feldon, 2017a). Instead, local authorities must first assess needs and determine if they are eligible before then considering how to meet those needs. Section 8 sets out a range of ways those needs *may* (not must) be met, which include the provision of information/advice (as set out in section 4) and social work interventions, in addition to care and support services either in a care home or in the community. This must all be understood in light of Paragraph 1.17 of the statutory guidance (DHSC, 2018a), which states *'neither these principles, nor the requirement to promote well-being, require the local authority to undertake any particular action'*. The statutory framework then for the relationship between assessment of need and the provision of services has changed considerably.

Section 9: Assessment of an adult's needs for care and support

Section 9 clarifies the local authority's duty to assess an adult where it appears they may have needs for care and support, which must take place regardless of the apparent level of need and regardless of the adult's financial resources (thereby closing the door to the previous common practice of avoiding assessment of potential 'self-funders'). Section 9(4) states the needs assessment must evaluate the impact of the adult's needs for care and support on their wellbeing as set out in section 1(2), identify the outcomes the adult wishes to achieve, and consider whether the provision of care and support could contribute to the achievement of those outcomes (see also *R (Davey) vs Oxfordshire CC* [2017] below). This resonates, to some extent, with the *exchange* model of assessment and the role of *empowering helper* outlined above. Section 9(5) specifies who must be included in the assessment and section 9(6) outlines a duty to consider interventions or provisions other than care and support that could contribute to the achievement of their outcomes and whether the adult could benefit from the provision of anything under sections 2 (prevention), 4 (information or advice), or anything in the community. Section 10 similarly outlines the duty to assess a carer where it appears they may have needs for support deriving from the provision (or intention to provide) care for another adult, which must take into account the impact of those caring responsibilities on the carer's desire or ability to work or take part in education, training or leisure (DHSC, 2018a: para 6.19). The process is broadly similar but with some difference in the detail regarding outcomes for carers (addressed in more detail elsewhere in this volume).

Section 13: The eligibility criteria

An assessment under the Care Act must identify the person's needs and then determine if those needs are 'eligible'. The determination of the eligibility of identified needs is a three-stage process, set out in the Care and Support (Eligibility Criteria) Regulations (DoH, 2015b) sections 2 (1) and 2 (2). Firstly it must be shown that the adult's needs relate to a physical or mental impairment or illness. Secondly, as a consequence of those needs, the adult must be unable to achieve two or more of the ten outcomes identified in the regulations, most of which focus on activities of daily living (e.g. 'maintaining personal hygiene'), with others more focused on social factors (e.g. 'developing and maintaining family or other personal relationships'). Finally, it must be shown how the inability to achieve these outcomes has a significant impact (DHSC, 2018a: para 6.108) on the adult's wellbeing. The interrelationship between these three factors (needs, impact on desired outcomes, and consequences for wellbeing) is critical to determining eligibility, i.e. whether the local authority must meet those needs by providing interventions in line with section 8 of the Act.

The term 'unable to' is further specified (regulations 2(3)a-d) in relation to: requirements for assistance; consequences in terms of pain, distress or anxiety; dangers to health and safety; and the length of time required to undertake a task. The regulations also give advice on evaluating fluctuating needs. This is all practically helpful but effectively emphasises a deficit focus to the application of the eligibility criteria, thereby highlighting aspects of both the *questioning* and *procedural* models of assessment noted above, and the unavoidable role of *agent of the state*.

The statutory guidance (DHSC, 2018a) further says that local authorities must consider the person's own strengths and capabilities alongside any support available from their wider network or community that might contribute towards achieving their desired outcomes (paragraphs 6.2 and 6.5). Indeed, strengths-based approaches have become the 'new normal' (Romeo and Hunter, 2017; SCIE, 2015b; Slasberg and Beresford, 2017b), despite the guidance saying little to specify what applying a strengths-based approach might involve (Feldon, 2017a). It ostensibly replaces 'care management' as a template for practice, although it is worth noting that three of the core tasks of care management (Department of Health, 1991), i.e. assessment (sections 9 and 10), care and support planning (section 25), and review (section 27), are now directly embedded in the statute. Indeed, Slasberg and Beresford (2017b) describe strengths-based approaches as 'the new elixir', and argue the problems this shift is meant to resolve are systemic and beyond the reach of a change of approach alone.

The 'whole family approach' (DHSC, 2018a: para 6.65 to 6.74) requires local authorities to identify how the adult's needs for care and support impact on family members (including children) or others in their social network, including whether a carer's assessment may be required. Indeed, the guidance routinely uses terms such as 'family or friends', 'family or other support network' (rather than 'family' alone) in a manner that indicates at least some awareness of the different ways adults' networks may be constructed (with important consequences for anti-discriminatory practice: see for example Crossland (2016) on working with older people in LGBT communities), the central principle being the requirement to see people not simply as individuals in need of care but to understand them in the context of their families and/or other support networks. The process of assessment is set out in the guidance as below:

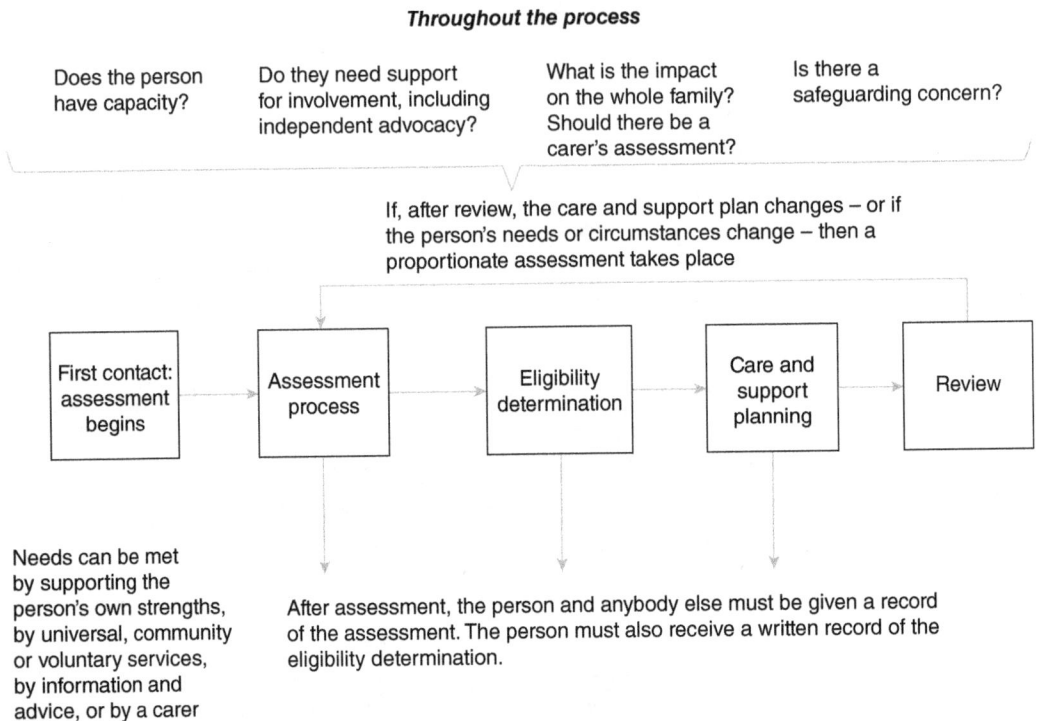

Throughout the process

| Does the person have capacity? | Do they need support for involvement, including independent advocacy? | What is the impact on the whole family? Should there be a carer's assessment? | Is there a safeguarding concern? |

If, after review, the care and support plan changes – or if the person's needs or circumstances change – then a proportionate assessment takes place

First contact: assessment begins → Assessment process → Eligibility determination → Care and support planning → Review

Needs can be met by supporting the person's own strengths, by universal, community or voluntary services, by information and advice, or by a carer

After assessment, the person and anybody else must be given a record of the assessment. The person must also receive a written record of the eligibility determination.

Figure 3.1 Needs assessment (DHSC, 2018a)

It is possible to map, if imperfectly, Milner et al.'s (2015) five-stage model (preparation, data collection, analysis, judgement and decision making/recommendation) to the process model outlined above, but the two central activities of data collection and analysis are not clearly delineated, reflecting the authors' observation that 'analysis' is often missing in policy guidance. Potentially, the two activities span the first three components of 'first contact', 'assessment' and 'eligibility determination', but it is important to consider the collection and analysis of data much more explicitly. What information are you collecting and to what purpose? What sources of information are you using? How are you balancing the potentially conflicting requirements of a deficit focus ('unable to achieve') on outcomes that must be related to a physical or mental impairment or illness, with the broader strengths/assets approach now also required? What sense are you (and the service user) making of the various types of information you are collecting?

Greater consideration should be given to techniques of assessment and tools for analysis within the Care Act's assessment process. For example, the Care Act's focus on assessing adults in relation to their social networks should be reflected in the use of appropriate analytical tools. Genograms and ecograms map people's relationships, providing a framework for discussing family (and other) relationships and identifying the nature and impact of important links in service users' lives (Dyke, 2016). It has long been known that the quality and type of social network has consequences for both health and wellbeing for older people (Litwin and Shiovitz-Ezra, 2010; Wenger, 1991, 1997) and yet these tools are primarily associated with practice in children's rather than adults' services. The focus on assessing adults in the context of their social networks would also suggest that a systems-orientated theoretical framework (Teater, 2010) could be helpful in guiding analysis in Care Act assessments.

In summary, then, the Act and its statutory guidance (DHSC, 2018a) create a statutory framework in which the assessor must identify, in a person-centred and proportionate process that takes the adult's wider social network into account, the following:

1. Any specific needs that arise as a consequence of a physical or mental impairment or illness. This requires knowledge of that condition, its general effects (potentially requiring the assessor to undertake some basic research), as well as the specific impact on this particular person in the context of their wider family, social network or community (identified appropriately and informed by anti-discriminatory practice). The decision of the Local Government Ombudsman in LGO and Northamptonshire County Council (2016) is instructive here, finding that an assessment process failed to take into account a particular individual's specific needs as a deaf adult.

2. Which outcomes (as specified in the regulations) are constrained ('unable to') by those needs. This requires linking or mapping those specific impacts to particular outcomes, and analysing data acquired through interview, observation, and/or reports from carers, other professionals or services, for example.

3. The extent to which the person's wellbeing (based on their own judgement of what is important) is impacted by the inability to achieve those outcomes. As Barnes et al. (2017) note, two people with the same needs in relation to specific outcomes could end up with a different assessment of eligibility. What is fundamental to one person's sense of wellbeing may be unimportant to another. If wellbeing is not significantly affected then the same 'need' can be ineligible for one person as may be eligible for another. There is considerable space for professional judgement in this component of a Care Act assessment. Tensions can also arise between the principle of respecting the autonomy of the service user and a professional duty of care, as identified by Preston-Shoot (2018) in his review of Safeguarding Adults Reviews. For example, the outcome 'maintaining a habitable home environment' (Care Act regulations 2(2)f.) can have very different meanings for different individuals, and must be understood in relation to the principles of the Mental

Capacity Act, including the right to an unwise decision. Judging what is good enough and what might be dangerous is both complex and critical in this phase and shades into considerations of safeguarding (sections 42–44), particularly in relation to self-neglect, an area that generated considerable comment and anxiety in this author's study too.

The Luke Davey judicial review (*R (Davey) vs Oxfordshire CC* [2017]) clarified that, under section 9(4), it is not necessary to ensure outcomes are achieved; rather there is a duty to assess whether the provision of care and support could *contribute to* achieving those outcomes. Before considering any such provision, however, the assessor must also determine whether the provision of either information/advice or preventative services could prevent or delay the need for care or support, before finally deciding which needs are eligible and recommending how those needs might be met in line with section 8. These are the core areas in which Milner et al.'s (2015) phases of preparation for the task, data collection and analysis, making judgements and recommendations must be undertaken in the process of assessment within the complex framework of the Care Act.

Professional judgement

In the only study to date of assessment practices in the context of the Care Act, Symonds et al. (2018) identified the difficult balancing of professional judgement with the nurturing of autonomy in the client as a key tension in their findings from interviews with thirty social care assessors across four local authorities. Assessors saw themselves as allies of clients (sic) but also felt they had to exert professional judgement in deciding on the needs of those who (in their view) lacked competence (rather than capacity) to decide on their own outcomes or needs (begging the question of why independent advocacy support was not considered), as evidenced by either an under- or overstatement of their needs and wishes. The social work role was portrayed in Symonds et al.'s study as an interface between client and system, occupying a position in which assessors' allegiances faced both ways (i.e. towards the client, but also as a representative of the system that shapes their practice) which they report can lead to feelings of powerlessness in relation to that bureaucracy. The authors suggest the social care practitioner can be best understood as interacting with both the client and the social care system, but positioned at the decision-making nexus between the two, where the skill of professional judgement is key.

Indeed, a social worker's professional judgement sat at the heart of Luke Davey's judicial review, which hinged on the interpretation of 'need' in relation to time spent alone. In that case, the social worker's view that spending periods of time alone would be beneficial for Mr Davey was agreed as 'reasonable' under the law. This was constructed as a 'need' to develop independence by the social worker, not Mr Davey, and accepted as such within the framework of the legislation by the judge, even though this was partly based on evidence given in court rather than entirely derived from the original assessment documentation. The judgement states:

> *That was a social worker's assessment which could not be regarded as Wednesbury unrea-sonable[2] and was a matter for her professional judgment ... I am satisfied that Ms Lovelock and Ms Collins did genuinely believe both that developing the Claimant's independence was a need and that spending more time alone was a way in which to achieve this end.*

How social workers approach their assessments can be significantly shaped by the paperwork they are required to use in their local settings. Local authorities may adopt a *defensive* (Harris, 1987) approach to assessment using documentation that itemises every outcome and dimension of wellbeing, for example, but which carries the risk of embedding a 'tick-box' process to assessment.

Other approaches can be more open-ended, examples of which would include the development of a 'conversation record' in Leeds that replaces the previous assessment documentation and has neither service-led nor needs-led questions (Romeo, 2018), and the 3 Conversations model (CareKnowledge, 2018), adopted in a number of different authorities. Strong claims have been made that the latter can liberate practitioners to return to a more relationship-focused approach whilst simultaneously reducing demand for formal care services. It is claimed that when the 3 Conversations model was applied to 100 people in a specific local authority area, the overall cost of care and support (£750k) was reduced by £100k (SCIE, 2017). The model focuses primarily on people's strengths and community assets, clearly locating it within the 'strengths-based' framework promoted since the passing of the Care Act (Romeo, 2018; Romeo and Hunter, 2017; SCIE, 2015b). The first conversation is designed to explore people's needs and connect them to any personal, family or community sources of support. The second conversation should be service user-led and seek to address levels of risk and any crisis contingencies that may be required. The third and final conversation should focus on long-term outcomes and planning, constructed around the service user's view of what a good life would look like and how best to mobilise the resources to support that, including any formal personal budget.

One of the risks with more open approaches derives from practitioners' reasonable anxieties that they may 'miss something', an issue that was indeed raised in this author's own small study (see below). Indeed, in the Luke Davey case, the judge confirmed that if, in the course of a needs assessment, the local authority does not assess the matters specified in s.9(4) (including the impact on wellbeing set out in section 1(2)), then there is a breach of the statutory duty. In addition, in the second judicial review (*R (JF) v London Borough of Merton* [2017]) the London Borough of Merton made a decision that JF had no need for a particular service he had previously received but the assessment that was undertaken made no mention of this. The only evidence given with regard to how the decision was reached was in a witness statement from a social worker, which simply stated the decision was taken following a process of consultation and advice, with no further information as to when, how and by whom. The court ruled that it was therefore not possible to determine whether the local authority had taken into account the factors it was obliged to under the Care Act and its regulations, and therefore the assessment was Wednesbury unreasonable and unlawful.

This does not mean that social care assessors have to laboriously ensure they cover all aspects of the Care Act (which could in any case fail the proportionality test) but it does mean that anything raised by the individual being assessed (at the time of assessment) that pertains to matters specified in the Care Act must be taken into account, responded to and documented appropriately. Assessors under the Care Act should be reassured by further comments in the Luke Davey judgement that recognise social workers are entitled to rely on what service users tell them at the time of assessment. It also clearly states that courts should neither subject social care assessments to overzealous textual analysis nor be prescriptive to the degree of detail in assessments or care plans. As a rule, social workers in adult services are less exposed to legal processes (although this is slowly changing) and this may be a useful area for further development in social work education.

Care and support planning

A local authority's duty to meet needs (section 18) depends on a number of conditions, including ordinary residence and an assessment of the individual's own finances, most of which are not fundamentally different under the Care Act. However, as previously outlined, how eligible needs can be met has changed quite significantly, with local authorities no longer required to provide particular services nor to determine whether individuals are in need of those specific services (Feldon, 2017a). In this respect, the Act has broadened the territory considerably in terms of how eligible needs can be met, removing the reliance on services in favour of other ways of supporting people to achieve their outcomes, whilst reinforcing that eligible needs must indeed be met. In addition, the requirements of a care and support plan have been written into the legislation for the first time (section 25), along with the concept of a personal budget (section 26).

Care and support planning maps well onto the decision-making phase of assessment identified by Milner et al. (2015). The plan must always specify: the needs identified in the assessment; which of those needs meet the eligibility criteria; how the local authority will meet those eligible needs (as outlined in section 8); the relevant outcomes to which this contributes; the amount of the personal budget (see below); information and advice on ways to reduce, delay or prevent needs both currently and in the future; and which needs can be met via a direct payment (section 25(1)a–f). The statutory guidance (DHSC, 2018a: para 10.31) further emphasises that local authorities should 'encourage creativity' in planning how to meet needs. The amount of the personal budget, i.e. the net figure (less any contribution following financial assessment) allocated to an individual to meet eligible needs, is central here and must be clearly formulated in relation to any specified eligible needs. An Ombudsman's decision against one Council (LGSCO and Haringey LBC (2017)) found fault because it was not clear what the Council considered Ms X's eligible needs to be nor why it would not fund support for certain specific dietary needs. The personal budget must be sufficient to meet those needs and reflect the cost to the local authority too. Indeed, how the personal budget was determined formed part of Luke Davey's judicial review, with the judge noting that the amount must be calculated in relation to the specific service options identified in the care plan.

A move away from a 'traditional service-led approach' (SCIE, 2010) that saw many adults receive standardised care services to resolve any difficulties, regardless of their fit to an individual's needs, predates austerity. Indeed, it was central to the whole thrust of personalisation policy (Department of Health, 2007). The current focus on creativity in care planning that builds on personal strengths and community assets can be understood as a continuation of that policy direction. However, in the context of austerity, it can also be reasonably interpreted as a desire to minimise expenditure on formal care services.

How effective these new approaches may be is contested (SCIE, 2017; Slasberg and Beresford, 2017b) and there is little formal evidence to date. The alarm has already been sounded (Humphries et al., 2016) that austerity policies could lead local authorities to fail to meet their legal duties, and at the time of writing both Northamptonshire and East Sussex County Councils have stated their intention to strip services back to the legal minimum. What is arguably not yet clear, given the small number of judicial reviews to date, is what that 'legal minimum' might mean. It is in this uncertain space that Preston-Shoot's (2000) argument remains cogent, that well-developed legal literacy can support social care assessors in navigating that tension between their roles as empowering helpers and as agents of the state (Nosowska, 2014), and in challenging overly narrow and potentially unlawful definitions of a 'legal minimum'.

Study findings: making sense of the Care Act in practice

This small-scale study was undertaken to inform one local council's training and development activities. The questionnaire, which set out a number of key components of the Care Act (e.g. prevention, well-being, assessment, etc.), asked respondents to indicate first whether they found those components 'easy or difficult to understand' and 'easy or difficult to apply in practice', with options for additional free text commentary. Around 43% of social care assessment staff took part. A series of semi-structured group interviews with senior practitioners explored issues that arose in practice more broadly.

Unsurprisingly, the constraints deriving from a lack of resources came up quite strongly in both components of the study. Just over 90% of respondents in the questionnaire said they were either 'very confident' or 'quite confident' overall with regard to the Care Act. Indeed, there was a statistically significant relationship between 'length of service' and 'level of confidence' in the responses, with the most experienced feeling most confident. Other findings, however, highlighted significant gaps between understanding the principles of the Care Act and applying them in practice. This came through strongly in relation to the interpretation of 'wellbeing', for example, with additional comments highlighting: concerns about the relationship between promoting wellbeing and the availability of services; a perceived lack of distinction between wellbeing and outcomes; service users' own difficulties in understanding what wellbeing might mean and how that might impact on their expectations. The difficulty in promoting wellbeing when service users are often already in crisis at the point of contact was also raised.

Respondents also struggled to apply 'prevention' in practice too, primarily citing resource issues. By contrast, the provision of information and advice was seen as largely unproblematic, although this was not mentioned as a way of meeting needs. 'How to meet needs' was, in turn, experienced as considerably more difficult to apply in practice than to understand in principle. This was partly because of available resources (particularly with regard to specialist needs, an issue that framed Ombudsman decisions in both Northamptonshire and Haringey) but also the challenge of responding creatively and not falling into service-led solutions. Resonating to a degree with themes in the Luke Davey case, respondents also raised the issue of differing interpretations of needs and wishes between professionals and service users.

In terms of assessment, the eligibility criteria were experienced as more challenging to apply in practice than to understand, with a good deal of uncertainty coming though in the comments, including how best to interpret the criteria in mental health settings. This aspect was framed in this authority by a recent change in assessment paperwork away from a highly structured format to a largely free text form. This was welcomed overall but also generated some anxiety about how to ensure assessments were compliant with the Act, as noted above. Respondents struggled with understanding 'ordinary residence' rules, describing the ongoing 'ping pong' between authorities, despite changes in the Act. They also seriously struggled with applying 'independent advocacy support' in practice, citing contractual difficulties and unclear criteria from providers, which may have been local issues but also highlighted the difficulties with implementing new duties in difficult financial circumstances.

Conclusion

Underpinning this chapter is the assumption that the law provides a framework for practice but does not prescribe what social workers and other social care assessors must do in each and every case. There is considerable space for professional judgement, which is recognised as such in case law to date. The legislation is still relatively recent and will continue to be shaped through its application in practice, including reviews of that practice by the Local Government Ombudsman and reviews of the lawfulness of that practice through judicial review. Whilst these are uncomfortable processes to experience as a practitioner, they are helpful to social work and social care in general in clarifying the legal framework. Assessors are acting on behalf of the local authority, to which the duties under the Act pertain. Social workers in particular, because of the extent of their education in social care law, can and should use that knowledge to ensure that they continue to act as empowering helpers and that, when acting as agents of the state, they are confident that their employing authorities are interpreting the legal framework in an appropriate manner, even (or especially) in a context of considerable financial restraint.

Case study: Barbara

Barbara is a woman in her sixties who since the death of her husband has lived alone in a housing association flat. She has a number of complex health problems, including ulcerated legs for which she receives community nursing visits. She drinks a fair amount of alcohol and is also a heavy smoker, which suppresses her appetite so she does not eat well and is quite underweight. When she has been drinking she can be incontinent and she has been hospitalised on a number of occasions following falls, fractures and burns. She refuses, however, to engage with any alcohol or smoking reduction strategies that are offered by her GP. On this occasion, she has been admitted to hospital and has agreed to a referral to the social work team to discuss having some support at home when she is discharged.

Commentary

It has already been recognised that Barbara appears to be in need of care and support, which is the low threshold for triggering assessment of need (section 9, Care Act 2014). Barbara appears to have consented to this assessment. Throughout this process, the aim should be to maximise her wellbeing (section 1), and particularly at the moment her choice and control over all aspects of daily living. Assessment should also be guided by the principle of personalisation, namely that she is best placed to judge her own wellbeing, with her views, wishes, feelings, beliefs and desired outcomes therefore crucially important. However, those involved in the assessment should discuss openly perceived risks and what might help to mitigate their likelihood and also their seriousness should they arise. Barbara should be supported to participate in the assessment, with an advocate (section 67) if this would facilitate her involvement.

Assessment should consider not only current needs but also future needs where these can be reasonably foreseen. It should focus on Barbara's strengths and capabilities as well as her needs for care and support, considering also any circles of support in her immediate family

$\longrightarrow$

and social context. With her consent, the social care assessment can be combined with other assessments, in Barbara's case principally by healthcare practitioners, to ensure a holistic appreciation of her circumstances. Sections 6 and 7 specify a duty to cooperate between the local authority and relevant partner agencies. A written record of the assessment should be provided.

Once completed, social workers must determine whether any of Barbara's needs meet the eligibility criteria (section 13). For her needs to be eligible they must arise from physical and/or mental impairment or illness, as a result of which she is unable to meet two or more specified outcomes, such as being able to make use of her home safely and managing her nutrition, with a significant impact on her wellbeing. If she has eligible needs, the local authority has a duty to provide care and support to meet these (section 18); there is a power also to meet non-eligible needs (section 19). To be lawful, the care and support plan (sections 24 and 25) must have a reasonable chance of meeting identified needs. The plan must be person-centred, reflecting Barbara's wishes and desired outcomes, with advocacy again provided if this would facilitate her involvement. Joint planning with healthcare practitioners in Barbara's case would also be good practice.

A personal budget (section 26) will set out the financial cost of the care and support plan, and a financial assessment will determine what Barbara must pay if the local authority decides to levy a charge (which it has the power to do). Barbara should be given the option of taking part or all of the personal budget as a direct payment so that she can purchase her own care and support. Once the care and support plan is in place, it should be reviewed within six months and annually thereafter.

Note: Barbara's story will be continued in subsequent chapters (those relating to carers, safeguarding, mental capacity and mental health) in order to explore further aspects of her situation.

Further Reading

Department of Health and Social Care (2019) *Strengths-Based Approach: Practice Framework and Practice Handbook*. London: DHSC. Available at: https://assets.publishing.service.gov.uk/government/uploads/system/uploads/attachment_data/file/778134/strengths-based-approach-practice-framework-and-handbook.pdf

Dyke, C. (2016) *Writing Analytical Assessments in Social Work*. St Albans: Critical Publishing. (See especially Chapter 2 (Genograms and Ecomaps) and Chapter 5 (Analysis). Despite being written with children's social care in mind, the book contains valuable lessons for social work with adults.)

Notes

1. It is important to note that the application of this concept, closely associated with Carl Rogers' person-centred approach to counselling, is contested with regard to statutory social work, specifically because of the lack of fit between the instrumentalism of the latter and a practice that is predicated on 'principled non-directivity' (Murphy et al., 2013: 708)

2. A decision is 'Wednesbury unreasonable' (or irrational) if it is so unreasonable that no reasonable person acting reasonably could have made it (*Associated Provincial Picture Houses Ltd v Wednesbury Corporation (1948) 1 KB 223*). The test is stricter than simply showing that the decision was unreasonable.

4 The Care Act: the service user's experience

Peter Beresford and Colin Slasberg

Introduction

The Care Act could scarcely have been launched with higher hopes for the people who rely on publicly-funded social care. Norman Lamb, UK Minister for Care at the time, proclaimed that the Act represented the *'most significant change for social care in 60 years'* (Department of Health, 2014a). It would do so by *'putting people and their carers in control of their care and support'*. Councils would be under a duty to make wellbeing the driving force of all that they did – the 'wellbeing principle'. When assessing the needs of individuals, councils would be required not only to make wellbeing the driving force, but to start with the person's own view of their needs in relation to wellbeing. The Act also required councils to be *'aware of current and likely future demand'* (para 5(2)(b)) and ensure *'sufficient services'* were in place to meet the demand (para 5(3)). The final icing on the cake would be that the longstanding problem of the unfairness of the postcode lottery of provision (Commission on Funding for Care and Support, 2011) would be solved by the introduction of national eligibility criteria.

Lamb was right in that this would indeed be a radical transformation for service users and carers who had long experienced a bureaucratised and disempowering assessment process, with large swathes of their needs being left unmet, and a postcode lottery of provision. Three years on from the Care Act are these changes on the way? In the following section, we examine the evidence.

The evidence of delivery of the Act's ambitions

Direct evidence of the service user experience

Think Local Act Personal, the body charged by government to progress its personalisation agenda, carried out a survey in 2017 of over 1,000 service users to test their experience of the

Care Act (TLAP, 2017a). One question in particular directly tested the intention to empower people in the process of assessing their needs and planning their support. In response to the statement 'the council has listened to me and understands what I want and need', 70% said the statement was true either 'never', 'rarely' or at best only 'sometimes' (2017a: 9). This finding seriously calls into question whether the Care Act has made a difference in this critical area.

This view is confirmed by the survey's findings about where service users did find satisfaction. This was 'amongst a small number of people using direct payments who organised their own support, stayed in control of recruitment and the management of day-to-day support plans' (p. 22). This, however, is no different from what had been the case since the 1996 Direct Payments Act. It is a group of service users with the skills, confidence, awareness, time and energy to purchase and manage their own support systems, mostly by employing personal assistants (PAs). Not only do they control their support system, they are more likely to control the assessment process that generates the level of support they receive. The number of people in this group has scarcely changed in the twenty years since implementation. As at March 2017, 155,000 of 550,000 people receiving long-term support used a direct payment. However, it is estimated that only 29% of direct payment users employ PAs (Skills for Care, 2018). This represents about 8% of all service users.

Inequity and inequality

A key source of evidence of the impact of the Act is likely to be the comparative spend of councils on service users. If resources are being allocated according to the wellbeing principle through a process that is fair and equitable, we would expect to see the level of support to service users to be within reasonably narrow parameters around the country (once allowances have been made for cost differences that arise from differences in land and property costs). If there were to be any significant differences, they might perhaps favour councils serving more deprived areas, on the premise that people in more deprived areas are more likely to have worse health and therefore higher care and support needs.

The data show the opposite to be the case. NHS Digital publish the returns in relation to spend and activity of each council in England (nascis.digital.nhs.uk/). This includes the gross spend on people with continuing needs and the numbers receiving continuing support throughout the year. In 2016–17 Salford spent £48.8m amongst 5,215 people, making an average of £9.4K on each. Wokingham spent £43.4m but among only 1,775 people, making an average of £24.5K. Once an adjustment has been made for regional cost differences, these figures become £10.5K and £23.3K respectively.[1] A service user in Salford can expect less than half the support that someone with similar needs living in Wokingham would get.

The Index of Multiple Deprivation in 2015 (www.gov.uk/government/statistics/english-indices-of-deprivation-2015) showed Wokingham serves the most affluent community in the country. By contrast, only twenty councils serve more deprived communities than Salford. Salford and Wokingham represent the two spending extremes. However, they are not outliers. The 10%

highest spending councils spent an average of £20.2K per service user and the lowest spending 10% £11.1K per service user.

The postcode lottery has remained a virulent problem. Compounding the injustice, given that the lowest spending councils serve the most deprived areas and people, is that the inequity is worsening health inequalities. A study by the Institute of Fiscal Studies (IFS) showed the austerity years affected councils very differently. This is because cuts in the government grant have had the greatest effect on those councils most reliant on the central grant. This tends to be the councils serving the most deprived communities. The worst affected 10% of councils reduced their spend by an average of 30%. The least affected 10% actually increased spending by an average of 10% (Phillips and Simpson, 2017). Whilst the Care Act cannot be blamed for this injustice, it has not been able to challenge or arrest it.

Failure to promote wellbeing

There is evidence that provision of support under the Care Act is failing perhaps its most critical test – to promote wellbeing:

- In 2016/17, councils were required to survey service users on the extent to which their support enabled them to have full quality of life. The scale goes from 0, which is no impact, to 1, where 'full quality of life' is achieved. The 10% of councils that spent the most on service users achieved an average score of 0.4, which was scarcely any different from the 10% of council that spent the least who achieved an average score of 0.39 (www.theguardian.com/social-care-network/2018/apr/23/are-social-care-services-improving-peoples-wellbeing).

- A survey by Ipsos MORI (Blake et al., 2017b) based on national, longitudinal data found no discernible relationship between the level of need met and wellbeing. In a related piece of work talking to some service users, they found older people in receipt of support for personal care because these were the needs deemed 'eligible', while their own priority was the need they had to promote social engagement. This was doubly damaging for wellbeing. People would have preferred to struggle to meet their own personal care needs and so retained the prized asset of feeling in control and independent. At the same time, failure to support them to access a social life directly undermined their sense of wellbeing.

- The sector is showing awareness of a widespread problem of the system creating dependency. A campaign championed by the Department of Health's Chief Social Worker to promote 'strengths based practice' (TLAP, 2017b) is seen as the antidote. Few would argue that creating dependency can be said to promote wellbeing.

Awareness of the extent of need

In 2018, a Parliamentary Inquiry into long-term funding of social care was surprised to learn that councils had no direct information about the extent to which needs were met. Earlier in the year, a Public Accounts Committee Inquiry into social care (PAC, 2018) was also surprised to be told by the Permanent Secretary to the Department of Health and Social Care that councils had all the resources they required to meet all their statutory duties under the Care Act.

There remains compelling evidence of great areas of need not being met. The Local Government Association (LGA, 2017), in a report to government, says there is both unmet need, meaning people excluded from the system, and undermet need, meaning people in the system but undersupported. The report identifies a number of case studies of people who are suffering as a result. They estimate it will require £5BN to meet these needs. However, the report had to rely on speculative assumptions to arrive at this figure as it had none from the field. This evidence suggests the Act's requirement for councils to be aware of all needs in their communities is not being delivered.

Summary

The evidence is strong that the transformational ambitions of the Care Act are not being delivered. The next step is to unpick what might be happening.

Why might the Act be failing?

Why has the duty the Care Act placed on councils to put wellbeing first not overcome these problems? In what follows, we argue that the core problem is the perpetuation of a longstanding way in which needs are assessed and resources allocated. We then go on to identify that national policy – expressed through the Statutory Guidance to the Act (DHSC, 2018a) – is the key. There are two major gaps that, between them, ensure the perpetuation of the ongoing resource-led approach to what is considered to be 'need'. The first is an absence of vision of what social care should achieve against which individual needs can be assessed. The second is an absence of guidance for how councils should control spending.

How are needs assessed and resources allocated?

If resources are not being allocated in response to wellbeing as the Care Act intended, what is at play? A vital clue lies in the huge volatility of spend and budgets found by the IFS as set out above. Whilst budgets were slashed in the worst affected, the annual budget survey carried out by the Association of Directors of Social Services (ADASS, 2017) reported that over-spending was less than 2%.

This shows that councils are able to adjust their spend closely to match their budget and are able to make the adjustment rapidly. Crucially they do so without leaving any trace of needs left unmet in the wake. This is made possible by the definition of 'need' being adjusted according to budget. It necessarily happens at a highly localised level, with individual budget managers creating their own eligibility policies. There are as many 'eligibility policies' as there are budget holders around the country. The eligibility decision is always expressed in the language of whatever happen to be the national eligibility criteria of the day. This gives an appearance of consistency, but one which is wholly misleading (Slasberg and Beresford, 2016b).

The resource-led definition of need explains why the Care Act requirement that councils should know the extent of need in their community, and therefore the scale and type of resources that should be in place, is not being delivered.

Absence of vision

The Care Act creates a duty to promote wellbeing. Thus wellbeing has become the measure of the extent to which social care is achieving its objectives. However, the Act does not attempt to define the extent to which wellbeing should be promoted. Until that is known, no vision can be said to exist. A person may be a mile away from having the level of wellbeing that is right for them. If a council provides resources that moves them a mere inch along that path, the council can say it has satisfied the Care Act. The legislature left the question of the extent to which wellbeing should be promoted – a standard of wellbeing – to the executive to address. The executive has chosen not to accept this challenge.

Absence of guidance about how to control spending

The process of controlling spend through highly localised eligibility policies determining what is 'need' requires any national policy to be inert. The statutory guidance to the Act (DHSC, 2018a) achieves this in two ways. The first is to ensure the national eligibility criteria are, in effect, not criteria at all. Under Fair Access to Care Services (FACS) (DoH, 2002) this was achieved by making the criteria so 'convoluted' (Commission for Social Care Inspection, 2008a) as to allow a very wide interpretation (Fernandez and Snell, 2012). The Care and Support (Eligibility Criteria) Regulations to the Care Act (DoH, 2015b) replaced FACS. They have achieved the same outcome by making the criteria so loose as to have no meaning. A need is a duty to meet if it has a *'significant impact on wellbeing'*. The statutory guidance illustrates how to implement this threshold by describing two cases, one eligible and one not (DHSC, 2018a: para 6.112). It is easy to see that the needs of the person deemed eligible have a more significant impact than those of the person deemed not eligible. However, no rationale is offered as to why the threshold should fall between these two cases, and why it didn't fall below both of them, or above both of them.

The second element required of national policy to ensure it is inert is an absence of any guidance as to how councils should manage demand against their budget. The only reference to taking the budget into account is the following:

> *In determining how to meet needs, the local authority may also take into reasonable consideration its own finances and budgetary position ... the authority may take decisions on a case-by-case basis which weigh up the total costs of different potential options.*
> (2018a: para 10.27)

While this means that a council can choose the least expensive option, it cannot compromise on meeting the need. However, good practice will already have achieved this. The statutory guidance (DHSC, 2018a) does not acknowledge the possibility that the cost of meeting all needs may exceed the budget. This leaves councils with no option but to use the latitude offered to limit what they define as 'need' to that which their resources can meet in order to deliver their legal obligation to ensure the resource offered will meet the need. It is delivered through managerial control of the practice supervisory process.

Acts of omission or commission?

These gaps could be considered an innocent act of omission but may have been a knowing act of commission. Certainly the government had the information to know that their assessment of the reasons for the existence of the postcode lottery was wrong.

- Fair Access to Care Services (FACS) had been in place since 2002. The policy identified four bands of need in order of priority. It was for each council to decide how many of the four bands it could afford. The government said it was the ability of councils to choose which bands they would deem eligible that led to the postcode lottery. But in 2008, the Audit Commission had reported that there were major differences in spend between councils (Audit Commission, 2008), but that the differences in spending levels were not explained by the numbers of bands each council had made eligible.

- By the time of FACS's demise in 2015, all but three councils had chosen the top two bands only. These three councils chose only the top band. These councils requested additional funding if they would be required under the Care Act to expand their offer to match everyone else's. The government's own impact assessment (DoH, 2014b), however, reported that these three councils offered no less support than all the others, and in some cases even more. Their request was refused.

Personal budgets

Norman Lamb's confidence in the Care Act would have been largely founded on the Act passing into law the transformative effect of *personal budgets*. It was believed they would enable people to choose their own support using an up-front allocation calculated by a Resource Allocation System (RAS). Personal budgets had been launched as national policy seven years previously, with the aim of there being 'personal budgets for all'. It was expected to sweep away all the old systemic barriers to personalised assessment of need and support planning.

However, the policy has proven to be undeliverable in practice:

- Various freedom of information requests for data that enable a comparison of the 'indicative' and actual allocations have shown there is no meaningful relationship between the upfront 'indicative' allocation and what people are actually offered (Slasberg et al., 2015). An average difference in the order of two and half times was found. This means that if an indicative allocation was £100, those whose actual allocations were less averaged an allocation of £40, and those whose actual allocations were more averaged £250.

- In 2016, a report to Parliament (National Audit Office, 2016) found not all councils were delivering an upfront allocation despite this being national policy. They also found that when councils did so, practitioners were not telling service users what their upfront allocations were as they were 'inaccurate and unhelpful' (2016: 12).

Two judicial reviews in 2017 (*Davey v Oxfordshire* and *JF v Merton*) where service users challenged their councils' level of support to them were seen as the first major tests of the Care Act. In two lengthy judgements, an RAS or upfront allocation was not mentioned on a single occasion. An upfront allocation was not relevant to the cases of the service users or the defence of the councils, nor was it of any interest to the courts (see https://socialcare.blog.gov.uk/2017/08/09/ten-years-on-what-can-we-make-of-personal-budgets/).

The Act did indeed introduce the concept of a *personal budget*; however, its definition was entirely different from the policy definition. The Act defined a personal budget as:

> ... *a statement which specifies ... the cost to the local authority of meeting those of the adult's needs which it is required or decides to meet...* (section 26)

This can only be known *at the end* of the process of assessing need and planning support once the person's unique needs and support requirements are known. While the phrase 'personal budget' has become an established part of the industry lexicon, it has been stripped of its transformative ambition and has only an administrative meaning.

Realising the ambitions of the Care Act

The preceding analysis leads to the conclusion that if the ambitions of the Care Act are to be realised, the following changes to national policy will be required:

1. A *strategic aim* must be set. It should take the form of a standard of wellbeing and it should drive the assessment of need at the individual level.
2. As long as social care continues to be delivered within a budget, *eligibility of need* must be replaced by *affordability of need* as the means to control spending.

A strategic aim

The concept of independent living as defined by Article 19 of the United Nations Convention on the Rights of Persons with Disabilities (www.un.org/development/desa/disabilities/convention-on-the-rights-of-persons-with-disabilities.html) can be seen as a standard of wellbeing if viewed through the lens of the Care Act. It is thus a readymade standard, and one that has international credibility.

Independent living was first developed by the Disabled People's Movement in the 1970s (Beresford, 2016). The movement was reacting to a care system built on people in need of support being seen as 'sick, defective and dependent'. The movement believed support should be built around an entirely different conception of disabled people. The right support should be enabling, so that people could *'do things for themselves, like anybody else'* (2016: 212).

The concept was given practical expression through the provision of direct payments to enable disabled people to design and manage their own support system, most often through employing personal assistants. The re-conception of the relationship between the person and the state that was the original inspiration behind independent living attached only to those able to manage their own support in this way, thus excluding the great majority (although there was an aspiration to establish a network of local 'user-led organisations' to support disabled people to do this).

However, the UN definition of independent living has been crafted in a way that makes applicability universal:

- Its definition of disability is inclusive, effectively including anyone with care and support needs as a result of impairment.

- Two concepts are central to the definition. The first is that people should have *'choices equal to others'*. This might mean nothing more than going to bed at a time of the person's own choosing or having their meal of choice. The second is to be able to *'participate in society'*. This might mean being able to offer their talents to the wider society, while for others it can mean just being able to continue as a valued family member.

The government did indeed consider adopting independent living as a matter of policy in the context of the Care Act. However, it was rejected on the grounds that the wellbeing principle was superior to what it called the 'abstract' concept of independent living (para 1.19).

Government thus viewed wellbeing as an alternative to independent living. But this is not the case. The concepts differ in that one is a relative term and the other absolute. People have more or less levels of wellbeing and so this is a relative concept. Independent living is an absolute state. They are in fact complementary concepts, not alternatives. Independent living can be used to describe the endpoint in the journey to promote wellbeing.

Replacing eligibility of need with affordability of need

If the achievement of independent living is the context for assessments of individual need, the ability to flex the assessment as the means to control spend is denied. If the assessment process establishes the least costly route to enabling independent living, this becomes the level of resource that is *sufficient*. However, whether the *sufficient* amount is also *affordable* would be a separate and subsequent decision. This is a major departure from the eligibility-based system which conflates sufficiency and affordability into one decision.

The idea of separating the sufficiency and affordability decisions is not new. In the early 1980s, the University of Kent led a project to find a new and creative approach to supporting older people with complex needs (Davies and Challis, 1986). They sought to free the practice process from being resource-led by making the offer cash-based to enable flexibility of options. Working with some 90 service users, they achieved highly encouraging results. Their work went on to become the basis of the concept of assessment and care management under the community care reforms of the 1990s. However, crucially, the project failed to address the issue of control of spending. For the project, costs were controlled by placing a ceiling at two thirds the cost of residential care. While this worked in a small-scale project, it was not a formula that could do the same in rollout. With no other ideas forthcoming, government reverted to the tried and trusted method of allowing councils to control the flow of needs to manage cost. Dalrymple and Burke (2006: 205) point out that the formal guidance to support for the 1990 NHS and Community Care Act '*recognises that needs are unique to the individual*' but that '*they have to be met within available resources*'. This doomed the service to continue with a resource-led approach to need. Assessment and care management, far from delivering the liberating process its creators had intended, became a totem of an oppressive regime.

Strategic implications

Separating the decision about sufficiency of resource from affordability of resource has major strategic implications.

The real gap between needs and resources will for the first time be known. Current estimates by sector leaders and think tanks of the funding gap run into a serious credibility problem. The Local Government Association in August 2018 estimated that some £5BN is required to meet needs unmet or undermet (LGA, 2018a). This figure was arrived at by estimating the number of people currently excluded from the system and multiplying this by the average cost of care. However, the argument has fatal weaknesses:

- There is a fundamental credibility problem in that the sector is asking for money to meet needs it currently deems are not of sufficient importance to warrant public expenditure.

- The report illustrated the problem of undermet need with a number of cases where the level of support is so low that wellbeing is very poor, leading to great distress. The methodology used by the report, however, would not provide any more resources for these people.

- On the other hand, the report identified a range of initiatives at council level to improve value for money, largely by addressing the tendency of the system to create dependency within the context of the move to asset- or strengths-based working. The report lays claim to very large savings by councils. However, no account is taken of reduced funding requirements if, as society might be entitled to expect, such measures are adopted across all councils.

It is unlikely such a case will survive the scrutiny of the democratic process even at its most dovish.

The uniqueness of need and high variability of cost makes it unknowable, in advance of making the change, what the cost would be. Unmet need would therefore become an inherent feature of such a system and a political reality. People's expectations would be raised and not fully realised. This would place social care on a similar footing to health where waiting lists act as a weather vane for the balance of need and resources, creating political pressure. Unmet need in social care would fulfil a similar function to waiting lists in health.

Operational implications

There would be major operational implications. A two-year project with a London Borough to personalise the mainstream assessment and support planning process – involving managers, members, practitioners, service users, carers, IT and finance leads – explored what these would be (Slasberg, 2017):

- A re-design of the assessment process to enable service users and carers to be in authentic control of the process. This meant the person's view would change its status from simply being regarded as their 'wishes' to a respected view of their needs. Key to this change was the realisation that 'need' in the context of assessing for eligibility has a quite different anatomy from 'need' in the context of wellbeing. The anatomy of need when assessing for wellbeing is one that ordinary people can relate to, while 'need' in the context of eligibility is a professional matter. When assessing for wellbeing, the professional role is to support people to develop their assessment so that it passes a 'fitness for purpose' test. The test would be whether the resulting support plan could deliver the level of wellbeing that would be right for the person and in the most cost-effective way.

- The budget holder's responsibility would become to decide how much of each 'fit for purpose' support plan could be afforded. This is a skilled decision that places value for money alongside equity as the key criterion for resource allocation. It may be more appropriate to fund a lower risk need that will have a greater impact through preventive potential than a higher risk need with less impact. The search for *greatest need* would be replaced by *greatest impact*.

- Both the greater number of decisions required and the level of professional grasp of each case to make the best decisions would mean that budget holding should be delegated to team manager level. This would also mark a movement away from the conflictual model between practitioner and manager that eligibility working creates to one based on roles that are different but complementary.

- New spend is funded primarily by case turnover. Information systems for budget holders would need to ensure continuous information about the state of the budget.

- The degree of equity between teams is determined by the level of budgets relative to assessed needs. Strategic reporting systems would be needed to create information to show the level of needs funded and the level unfunded. This would enable decisions about the appropriate allocation of the budget between teams. At the macro level, this information could also ensure that the council would know the level of resources it required so that it could enable all those involved to have the wellbeing that was right for them.

All the above crucially depended on replacing the policy of only meeting needs that are a duty to meet, with one whereby the duty to meet needs comprises only a floor or minimum guarantee, and with all other assessed needs coming under a power (Slasberg and Beresford, 2017a). The Care Act makes this possible. It would have required the council to apply a corporate standard to the phrase 'significant impact on wellbeing'. This would have meant going against the statutory guidance, which says none should be applied. In the end, the participating council decided against taking the risks this would entail.

Conclusion

The evidence shows that the Care Act has yet to make any impact for service users. It has, however, created the legislative context for real and transformative change. Those changes have yet to take place. For them to do so this will require national policy in the management of the tension between needs and resources to change.

Two things need to happen. Social care needs a strategic aim, and it has to be able to assess and cost individual needs against this aim, unhindered by a requirement to make 'needs' fit resources. The gap between needs and resources must become a transparent reality whereupon it will become a political responsibility to address. This would place social care on a similar footing to health. The goal of securing the best level of wellbeing would then be able to stand alongside securing the best health of mind and body. With social care having lead responsibility for the former and the NHS the latter, therein could lie the key to an authentic integration of effort between equal partners.

Further Reading

Beresford, P., Fleming, J., Glynn, M., Bewley, C., Croft, S., Branfield, F. and Postle, K. (2011) *Supporting People: Towards a Person-Centred Approach*. Bristol: Policy.

Slasberg, C. and Beresford, P. (2015) Building on the original strengths of direct payments to create a better future for social care, *Disability & Society*, 30 (2): 305–9.

Slasberg, C. and Beresford, P. (2017) The need to bring an end to the era of eligibility policies for a person-centred, financially sustainable future, *Disability & Society*, 32 (8): 1263–68.

Note

1. The methodology for the adjustment was as follows. The impact of regional cost differences stems largely from land and capital costs. This primarily affects services requiring substantial premises. Residential and Nursing Home costs make up about 50% of the gross spend. The adjustment to spend for each council was delivered by dividing 50% of the gross spend by the regional average unit cost for each council, and then multiplying by the national average unit cost.

5 Carers and the Care Act: promise and potential

Jill Manthorpe, Jo Moriarty, Nic Brimblecombe, Martin Knapp, José Luis Fernández and Tom Snell

Introduction

In every area of practice, social workers are working with carers. Examples could be:

- a lone parent supporting a child with a learning disability;
- a young carer supporting a parent with a mental health problem;
- an adult child ensuring care is delivered to a parent with dementia;
- a middle-aged person supporting a life partner with a long-term condition;
- a sister supporting her brother with substance misuse and psychosis;
- an older person caring for a dying spouse.

This chapter introduces the context of social work with carers following the Care Act 2014. The legal changes are summarised relating to carers, with some discussion of the developing case law and administrative redress in this area. The prevalence of family care in contemporary England is outlined, along with demographic trends that are suggesting changes in patterns of care within families and social networks. Outcomes of social work with carers, in particular provision of information and advice, support with care planning and accessing services, and social work effectiveness when providing interventions to carers, are then presented. The use of research evidence around the meeting of different carers' wishes, needs and difficulties by social workers is next considered. Social work good practice points are suggested. We next outline the impact of personalisation on work with carers under the Care Act 2014 to make the case that while the law may have changed there is much continuity. Finally we point to ways in which meeting the high expectations of the Care Act among carers can be analysed.

Any discussion of the Care Act 2014 needs to acknowledge the accompanying changes in publicly-funded social care funding and the eligibility criteria that affect people with care and support needs and carers. Proportionally fewer people are now eligible for social care support. Nearly 1.2 million people aged 65 years and over do not receive the care and support they need with essential daily living activities, equating to nearly one in every eight older people living with some level of unmet need (Age UK, 2017a). The impact of this is that not only do some people not receive any services but also that more people are depending on family carer(s) (often themselves older people). The increasing pressure that this brings is highlighted by carers' organisations such as Carers UK and the Carers Trust. Such pressure may take many forms; many carers are out of pocket, their health and wellbeing are negatively affected, and they become socially isolated. For some there are long-term negative effects – on relationships, employment and mental health. Social workers are often well aware of the complexities of caring – many of them have caring responsibilities and their personal and professional worlds may collide (Manthorpe et al., 2012).

There are also other dimensions to care. Forbat (2005) observed that the distinctions between carers and those they care for are not always clear; for example an adult with learning disabilities may be providing support to their parent(s) more than previously. And carers' support organisations are increasingly arguing that it is important to recognise that caring can have a positive side:

> Having a family member with severe learning disabilities brings positives to family life, from the pleasure of spending time with them and seeing their achievements, to new experiences and opportunities for your family. People may become tougher, more assertive, but also more understanding and kind. A lot of family carers develop new skills in communication, organisation, or even creativity! (Challenging Behaviour Foundation, 2018: 7)

Overview – the powers and duties of the Care Act 2014 in relation to carers

In England 'A carer is anyone who cares, unpaid, for a friend or family member who due to illness, disability, a mental health problem or an addiction cannot cope without their support'. Anyone can become a carer but carers generally do not choose to become carers; it happens. Indeed, many 'carers' do not recognise themselves as carers and so do not get support for themselves or see themselves as entitled to it. In this chapter we avoid using the word 'carer' when referring to paid workers; although some carers may be paid by the person they are supporting using their own or public funds; in other countries the term 'caregiver' is often used instead of 'carer'. We also use the term 'local authorities' (unless the term 'councils' is used in a quote). This chapter concentrates on England but some references are made to relevant Scottish resources.

The United Kingdom (UK) was one of first countries to recognise carers' rights, firstly through the benefits system (in 1992), then through rights to an assessment (1995) and then services in their own right (2004). Central government strategies (Department of Health, 1999, 2008, 2010), most recently a Carers Action Plan (Department of Health and Social Care, 2018b), set out the national policy context. While the Care Act 2014 is the main legislative framework for social work practice with adults, practitioners also need to be mindful of the provisions of other legislation that affects carers in their roles as family or friends; this includes the Human Rights Act 1998, the Mental Capacity Act 2005, and the Equality Act 2010.

Local authorities in England are under a responsibility to assess a carer's own needs for support under the Care Act (section 10). Assessment should be triggered by the appearance of any needs – not the application of eligibility criteria in advance. Criteria such as providing regular and substantial care are no longer relevant. They must consider the impact of caring on a carer and the carer's own wishes (employment, leisure and so on). They must also consider the importance of preventing or delaying the development of needs for care and support among carers, for example, by considering 'prevention' options, such as a short break from care to forestall a breakdown of care.

The Care Act extended carers' rights and local authorities' duties. In the parliamentary debates on the progress of the proposed legislation there was much consensus that the new provisions were timely and would provide greater clarity when assessing whether a carer is 'eligible' for support, in ironing out variations in response to carers between different parts of England, and in linking up support for carers/parents of disabled children who are moving to adulthood (see Manthorpe et al., 2019). From April 2015, this new legislation came into force. One substantial change was the allocation of responsibility for 'meeting needs' that became a core legal duty. For the first time, as was often summarised by politicians, carers were to be as recognised in law as those they cared for. These changes were intended to lead to more carers getting the support they needed (echoing the theme of choice currently popular in policy). Such changes were further intended to put carers in control of the help they received (echoing the equally popular theme of control). The Care Act is not applicable to young carers (under the age of 18 years who care for others); instead the legislation covering the rights of young carers and parent carers to be assessed is the Children and Families Act 2014. The Care Act 2014 gives the right to the young carer to plan the support that they may need once they reach 18 under a 'transition assessment'. This applies also to adult carers of children (in the main parents) where the adult carer may appear to have needs for support once the disabled child reaches 18.

The Care Act introduced an assessment and eligibility process that acts as a key interaction between the local authority (often in the persona of a social worker) and the carer. This can be seen as a social work intervention in itself that may help carers address their situation and the use of helping resources.

The National Eligibility Criteria for supporting carers set the threshold to determine whether a carer meets eligibility criteria. The concept of carers' outcomes has parallels with outcomes for care users. A carer's assessment addresses possible tasks that the carer is unable to 'achieve' because of caring responsibilities (referred to as 'outcomes'). They include physical, mental and emotional wellbeing outcomes. Key question areas may cover the following:

- Does the carer provide or intend to offer care provision for another person? As a result, is there or is there likely to be a significant impact on the carer's wellbeing?

- Is the carer unable to perform the outcome (their wellbeing) without support? This involves where the carer would be unable to achieve an outcome even if support was offered.

- Is the carer able to achieve the outcome without assistance, but doing so causes the carer significant fatigue, distress or anxiety?

- Can the carer achieve the outcome without support, but does this place them in danger or risk endangering their own or others' health and safety?

More practically assessments can cover whether the carer's physical or mental health is, or is at risk of, deteriorating and consider their social context. The Care Act guidance (termed the Care and Support Statutory Guidance) (DHSC, 2018a) is the key practice resource, although local authorities are entitled to organise systems in their own way.

How common is caring in England?

The prevalence of caring has remained fairly stable over time. NHS Digital's (2017a) analysis of the Survey of Adult Carers in England (SACE) showed most carers (those in touch with local authorities) are women and the greatest number of them are over retirement age. However, a growing number of people are needing support over the lifetime and so more parents are caring for children over the life course. Indeed the idea of 'sandwich' carers who are caring for parents and children has been gaining common currency. These have probably always existed but the growing trend to having a first child at a later age, and fewer of them, means there are more 'beanpole' (young children, parents, grandparents and great grandparent or beyond) families than in the past.

In such circumstances, people often see themselves as a partner, a child, a parent and so on, but O'Connor (2007) talks about people 'positioning' themselves as carers and this may be increasingly happening with the greater media attention being paid to carers and the activities of carers' organisations such as Carers UK (see for example Carers UK, 2018a). The heterogeneity of carers is also increasingly recognised, as outlined below.

Demography and caring relationships

Glover (2018: 48) estimated that, given that 12% of the population are carers, in 2018 there were an estimated 7,980,000 carers in the UK. Social work contact is only with a minority but this is likely to be with carers under particular pressure or in crisis. Given the wide variety of roles in social work with adults, there are some social workers who work intensively with carers, whereas others may be more frequently encountering people who are now on their own.

An important consideration in terms of social work research is to consider when it is helpful to look at provision in its entirety and when it is important to differentiate between different forms of social work practice. For example, carers from minority ethnic groups are less likely to identify as a 'carer'. There is considerable evidence that people from black and minority ethnic groups are disproportionately likely to be detained under the Mental Health Act 2007 (Gajwani et al., 2016), which means that they and their family members are likely to be over-represented among people aged 18–65 in contact with statutory mental health social workers. By contrast, research has found that levels of awareness and information about dementia are lower among people from black and minority ethnic groups, and that older people from several black and minority ethnic groups present later to services, when their dementia has become more severe (Moriarty et al., 2011; Mukadam et al., 2011). This means they are more likely to be under-represented in the data about the Care Act and other provisions for people with dementia and their carers.

One difficulty in analysing adult social care data and practice accounts is that the population of people receiving adult social care services, and of them the minority in contact with social workers, is not representative of the general population. This makes it much harder to explain apparent differences in the under- or over-representation of people from minority groups among those in touch with local authorities or those organisations acting on their behalf.

This may explain the differences in satisfaction with social care and social work between people from black and minority ethnic groups and their white counterparts which have been reported for several years (Blake et al., 2017). Research consistently shows that ethnic differences in satisfaction often arise from stereotyped assumptions about the nature and amount of family support available to people from ethnic minority groups. However, levels of stigma (particularly about mental health and some physical disabilities and learning disabilities) seem to be higher among some ethnic groups than others. There is also evidence about language and other barriers in terms of accessing information about what is available and that sometimes services are not provided in culturally sensitive ways. Finally, there is evidence of differences in cultural expectations about care (Moriarty and Butt, 2004) from the emerging literature showing that carers of people from black and minority ethnic groups who are considering social care services are often caught between cultural expectations that they will provide substantial amounts of family care and service assumptions that they are willing to do this (Ismail and Mackenzie, 2003). The Care Act Guidance itself makes several references to practice imperatives needing to address individual and contextual strengths and needs.

When studying the continued implementation of the Care Act, it is important to look at local authority data in context. Using the ASCOF (Adult Social Care Outcome Framework) data on outcomes (NHS Digital, 2017a), there seem to be some unusual differences in the number of responses by different ethnic groups within each local authority. Social workers acting as research advocates are in a good position to scrutinise local data when commenting on their employer's plans or strategies. They can also assist in building the evidence base for their practice by considering case study reports, contributing to quality assurance and inspections, and working with researchers to identify and address research priorities.

In terms of research gaps about social work and carers, research into the areas that currently have the smallest evidence base might be highly useful in practice. These could include:

- the interface with social care services and housing – in particular, experiences of people and their carers in supported living and extra care housing so that social workers can advise carers about such options;

- the experiences of people with learning disabilities from black and minority ethnic groups that are especially lacking, and patterns of commissioning and practice in this area (including their carers' and other family members' expectations and experiences) which remain under-explored for their impact on outcomes;

- barriers and facilitators to asking for a carer's assessment and addressing the results of this assessment (e.g. the use made of information or care planning), again by families where a member has learning disabilities/complex needs in particular;

- the operation of local markets and provision of culturally-, geographically- (e.g. rural) sensitive and acceptable services for service users and for carers, at times of crisis in particular.

Satisfaction levels are likely to be influenced by expectations among all carers, whatever their ethnicity, class, gender or sexuality, because several intra-group dimensions often need to be taken into account. Greenwood et al. (2015) found that studies rarely differentiated between men's and women's views or between different ethnic groups, and this may be very relevant to carers who encounter family expectations about their role (which could include providing care or not providing care).

Risk factors for carer distress and problems

Under the Care Act a local authority has to determine whether a carer is:

- unable to perform the outcome without support – this involves where the carer would be unable to achieve an outcome even if support was offered;

- able to achieve the outcome without assistance, but doing so causes the carer significant fatigue, distress or anxiety;

- able to achieve the outcome without support, but doing so puts her in danger or is likely to endanger the health and safety of the carer or others.

We need more evidence about the operationalising of 'fatigue, distress or anxiety'. Does this include, for example, loneliness which may be triggered or made significantly worse by changes such as becoming a carer? Caring can bring physical, psychological, social, financial and emotional changes – at what point does a carer reach 'significant' fatigue, distress or anxiety? The Care Act makes it clear that this has to be considered individually.

Beyond the individual and their resources or resilience are social contexts of ambivalence which see carers as 'saintly' or somehow to blame for their circumstances. Among some carers there is a combination of caring difficulties, family conflicts and tensions, and stigma – associated with the circumstances of the person they are supporting or the context of care. Overall we probably underestimate the proportion of carers caring for someone with continence problems, for example, and there is very little evidence on what helps for carers and what sort of advice they are given about managing this (Drennan et al., 2013). For some carers, it may be significant in its distress. Incontinence is an example of how stigma can make a practical problem seem worse but social work has generally neglected this subject. Other evidence in relation to family members of people with intellectual and developmental disabilities (such as autism) has recently reported that the stigma they experience is multidimensional and encountered by many (Mitter et al., 2018).

Carers and the Care Act – evidence of early changes

There are currently two important sources of information about the impact of the Care Act on carers and these provide valuable insights for social workers. The first source draws on the expertise and insights from carer groups; the second is from case law and other findings related to complaints and their redress.

The former set of analyses draws on carers' experiences – surveys and calls for evidence being the prime methods of accessing data. However, other research has explored subjects such as the availability of information and advice by other methods. For example, in scrutinising local authorities' compliance with the duty to provide information by consulting its websites, Independent Age (2016) concluded that these were generally 'Care Act compliant' but offered the minimum. Glover (2018) observed the reliance on carers to self-identify, meaning that accessing support is largely up to the carers themselves. For some this may not be a problem, but he noted that fewer than half of the people who care for someone with cancer identify as a carer (also male carers, carers of older people and those who provide less intensive care are all least likely to identify as a carer).

One of the first main surveys following the Care Act implementation was undertaken by the Carers Trust (2016a). It set up a commission to assemble evidence about the impact of the Act on carers (hearing from 624 carers). Briefly this reported that:

- 21% of all respondents (not just the carers) said that things had changed for the better under the Care Act;

- 31% of carers told us that they had had an assessment, of which the quality of assessments was largely good;

- 74% of these had been face-to-face assessments;

- 52% of these carers felt that the assessor was 'knowledgeable';

- 26% had received a letter and a support plan after the assessment;

- 34% found their assessment helpful.

Later, Thorlby et al. (2018) reported that carers continue to absorb the bulk of the pressure of limited local authority resources; in their survey three-quarters (75%) of carers said they had not received any support or service which allowed them to take a break of between one and 24 hours from caring in the last 12 months.

Healthwatch (2018) also found that many carers were waiting for an assessment (an average of 28 days) and a further 29 days for services following an assessment, even those in crisis. It concluded that few local authorities were able to estimate the numbers of carers in their localities and so remain unable to plan how to meet carers' needs.

These early studies are being augmented by reports drawing on other national data from more general populations. The Nuffield Trust's (2018) further analysis of the biennial Survey of Adult Carers in England (NHS Digital, 2017a) (covering over 50,000 carers) found a drop in satisfaction among carers with the support and services they receive, such as services that carers receive themselves (such as advice and information), as well as the support for their family member including home care or a short break. The latest survey charted a decline in carers' satisfaction over the last five years. The proportion being either extremely or very satisfied with the support and services they received fell from 43% in 2012/13 to 41% in 2014/15, and to 39% in 2016/17. The Trust commented that, while the drop may not be substantial, carers' satisfaction was already low and there remain consistent reports of having no encouragement and support, being worried about personal safety, self-neglect, not having enough time to care, and feeling socially isolated.

From such studies we have reliable evidence about what carers value, such as financial help and the ability to work. Carers with financial difficulties (due to their caring work) are nearly four times more likely to be dissatisfied with their social care than those without such worries (30% compared to 8%). Those who have been supported to stay in employment, and who have their employers' backing when it comes to their caring responsibilities, are more likely to be happy/happier. For social workers this underlines the importance of putting carers in touch with expert financial advice and assistance that can cover caring-related finances, but also possible family debt and the need to maximise income benefits since caring has severe financial consequences particularly if caring long term (Carers UK, 2018b). In respect of employment, local advice on work options should be accessible and contacts made between social work teams and relevant agencies (Brimblecombe et al., 2017).

As the Nuffield Trust observed, more care and support helps carers, ranging from the ability to take a break at short notice or in an emergency, as well as access to longer breaks, home care and meals services. Those carers with access to support groups and good quality advice and information services were more satisfied than those without. This area is perhaps one where there is room for cautious optimism: 72% of carer respondents found it easy and helpful to obtain information and advice (and were very or extremely satisfied), while 12% found information difficult to find and 8% thought it was unhelpful. Social work may have a particular role in helping that 12%.

These are also potentially discouraging findings – of a gloomy picture that, despite commitments made in the passing of the 2014 Care Act, the situation for carers has deteriorated in recent years. As several commentators have noted, it may be the gap between needs and resources rather than the Act itself that is problematic. For example, the disability organisation In Control (2016) acknowledged that the Act arrived just as local authorities were experiencing profound budget cuts and the Independent Living Fund closed and elements passed to local authorities (a major source of funding for some disabled people). Just over a third (38%) of their respondents (mainly disabled adults) reported that the support they were receiving from friends or family had increased or increased significantly in the previous year (2016: 14).

Other early surveys, such as that conducted by Think Local Act Personal (TLAP, 2017c), and completed by 1,181 adults (391 people needing care and support, 643 carers), found that carers were less likely than people receiving care and support to feel they were listened to (74% compared to 65%), and just over half (54%) of carers felt they were involved as much as they wanted to be in arranging care and support (2017c: 11).

The second group of evidence comes from case law and complaints (such as those covering maladministration and service failure). These are important developments for social workers and local authorities, prompting change or amendments to practice, procedures and policies. The report of the Local Government and Social Care Ombudsman in LGSCO and Wiltshire (2018), for example, covered the following:

> *Mrs N cares for Mr P, her son. She complains the Council has wrongly cut the respite care provided for her son and has wrongly asked her to pay towards the cost of her son's transport between home and day care.* (2018: 1)

Taking just two elements of the Ombudsman's findings (in which the term 'fault' is used in the context of 'fault found causing injustice'), the Ombudsman declared:

The Council says the family is receiving care 'at the top level'. This approach does not accord with the Care Act which requires councils to assess and meet eligible needs. The Council cannot set maximum budget levels. The Act says eligible needs must be met, no matter what the cost.

{and further}

The Council's decision to ask the family to either fund or provide one day's transport per week appears to have been part of a general withdrawal of provision and a cost cutting exercise. It was not based on assessments of need and was therefore in breach of the requirements of the Care Act and was at fault. (2018: 3)

Other instances where the Local Government and Social Care Ombudsman has found 'fault' also cover situations where frontline staff seem to have been at risk of having their professional judgement overshadowed by financial pressures. The Ombudsman reported examples where local authorities had missed out the needs assessment stage altogether, and assessments had been used to justify funding-driven changes in care. LGSCO and Kent County Council (2016), where a mother was caring for her disabled 17-year-old child, illustrates that such pressures affect carers of young people nearing transition. The local authority had introduced a new Direct Payments policy:

It decided it would not provide payments to support carers who were also going out to work. The council did not properly consider the individual circumstances of the case or the impact of a reduced budget on the family. It assumed the carer would take time off work, but she could not do so. (LGSCO, 2018c: 6)

In other cases access to assessments was found at fault, with the Ombudsman in LGSCO and Merton LBC (2017) (para 10) summarising the statutory guidance thus:

The carer must be involved in the planning process. Provided the carer remains willing and able to continue caring, the local authority is not required to meet those needs. However, the local authority should record the carer's willingness to provide care and the extent of this in the plan. Where the carer also has eligible needs, the local authority should consider combining the plans of the adult requiring care and the carer, if all parties agree, and establish if the carer requires an independent advocate. (Care and Support Statutory Guidance, 10.40)

In this case concerning the London Borough of Merton, the Ombudsman found that the local authority had both failed to properly assess the care needs of Mr E and his sister/carer Miss D and provide care plans. It had also not provided indicative personal budgets as the Care Act guidance (DHSC, 2018a) suggests; indeed its decision to cut Mr E's services had been going back several years. The Ombudsman concluded that these decisions were motivated by a desire to save money and its failure to create care plans meant neither Mr E's nor Miss D's (his carer) needs were met:

> *For example, Mr E did not attend courses at college because of his behavioural problems, and alternatives such as internet-based tutors were cut. After our investigation the council reassessed needs, paid a financial remedy and reviewed its procedures to provide indicative personal budgets. It has also created a new forum to help support staff meet statutory duties and focus on eligible need so support plans correctly promote independence, wellbeing, choice and control.* (as summarised in its overview report, LGSCO, 2018c:17)

What was not in the Care Act is also important to note. Parliament decided that it would not mandate the NHS with responsibilities to identify carers (see Manthorpe et al., 2019) and assurances were given by Parliament that the NHS was addressing this subject. However, Glover (2018) and others have argued that more needs to be done by the health services in this regard and recommended that they take steps to better identify carers.

Good practice points

There are many encouragements to good practice with carers, most of which pre-date the Care Act and are hard to distinguish between good practice with service users or civility in professional life. Putting the rhetoric of giving information or 'signposting', advocacy, 'being there', 'providing a listening ear', counselling, care or case management, into practice can seem an over-general demand. The much over-used word 'support' exemplifies this. Ways of operationalising such injunctions are being developed and might be more broadly useful in practice. For example, the Scottish Carer Support Planning Toolkit (Scottish Government, 2016) contains a set of conversation and planning tools to help carers and their supporters (such as social workers) complete the support plan under the Carers (Scotland) Act 2016. Using the toolkit with a carer may help them reflect on what might be best for them and it avoids the generally off-putting language of assessment. There will be much to learn from the implementation and outcomes of this legislation more generally – echoing the general optimism that across the UK there is also much to learn from each other's practice perspectives.

Such developments chime well with the moves to encourage self-assessment by carers which is not the same as self-assessment of eligibility (that is up to the local authority). What a social worker can do is help a carer in a self-analysis of his/her needs as presented in the Scottish toolkit (mentioned above). This means that a social worker might offer to go through the questions that would be asked in advance with a carer on the phone, for example, or a peer supporter or navigator might be able to help get the information organised in a way that will minimise repetition and cover the items that matter. Knowledge of the resources and skills available in local carers' services or centres is important to good social work practice (part of asset-based approaches) and reflects social work interests in community-based, strengths-based and place-based social work. In some areas the local authority has contracted with the voluntary sector to provide information and advice, including self-assessment and assistance, as this example from a Carers Trust UK (2016b) report suggested:

> Wigan Council: "We have focused our resources externally, moving from having an internal Carers Support Team to outsourcing the statutory function to Wigan and Leigh Carers Centre. The centre's knowledge-base as well as being the central hub in the borough for carers makes them the ideal group to carry out this function. Additionally, the equality of status permits much more personalised support for carers and has allowed Wigan to move away from the standard sitting service model of support to genuine carer-focused support and services. Basically speaking, the Care Act has encouraged Wigan Council to be more creative in its approach to supporting carers and this is getting some really positive results.

In Scotland relationship-based practice (RBP) is offering a potentially new dimension to work with carers:

> While RBP does not require a sophisticated understanding of the psychology behind this, effective social work requires that a worker tune into the emotional world of a client and be able to communicate this understanding within the relationship. (Ingram and Smith, 2018: 25)

This more therapeutic approach also needs evaluating for cost-effectiveness.

Caring and personalisation

Personalisation is far more than personal budgets although the Care Act 2014 confirmed the primacy of this mode of financial transaction in social care. Indeed some of the principles of personalisation (outcomes, wellbeing, individualism or person-centredness) may be said to be fundamental to the Act.

Here we touch briefly on the support planning process which may underpin how a carer's needs will be met, not just their financing. Social workers can assist a carer in preparing a support plan to outline the carer's needs and how they will be met. As part of this support plan, an eligible carer should be given a personal budget describing the overall cost of meeting these needs including what the local authority will meet. This reflects practice prior to the Care Act but there is greater specificity of carers' eligibility criteria. Support planning, which may also be set in the context of self-directed support, is a role and task that is not confined to social work professionals; indeed it may be part of the Care Act-related activities that are contracted out to the voluntary sector. Social workers may be involved in particular cases of complexity (as outlined in the final chapter).

Conclusion

The response to carers

Writing in 2013, before the Care Act was enacted, Dame Philippa Russell, Chair of the Carers Standing Commission, stated:

> The Care Bill in many respects marks a quiet revolution in our attitudes towards, and expectations of, carers. At last, carers will be given the same recognition, respect and parity of esteem with those they support. Historically, many carers have felt that their roles and their own well-being have been undervalued and under-supported. Now we have a once in a lifetime opportunity to be truly acknowledged and valued as expert partners in care. (Department of Health, 2013b: 1)

These would always have been difficult aspirations to meet but the statement gives a flavour of the high level of expectation among the carers' movement about the Act. More specifically, in 2016 the Carers' Trust identified six litmus tests, at a minimum, for judging the success of the Care Act 2014, these being the following:

1. That carers report satisfaction with the assessments and personalised support they receive, have access to the services they need and have an understanding of their rights under the Care Act.
2. That social workers and other care practitioners can evidence that they are applying the wellbeing principle in all their adult social care decisions.
3. The number of assessments in 2018 has reached at least 360,000 in line with the Government's own estimate.
4. Social workers and other care practitioners can show that tailored support plans are routinely co-designed and kept under review with carers.
5. If a carer is facing a crisis they know how to access a rapid response service to assess and respond to their need.
6. The CQC (Care Quality Commission) routinely includes carers in its key lines of inquiry for inspections of adult social care, and health services. (Carers' Trust, 2016: 25)

These are helpful in respect of practice and system scrutiny – offering some guidance for self-audit (or others) of practice, the workings of a multi-disciplinary team or partnerships across sectors. As is often the case in social work, sharing the effectiveness of interventions is needed which involves making sure research and consultancy evaluations have clear evidence of the social work components of practice. This can be hidden, even when considering subjects such as hospital social work where studies often do not clarify the memberships of hospital liaison teams that work with patients and carers (see Moriarty et al., 2019).

Social work with carers brings great professional satisfaction and will increasingly be part of mainstream practice if only because the number of carers has been growing faster than the growth in the population over recent years. Paradoxically we will need to be better at identifying under-represented and under-recognised carers. The Care Act 2014 provides a legal framework for practice in the statutory sector, emphasising that social workers will need to continue to help them access the right help at the right time.

Case study: Barbara

In Chapter 3 (Implementing the Care Act: Assessing Need and Providing Care and Support), you met Barbara, whose care and support needs were assessed under section 9 of the Care Act prior to hospital discharge, resulting in a care and support package at home. This case study continues her story.

Barbara, who lives alone, has complex health needs and is a heavy drinker and smoker, has now for six months been receiving a daily care and support visit for personal care each morning. The local authority is now reviewing the arrangements. At the review visit it becomes clear that Barbara's health and personal care have deteriorated and that her son Robert has moved in with her. Barbara appears to rely on him for many of her daily needs, but he is finding it difficult to juggle his work commitments with these responsibilities.

Commentary

Barbara's care and support plan should be reviewed after six months and annually thereafter, but also when there has been a significant change in her circumstances (section 27, Care Act 2014). Any change to the care and support plan must have a reasonable chance of meeting the needs identified.

Barbara's son Robert appears to be providing her with care and support. Accordingly he is entitled to and should be offered a carer's assessment (section 10) since it would appear that

$\longrightarrow$

he too has needs for care and support. This would be the case even if his mother had rejected either an assessment or a care and support plan. It will be important to establish whether he feels able and willing to provide care and support for his mother, the impact of being a care provider on his wellbeing, the outcomes he wishes to achieve and whether the provision of care and support could contribute to those outcomes.

Barbara can be involved in this carer's assessment if Robert consents. Again, advocacy should be considered if this would help him to engage in the assessment (section 67). Once the assessment is complete, the eligibility of his needs must be determined (section 13) by considering whether the needs arise from providing necessary care for her, whether his physical or mental health is deteriorating and/or whether he is unable to achieve specified outcomes, such as engaging in work or recreational activities, as a consequence of which there is a significant impact on his wellbeing.

Should the assessment conclude that Robert has eligible needs, a support plan must be prepared (sections 24 and 25). This should outline how his needs will be met, the outcomes that the support plan is designed to achieve and the personal budget. As Barbara's son he can request a direct payment.

If the local authority wishes to charge Robert for any support provided, they must conduct a financial assessment (section 17) to establish how much he might have to pay (although the statutory guidance (paragraph 8.50) provides a number of reasons why it might be a false economy to levy such charges). The support plan should be reviewed, at least annually and when there is a significant change in circumstances (section 27).

Further Reading

Keating, N. and Eales, J. (2017) Social consequences of family care of adults: a scoping review, *International Journal of Care and Caring*, 1 (2): 153–73.

Larkin, M., Henwood, M. and Milne, A. (2018) Carer related research and knowledge: findings from a scoping review, *Health & Social Care in the Community*, 27 (1): 55–67.

Moriarty, J., Manthorpe, J. and Cornes, M. (2014) Reaching out or missing out: approaches to outreach with family carers in social care organisations, *Health & Social Care in the Community*, 23 (1): 42–50 (open access). Available at: https://onlinelibrary.wiley.com/doi/full/10.1111/hsc.12119

Acknowledgements and disclaimer

We acknowledge funding from the National Institute of Health Research (NIHR) Policy Research Programme under its programme of work evaluating the Care Act 2014. The views expressed in this presentation are those of the authors and not necessarily those of the NIHR, the Department of Health and Social Care or the NHS.

6 Caring: a personal perspective

Imogen Taylor

Introduction

It was very difficult to get this chapter started, probably more so than any other writing I have done in my career. I wanted to write a personal story rather than take a conventional academic approach and discovered that I really only knew how to write academically. Furthermore, exploring my recent experiences of caring for my parents and my various 'data sources' generates emotionally laden and sometimes difficult memories.

Why write this chapter? The Care Act 2014 places strong emphasis on the experiences and needs of carers. Writing offers the opportunity to make sense of my experience of caring for my parents in their very old age and to see what if anything might be learnt that could be of use to others, or indeed for myself as my caring work might not be over and I might need care myself. I am interested in our experience as self-funders, having become aware that older people are the largest group of self-funders of social care and among those most likely to experience difficulties accessing and managing their own care, yet we are largely invisible (Tanner et al., 2018). During intensely challenging phases of caring work, there were times when I would privately rail against the problems I was encountering and imagine writing for *The Guardian*, but there was never enough time for this. I was a Professor of Social Work, with extensive work commitments and responsibilities, not fully retired from my university until 2014. My father Albert died in 2012, aged 97, and my mother Sarah died in 2014, aged 94.

In 2018, on Sarah's birthday, I began sorting boxes that might be relevant for this chapter, largely untouched since moving them to my home following the sale of the family home in 2015. I noted, 'Getting started finally is a relief and has resulted in a surge of energy – anticipating unravelling the puzzle of memories about the experience of caring'. So, what are my 'data'? Sarah's diaries and letters go back to World War 2, but I decided to focus this chapter on the acute caring period, from May 2011, when my carer notebooks began, until 2014 when Sarah died. They are mostly handwritten: Sarah's diaries for 2012–2014; my three 'caring notebooks'; and three notebooks of daily carers' records for 2013–2014. Miscellaneous health and social care documents include handwritten paramedic reports from Ambulance Emergency callouts generated by falls at night (2012), written NHS and Adult Social Care communications, and finally the palliative care plan for Sarah (2014).

Thumbnail sketches

Both parents had very long lives, and these 'thumbnails' are to contextualise the caring story. Albert, born in 1915 to a working-class family in London's East End, was the youngest of three. His father worked at night as a typesetter, his mother 'did the books' for local small businesses. Albert, an avid reader, achieved a grammar school scholarship and nurtured ambitions for university and becoming a writer, but the Depression meant leaving school at 16 to become a clerk. Sarah, born in 1920 in rural Sussex, was expected to look after her frail mother; her older sister, the first in the family to attend university, became a teacher, and her older brother was to look after the family farm. Sarah's ambition was unequivocally to be an artist, inspired by her love of the countryside. In 1938 she negotiated that if she could attend art school she would look after her mother. This plan was curtailed by the outbreak of war and she became a land girl on the family farm.

In 1942 Sarah and Albert met in a soldiers' canteen and discovered a shared passion for literature, the countryside and politics. Three months later they married. Albert, away for most of the war, was demobbed after Imogen was born in 1946; a sister and brother were to follow. Being a 1950s housewife and mother was hard for Sarah, who experienced several depressions, mitigated once she began to establish herself as an artist. She was later to become known for her batiks.

Post-war, and keen to establish family life, Albert turned down a university place in favour of the security of fast-track teacher training. In 1958 we moved to Sussex for Albert to take up special needs teaching, and in 1962 to the village home where Sarah and Albert were to end their days. An inheritance enabled Albert to take early retirement and try writing, but sadly his work remained unpublished, and life revolved around the family, books, and being outdoors. He dabbled in investments – hinting that this income (of which we knew little) was to fund their future care. They added Sarah's studio to their home and Albert actively supported her career. Sarah was community oriented, an early member of the Sussex Guild, a leader in art for hospitals, and active in women's, writing and book groups. She learnt Greek for their holidays and monitored their diet and health.

My journey into caring

Caring for my parents was a positive choice, supported by my partner who had known my parents for almost fifty years. 'Choice' was influenced by my gender, birth order, family history, and career in social work. Looking back over three generations, I am struck by the caring tradition. My parents cared for my paternal grandparents in a small cottage next door to our home. My maternal grandmother, widowed in her seventies, had dementia, and was cared for by a 'live-in'. My partner's maternal grandmother lived with his family from wartime until her death at 94. My in-laws moved to a purpose-built cottage beside our then home where my mother-in-law died following an illness, preparation for my own parents dying at home. Two years later, my father-in-law unexpectedly died of an infection following elective surgery, reinforcing our concern that hospitals are potentially dangerous for older people.

Given this history, it is perhaps unsurprising that I have researched and written about caring. Initially at the University of Toronto, I wrote about caring and domestic violence (Taylor, 1991), influenced by Finch and Groves' (1983) concept of caring as *love* and *labour* and Dalley's (1988) concepts of caring *for* (services) and caring *about* (love and affection). Following my appointment at the University of Bristol, I undertook with Mike Fisher research into carers and carer support workers in rural Somerset (Taylor, 1999), also exploring reciprocal caring in long-term relationships (Fisher, 1994).

Framework for this chapter

When debating how to approach the data, 'Making Safeguarding Personal' (MSP) (Cooper et al., 2018) appeared in my inbox and appealed to my values of supporting participation, choice and control. Here, I adapt the challenges to MSP that they identified, through my lens as a carer:

- Early support of continuing independence.
- Sustaining choice and control under intense and fluctuating pressures.
- Responding to changes in ideas of selfhood and interdependencies.
- Building collaborations around cared-for persons.

Key examples of caring for Sarah and Albert have been selected to illustrate discussion. Although too late for them, the experience of caring is discussed in light of the Care Act (2014), which repealed previous legislation and introduced a duty on local authorities to promote an individual's wellbeing. It entitles carers to assessment if they appear to have support needs, and to support if as a result of caring they are unable to achieve certain personal outcomes and there is a significant impact on their wellbeing.

My aim is to explore the above themes within a temporal framework, as the caring work significantly changed over time. Like Cooper and colleagues, I was influenced by work on the ethics of care (Tronto, 1993) and the fundamental attributes of attentiveness, responsibility, competence and responsiveness.

Early support of continuing independence

In early 2011, Sarah and I had a pivotal discussion about their increasing needs. Albert, diagnosed with dementia in 2008, attended appointments to monitor his medication but did not acknowledge the disease or its implications. He still gained pleasure from his daily activities. He received an Attendance Allowance, and Sarah appreciated the recognition that being a 'carer' conferred. However, caring for Albert was increasingly demanding, and combined with changes in her own health, it was affecting Sarah's wellbeing. She was ready to hand on the carer role.

Sarah needed more practical support and she thought Ellen, who lived in the village, might be available to cook, shop, clean, and drive them where they wanted to go. Ellen agreed to work three days per week; furthermore, her adult son would look after Sarah's beloved garden. Ellen, who had cared for her own mother in the village until her death, was to become someone I would work in partnership with, almost another family member. However, we soon needed to take further steps to address Sarah and Albert's wellbeing, and I found that when caring for frail elderly people, nothing stays the same for long.

Driving the car

Much as we wanted to continue to support their control over their everyday life, Sarah and Albert's use of their car was becoming a worry and became an early test of balancing wishes and views with the need to keep them safe. The car was essential to independent living in their rural location. Sarah had been driving since her teens, Albert had failed a series of driving tests. In 2011 Sarah's driving competence was questioned when, driving up the familiar lane to their home, she hit a council hedge-cutting vehicle. Albert could not recall the incident and insisted Sarah was competent to drive; she did not dispute this view yet always preferred others to drive. There were differing views within the family about whether she should immediately stop driving. I proposed we aim to minimise her driving by a carer or family member doing so. Her driving diminished, the car remained parked as always, with keys out of view. I was to discover that there was never a fully comfortable position in balancing risks, particularly as Sarah's and Albert's wishes were increasingly divergent, challenging notions of choice and control embedded in the personalisation agenda (Woolham et al., 2016, cited in Tanner et al., 2018).

Adapting daily living

After almost fifty years Sarah and Albert were embedded in their home and community and moving to housing more suited to their changing needs was not on the agenda. During 2011, discussions intensified about adapting their home: they were both experiencing problems safely using the bath with Ellen, her son, or neighbours being called to help (I lived 30 minutes away by car). In June 2011, supported by the Memory Clinic monitoring Albert,

Sarah contacted Adult Social Care (ASC) for advice about bathroom safety and a stairlift, resulting in advice from Occupational Therapists (OTs) who Sarah liked and Albert tolerated. I was grateful for early advice that stairlifts are unsafe for people with dementia. It emerged that Sarah, influenced by newspaper advertising, was already contacting installers.

Discussions focused on converting Sarah's ground floor studio into a bedroom, and the downstairs cloakroom to a fully adapted shower room and toilet. Initially, she strongly resisted – the loss of her bath as a retreat, and her studio, core to her artist identity, was too much to bear. Albert denied the need for such a move; his capacity to retain new information was declining. We tried to engage his participation in moving downstairs as being in Sarah's best interests, but his capacity to integrate a complex perspective was declining. The OT assessment led to taking our first visit to a Disability Association warehouse-shop. We were quite overwhelmed by the sheer range of unfamiliar products but, with OT advice, various pieces of kit began to be acquired. Sarah particularly enjoyed the support of a three-wheeled 'pusher' outside the home; Albert preferred his stick.

By December 2011 Sarah and Albert still slept upstairs, but there was an urgency to act before the health of one or both declined further and events overtook us. Work on the downstairs shower room began, and once it was ready the family joined efforts together with Ellen to support Sarah and Albert's participation in moving into the studio bedroom. This was a huge and disorienting change for them.

For the first time access to Albert's investment income was essential, and by then he had begun to trust my partner to help manage the bank accounts. The three children had registered an Enduring Power of Attorney (EPA) for Sarah and Albert before the Mental Capacity Act (MCA) (2005), but had not appreciated the implications that, although the EPA conferred powers over property and finance, it did not address health and welfare.

Fluctuating and diminishing capacities

The above period was essentially one of planned change with time to engage Sarah and Albert's participation. In contrast, in the first half of 2012, I felt I was always running to keep up. Albert's capacities were significantly diminishing. We introduced a second woman carer from the village, a friend of Ellen, to cover when Ellen was not available, and a cleaner to free Ellen for cooking, shopping and taking Sarah and Albert out. A key-safe was installed. Recognising the challenge of co-working, Ellen was the designated 'care co-ordinator' accountable to me. I was the family member who had chosen to assume caring responsibility, and by this time either myself and/or my partner were going to the house most days. I was feeling increasingly burdened and sought practical support from my siblings, specifically at this time to share responsibility for Sundays with our parents.

Over this period, my somewhat chaotic notes are dominated by concerns about Albert's diet, medications and unexplained bruising. Both parents were falling, and at least nine calls (throughout 2012) were made at night via Lifeline to paramedics to help one or other get back to bed. Albert was usually recorded as 'uncooperative', refusing hospital for further investigation. Sarah tended to 'slip' down and did not incur evident bruising. Albert was also experiencing incontinence and infections, and was prescribed a maintenance prophylactic antibiotic. A potentially serious muddle occurred between surgery and pharmacy regarding a prescription for Albert. I felt buffeted by events.

Worried about the risks when there was no carer in the house, in March 2012 I made my first enquiry of a private live-in agency. I was treading on unfamiliar territory and feeling I needed professional advice about setting up 24-hour care; I left a message with ASC but it was never responded to. On reflection, I was probably ambivalent about help seeking from ASC, as on an earlier occasion when I had phoned, an ex-social work student from my university had answered. Again, I used my own networks for advice and recommendations.

Sustaining choice and control under pressure

Treating others with dignity and respect and supporting choice and control underpinned my commitment to support my parents to remain in their own home as long as they wished. In general they treated each other with dignity and respect, but Albert could become angry and emotionally controlling with Sarah if his wishes were thwarted. He continued to resist outside interventions, with the exception of his long-standing GP and to some extent the village carers who had found a way to chivvy him along. Adding live-in carers into this mix was never going to be straightforward, and most problematic Sarah wanted live-in care and Albert did not.

Albert and diminishing control

In August 2012, our first experience with a live-in carer was a near disaster. Ellen was present when Susan arrived. Ellen phoned to advise that Albert was threatening Susan who, afraid he would hit her, had locked herself in her room; he had snatched food from her when she was making her own tea, accused her of stealing, and threatened to call the police. Susan was black and accusing Albert of racism. He was flushed and energised when I arrived, unable to remember what had happened. Albert, who normally greeted me warmly as 'dear', accused me of lying to justify the need for a live-in and orchestrating plans against his wishes. He did not accept that his memory was letting him down. I sought telephone advice from the Alzheimer's Society, who provided constructive and relevant information about how to manage such aggression.

A GP, not our preferred one, diagnosed a urinary tract infection and warned that Albert would 'end up in a nursing home' if we were unable to manage him. Albert ruminated 'I am the villain ... others can be infected by me'. I agreed that his paranoid responses were likely due to a combination of the major change in his environment, dementia, an infection, and possibly a head injury from falling. The GP agreed to seek a full assessment for Albert and in the meantime proposed anti-psychotic medication as a temporary intervention.

Albert was never so intensely angry again. On one occasion when I arrived he greeted me with 'We've got trouble' – the closest this very proud and independent man came to help seeking. There had been an incident in the night that disturbed them both, and not long after Albert went rapidly downhill. He regularly reminded us that he would live to 100 and had consistently refused to discuss an Advance Decision to Refuse Treatment (ADRT) (Mental Capacity Act 2005). However, the ADRT would have been redundant as he died peacefully at home in November, supported by the family, GP and district nurses.

Sarah and diminishing control

It had briefly seemed possible that in surviving Albert, Sarah might benefit from not competing for attention, but she was often lonely, even though not alone. I admit to some relief in being able to focus on one parent, and Sarah was receptive to support during her final two years when dealing with the intersecting problems of breast cancer and dementia.

Breast cancer

Sarah was first diagnosed with breast cancer in 2005 when a mastectomy was proposed but firmly rejected by Sarah due to the link between anaesthesia and dementia. She was prescribed Tamoxifen, regularly monitored, and the tumour shrank, but in 2011 the medication was stopped as it was assessed as causing undesirable side effects. The tumour returned and in late 2012 a mastectomy was strongly recommended: the tumour could cause discomfort, skin ulceration and fungation. Sarah and I talked the decision over with the family, the Breast Clinic nurse, anaesthetist, GP and herbalist, and she decided to proceed. The health team was very supportive and not ageist. Sarah was 92.

The hospital experience was unexpectedly positive. Sarah discovered that her 1990s Hospital Arts Project had resulted in art that was still on the walls twenty years later, including her own work. She proudly told the nurses this when on the trolley to the operating theatre. On discharge 24 hours later Sarah was told she was 'a trooper', but by late 2013 the tumour had returned and radiotherapy did not contain it. After the final meeting with the team (July 2014), the oncologist noted 'Sarah is happy and unconcerned emotionally and physically by her progressive disease'. Indeed, she did not remember that she had cancer and reminding her seemed cruel and unnecessary. The oncologist predicted that she might live for many months and recommended referral to district nurses (DNs) for skin management and the Hospice Community Palliative Care Team for 'all parties', particularly if admission for symptom control or respite was needed. The DNs were attentive, caring, and mostly competent. Sarah was in general comfortable. By this time, initiated by my sister, Sarah had acquired a new interest, a cat she named Whiskers.

Dementia and depression

Sarah, after her early depressions, in later life sought out and enjoyed support from a counsellor. She dreaded dementia but accepted the GP referral (November 2012) to a community mental health nurse (CMHN). The CMHN found sufficient short-term memory loss for referral to the old age psychiatrist and met weekly with Sarah in the meantime, monitoring medications and supporting her during the weeks of acutely restless and distressed behaviour following Albert's death. Sarah and I both found the CMHN interventions helpful and I particularly welcomed her view that she expected to become the key worker. Over this period of acute distress, we brought in a waking-night carer service to support the live-in carer. Sarah's beliefs were difficult to shift, for example that foreign students were living upstairs. Once again, my notes are dominated by the ever present myriad of issues, including discussions about medications, the question of sedation, and the challenge of Sarah eating enough.

In February 2013, I took Sarah to the same memory clinic that she had taken Albert to. The psychiatrist diagnosed Alzheimer's, vascular dementia and a recurrence of depression. In May 2014 he noted that although still poor there were improvements in her memory, and also in her mood and cognitive processing, and she had a 'normal capacity to consent to treatment'. We shared frustration at the lack of activities for people like my parents who have had a rich intellectual life – he suggested I might volunteer to run a group for academics with dementia! As Sarah's dementia developed, she at times looked for Albert, asking us to find him as she did not have much longer to live and wanted to say goodbye. Thankfully she always remembered her children.

Changes in selfhood and interdependencies

Sarah's handwriting, of which she had been proud, had become fragmented with crossings out and this embarrassed her. Nevertheless, when I put together her jottings made during the year before she died, they eloquently recorded her feelings about changes in herself and her life. Poignantly at times she thought she was the only resident in a care home and her real home was her childhood home:

> *30.12.13 Looking back – I would never have expected such a big change in my lifestyle, but there it is! Me, dependent on a regulated lifestyle, dependent as it is now on the support of a team of carers, who have become very much part of the remaining life that is left to me ... I should like to have more contact with some family members but I respect their need to be concentrating on their work, as long as they keep in touch with me, which I believe they will and I know how busy they are.*

> *31.12.13 I am fitting in to a life of an institution here which is something I would never have expected to do.*

6.1.14 I must try and write something intelligently every day. Yesterday I had a near clash with my carer – only narrowly avoided but warning me to avoid at all costs or life would become impossible in such a situation, when we are both shut up together. It was about our meals.

26.1.14 Imogen came on her own. It has been a good day. We went down through the village as far as the church. Everywhere is so familiar. Only met two people but our talk was memorable as we looked at graves and I told her I wanted to be buried in the churchyard there. Then we went to the Nursery and bought some plants; it is so familiar there. I felt so at home … I am thankful that we have a solid financial backing and I do not have to worry about the financial side of all this. Also that I have the huge geographical advantage of being in fairly easy reach of (daughters). Also I am situated in a pleasant rural place which suits me. I could do with mixing more with other people but that cannot be helped – it is better than being shut away in a home for old people like myself.

10.3.14 I am scrubbed clean by my cleaner and it is a bright, sunny morning. To do what? I would like to go for a walk in the sun but I am not allowed to go on my own. Oh dear!

21.3.14 I want to do some creative writing but cannot decide what… I have the perfect situation – a quiet room to myself, it is also a room in which the walls are covered by my work. So what? I was once a creative person – am I no longer then? Can an artist or writer force creativity?

4.5.14 My carer took me to buy some plants for the garden. I am beginning to feel like a guest who is staying at a boarding house and not a member of a family, which I do not feel happy about. But what is the alternative?

9.5.14 A memorable happening today has been that my carer suggested I walk with her across our field to our wood. I enjoyed doing it because it had been put off as I had no-one to go with in case I fell.

15.6.14 I am not happy but how to change my situation is a big problem. Is this a partial escape? I think maybe. This may be my house but does that mean I am in charge, or that I can be bossed around? No, it doesn't.

In the last few months of her life it became easier to find activities that satisfied Sarah – a favourite would be weekend visits from my brother. She enjoyed woodland visits to see bluebells, short drives to places with special memories, Sunday lunch at our house and being driven through her beloved Downs. She liked to wheel her pusher along the promenade and sit on a bench overlooking the sea; or she transferred to a wheelchair so that she could see less accessible favourite views such as the Seven Sisters. Her capacity to concentrate was diminishing, affecting her interest in reading and classical music. Finding TV programmes she liked was a challenge – one carer managed to successfully introduce her to *Mr Bean*, new to Sarah who previously had eschewed comedy.

Building collaborations around cared-for persons

I was committed to building collaborations to support, stimulate and energise Sarah and Albert, as well as keep them safe. The most significant for both of them was the family, particularly the three children, their partners and the grandchildren. All were engaged at one time or another in the emotional and practical labour of caring and their support meant a great deal to Sarah and Albert and was invaluable to me. Between the three children, there were different visions of care, a different willingness and capacity to deliver it and different aspirations. There was an acceptance that caring for Sarah and Albert was my choice, and I was responsible for it. There was also another view that they should be 'in a home'. Exploring these dynamics is another discussion; suffice it to say here, today we are good friends.

Carers' collaborations

The local carers collaborated well with each other and with me. My initial ambition was for long-term agency care-workers, essential to continuity of care. However, I soon learnt that carers were placed for up to two weeks with no guarantee of returns, and that the carers were self-employed with contractual obligations to their agencies. The plan to retain Ellen in a co-ordinating role – orienting new carers, overseeing changeovers and so on – led to concerns by some carers about too many bosses. At times, it felt like a dysfunctional family.

There were some very competent carers but too often I was concerned about the quality of care. Several incidents particularly raised my concern about agency selection processes and a lack of ongoing support for the carers. We requested on three occasions that carers be replaced. I was contacted by an ASC Safeguarding Manager, on receipt of a complaint that a carer was 'verbally and physically abusive' to Albert. She had already left at our request. I pointed out the irony that a complaint had triggered an immediate response from ASC, whereas I was still waiting to hear about my request for ASC support. An alarming example was when I learnt that the care agency suspected an imposter carer was imminently due to arrive at the house late on a winter afternoon; a manager arrived, and intercepted the arrival of the 'carer' outside the house and she immediately left in the taxi she arrived in. Another kind of problem was highly anxious carers, including one who was doing far too much unnecessary washing (using a litre of fabric softener and packet of washing tablets each week). When she was unable to change her behaviour, we asked her to leave.

Agency collaboration

I was well versed in research about failures in collaboration between health and social care, and the Care Act 2014 (sections 6 and 7) makes it a statutory requirement for local authorities and relevant partners to co-operate together when exercising their respective functions in relation to people with care and support needs and to carers. Social care services were restructured at least once over the period we were working with them, manifested in changes of OT, with whom individually collaboration worked well. Collaboration between health services, including with me as the carer, generally worked reasonably well. We experienced invaluable continuity from the GPs, the Breast Clinic team and the Memory Clinic, even if at times communication between them seemed slow. For example we might be advised of an outcome during a contact, yet it could take days and sometimes weeks for the communication to be formalised between the services, delaying action. If quick action was needed, it was usually possible for me to be the messenger. The district nurses were restructured while we knew them and their leadership changed; when they visited almost daily, cracks in the system became clear. For example, there were disagreements between them about the use of a certain kind of honey in bandaging, or they did not always follow the same protocols and were challenged on this by the hospice worker. There were evident tensions between the local surgery and pharmacy and both appeared to be significantly overloaded, affecting the capacity of systems to keep pace with change. I formally complained twice: for example, when two prescriptions for Albert's antibiotics were issued at the same time and an apology from the surgery was received; and again when the psychiatrist issued Sarah with a prescription for another patient, complete with the latter's identifying details. I felt I could never relax my vigilance.

Regrettably, there was poor collaboration at the boundaries between social care and health. Examples included: the GP expressing different views from the OT about the risks of bed rails, leaving me unclear about which way to proceed; a disagreement about who should assess Sarah's capacity, delaying the assessment; and confusion about the key worker role, with advice from the CMHN that she would be the key worker, to be advised weeks later that this was only possible if Sarah's dementia was 'primary' and somewhere a decision had been made that the cancer was 'primary'. Regrettably, the latter was not a decision that we were consulted on.

It was a relief when the Hospice Community Palliative Care Team became involved and there was an identified key worker whom I could turn to about anything. She initiated interventions: on her first home visit she observed poor practice by a district nurse and insisted with the head DN that this be corrected immediately; she stopped a medication that could be having serious side effects, and arranged a medication review; she amended Sarah's diet; and she insisted that the local council must pick up clinical waste from the house. No issue was too big or small for her to deal with and notably she carried authority with both health and social care and made things happen. I felt supported practically and emotionally through Sarah's final stages of life, and finally able to focus my energies on Sarah and relax my hyper-vigilance about the surrounding systems.

Final reflections

Sarah and Albert might be seen as enjoying an optimum situation – a supportive family, living in their own home in a community that cared for and about them, and in a position to self-fund and purchase social care services. Self-funding is far from a 'magic bullet', and conceivably it led to us being under-served due to assumptions that we were coping. Managing care for older people with multiple needs is a 'complex equation involving multiple variables and interactions ... our findings refute the notion that older people's wellbeing can be viewed as a product of individual purchasing power and consumer choice; rather it has to be understood as generated through relationships with others' (Tanner et al., 2018: 278). Following Sarah's death, her GP commented that I was 'brave' and on reflection I agree! Crucially, I had to sustain confidence in myself as the catalyst, ensuring that the relational work was doable and managing my anxieties about the complex range of tasks and risks involved. Others might have said that I was foolhardy given the risk taking, as well as the sheer labour of the project over more than two years. I would not have managed without support, in particular from my partner.

Writing this chapter has helped me make sense of the caring experience. On reflection and with the benefit of hindsight and the Care Act (2014), I would do three things differently. I offer these as learning points also for health and social care practitioners.

Firstly, I would have the confidence of my convictions and aim to sustain continuity of 24-hour care in the form of at least two privately employed carers, backed up by relief care from the village. It was important for Sarah and Albert as well as the family to come to know and trust their carers, and for this relationship to be reciprocal. We instituted this model when we terminated our contract with the first agency and negotiated privately with two of their best carers. Our model relied on a stable core of highly competent carers willing to work outside the agency, and being in a rural area, willing to drive. When one of the privately employed carers needed to take indefinite sick leave in the last few months of Sarah's life, we negotiated with an agency to provide the second core carer, in addition to continuing to draw on complementary local support. I would seek ASC support and monitoring for this plan. The Care Act statutory guidance (DoH, 2018) states that local authorities, as part of their market-shaping duty (section 5, Care Act 2014), should have a better understanding of the needs of people who self-fund their care, and should support and empower them to make effective purchasing decisions. My experience was that ASC were only interested if there were safeguarding issues.

Secondly, I would seek a named keyworker with sufficient authority to work across health and social care, a role that in the Care Act might be secured by the GP or ASC. My first choice would be for this being the GP, as key tasks would be to enable 'health' activities such as: i) regular medication reviews in a context where a number of medications were prescribed, and frequent changes made by prescribers; ii) nutrition reviews in light of the significance of eating well in very old age, yet the complex challenges to this; and iii) complex treatments such as bandaging, carried out at home by health professionals. There were brief glimpses of the value of such support, when the community mental health nurse became involved following Albert's death, and again when the community palliative care team worker became involved with Sarah. Significantly, this worker also made things happen with the local authority.

There is a different case for an ASC key worker. The local authority's duty to undertake care and support needs assessment (section 9, Care Act 2014) applies regardless of the individual's ability to pay for their assessed needs to be met, and in the early stages for Sarah and Albert this was for OT support. The LA also has a duty (section 10) to undertake a carer's assessment, and to provide proactive support if the carer's caring role prevents them from achieving personal outcomes and there is a significant impact on their wellbeing as a result. There were significant stress points for me in managing the care team, and I would have welcomed social work support to monitor and review our course of action, and in addition perhaps provide an opportunity for the family to explore diverse views about ways forward.

Thirdly, I would seek a GP referral to the Community Palliative Care Team prior to Albert's death. One of the most challenging periods was in the months before he died, particularly after the upheaval of introducing live-in carers when his mental and physical capacities were rapidly diminishing. It was not until Sarah's final visit to the Breast Clinic and the ensuing recommendation for community palliative care that I became aware such a service was available, accessed through the GP. It had not been suggested for Albert, a matter of some regret to me now as my energies were spread too thinly over his final weeks.

The last words here must go to Sarah, also reflecting on whether she could have done better, given another chance. She begins with the term 'ambushed', one that she had read (Lively, 2013: 3) and which strongly resonated for her:

> 'Ambushed by old age. After all those years, like a cupboard door that has never been opened – in case it was discovered to be, yes, unwanted, not fair, not deserved even. Yes, I know – No good thinking that! I have done my best surely haven't I? It hasn't been easy. All those careful diets, all those carefully chosen habits, all that exercising? So how has it let me down? Am I not allowed a re-run? Do I not have a second chance? What have I done wrong? No – it seems I cannot learn from my mistakes. That's not fair surely? Is it too late to start again? I'm sure I could do better next time. But there it is. No, I shall not have a second chance. It is not allowed'. (November 2013)

Further Reading

Baxter, K. (2016) Self funders and social care; findings from a scoping review, *Research, Policy and Planning*, 31 (3): 179–93. This scoping review maps a robust, research-based context.

Henwood, M., McKay, S., Needham, C. and Glasby, J. (2019) *From Bystanders to Core Participants? A Literature and Data Review of Self-Funders in Social Care Markets*. Birmingham: University of

Birmingham Health Services Management Centre. (I like the use of realist review research, the quality of the theorising, and the concept of moving from 'bystanders' to 'core participants'.)

Mangano, A. (2016) Self-funded elder care and the Care Act 2014: insights from a qualitative study of family carers' experiences, *Working with Older People*, 20 (3): 157–64. (Although a small study, I like the focus on the experience of family carers, and the particular emphasis on attitudes to 'public intervention'.)

7 Adult safeguarding

Suzy Braye and Michael Preston-Shoot

Introduction

For the first time in England, adult safeguarding powers and duties have been codified in primary legislation. As recommended by the Law Commission (2011), the Care Act 2014 gives lead co-ordinating responsibility for adult safeguarding to local authorities, with Clinical Commissioning Groups (CCGs) and the police as statutory partners. The statutory guidance (DHSC, 2018a) defines safeguarding as '*Protecting an adult's right to live in safety, free from abuse and neglect. It is about people and organisations working together to prevent and stop both the risks and experience of abuse or neglect, while at the same time making sure that the adult's wellbeing is promoted including, where appropriate, having regard to their views, wishes, feelings and beliefs in deciding on any action*' (para.14.7).

It is timely to review the evidence emerging about the implementation of these new provisions, drawing on national data that local authorities submit annually to the Department of Health and Social Care, on research reports, safeguarding adult reviews (SARs), judicial review decisions, and judgements following investigations by the Local Government Ombudsman and Information Commissioner. The potential for judicial and investigative scrutiny of adult safeguarding practice should remind local authorities and their statutory partners of the importance of adhering to standards contained within administrative law (Preston-Shoot, 2019).

This chapter reviews the key adult safeguarding provisions embedded in Act, critiquing the powers and duties contained in sections 42–47 and amplified in the statutory guidance (DHSC, 2018a), which together provide an overarching framework for the safeguarding process (Bows and Penhale, 2018). It evaluates available evidence on implementation of the duties to enquire, to establish Safeguarding Adults Boards (SABs), to commission SARs, and to share information. The statutory guidance makes it clear that Making Safeguarding Personal (MSP) should underpin adult safeguarding practice, alongside duties on statutory agencies to promote wellbeing and co-operate. The chapter explores currently available outcomes evidence in relation to these requirements. It further considers the requirements for advocacy and, finally, considers potential gaps in the legislation, in so doing offering a comparative perspective of adult safeguarding law in Scotland and Wales.

Section 42 – duty to enquire

Where a local authority has reasonable cause to suspect that an adult

- who has care and support needs (regardless of whether those needs are being met),
- is experiencing or at risk of abuse and neglect, and
- as a result of their care and support needs is unable to protect themselves,

the authority must conduct an enquiry (which it can delegate to another agency) and decide what action should be taken, if any, and by whom. There are no additional eligibility or threshold criteria; it is sufficient that the three core criteria are met in order for the duty to be engaged.

The duty to enquire covers all types of abuse and neglect, as listed in the statutory guidance (DHSC, 2018a). This includes well-recognised circumstances such as physical, sexual, psychological/emotional, financial/material, neglect and acts of omission, and is broadened to include organisational and discriminatory abuse, modern slavery, domestic abuse and self-neglect, although the guidance makes clear that this an illustrative rather than an exhaustive list. Confusingly, however, and perhaps reflecting ambivalence about the inclusion of self-neglect in adult safeguarding, the statutory guidance (DHSC, 2018a) states that self-neglect may not always prompt a section 42 enquiry; that will depend on the person's ability to protect themselves *'by controlling their own behaviour'* (para.14.17), and whether they need external support to do this.

Recalling administrative law standards, practice must be lawful and timely, decisions must be reasonable and rational, and relevant people should be consulted. Investigations have found fault where local authorities have failed to follow the statutory guidance or investigate in a timely, unbiased and focused manner. Similarly they have criticised delays, and failures in maintaining adequate records of assessments, reaching rational and reasonable decisions, following national guidance, and involving relatives and other relevant people (LGO and Oxfordshire County Council (2016); LGO and Bath and North East Somerset Council (2017); LGO and Hertfordshire County Council (2017h)).

Thematic reviews of SARs (Braye and Preston-Shoot, 2017a; Preston-Shoot, 2017a) have reported examples where referral opportunities for section 42 enquiries have been missed, or where referrals have been inappropriately screened out. Reviews have concluded that not all staff have been aware of safeguarding criteria and referral pathways, with consequent missed opportunities for multi-agency information-sharing and risk management. Reviews have also found that, mistakenly, the individual's consent was assumed to be required prior to a section 42 enquiry, contrary to statutory guidance. Noteworthy too is that there is no equivalent in the Care Act 2014 to duties elsewhere in the UK to report when an adult is suspected of being at risk of abuse, neglect or other harm (Adult Support and Protection (Scotland) Act 2007, section 5; Social Services and Well-being (Wales) Act 2014, section 128).

There have been cases where individuals, in the name of safeguarding, have been unlawfully removed from their home and deprived of their liberty, with breaches found of Articles 5, 6 and 8 of the European Convention on Human Rights (ECHR). These cases have been characterised by disregard for the legal rules, inadequate adult safeguarding investigations and a failure to involve the Court of Protection (see for example *Somerset County Council v MK* [2014]; *Milton Keynes Council v RR* [2014]). These are a timely reminder of the importance of legal literacy in safeguarding practice.

Making safeguarding personal

Ombudsman investigations, SARs and judicial findings are timely reminders too that section 42 enquiries, as with all adult safeguarding work, must be underpinned by a twin focus on wellbeing and MSP. Running as a sector-led improvement project since 2010, with extensive piloting, toolkits, guidance and positive evaluation (Lawson et al., 2014; Pike and Walsh, 2015), MSP entered the mainstream with implementation of the Act. Its principles require safeguarding to be person-led and outcome-focused, aimed at enhancing the person's involvement, choice and control, whilst also improving their quality of life and safety (DHSC, 2018a). It *'aims to: enable safeguarding to be done "with", not "to", people and shift practice from a process supported by conversations to a series of conversations supported by a process'* (Cooper and Bruin, 2017: 212).

The use of the term 'enquiry' in s.42 shows its influence; drawing attention to previous evidence of disempowering safeguarding processes, the Department of Health notes: *'Enquiries is a term that emphasises the need for discussion, reflection and a process that gives importance to the subjective experience of the individual as well as the views of the professional and the objective "facts". It also recognises that the enquiry, the discussion itself, is part of the intervention'* (Crawley, 2015).

MSP has required a fundamental culture change but has been broadly welcomed. Open discussions, while requiring more time, are seen as making safeguarding more effective, and potentially reducing the overall life cycle of the process (Butler and Manthorpe, 2016). A survey of implementation in local authorities (Briggs and Cooper, 2018; Cooper et al., 2018) found first steps completed: staff were trained, systems had been modified. A second stage of embedding MSP culture in practice was in progress but transfer of MSP to partner organisations was yet to take place. MSP was being strongly driven by frontline practitioners, by whom it was seen as a welcome return to strengths-based practice and core social work values, but taking place against a backdrop of bureaucratic systems, organisational inertia and funding shortages. MSP is also seen as part of the broader development of strengths-based and assets-based approaches in social work (Department of Health, 2017) and as having synergies with adult safeguarding models based on a Signs of Safety approach, aiming to mobilise person-led and person-centred practice (see for example Stanley, 2016).

While MSP is clearly indicative of positive changes to practice, it may not be consistently applied. Lonbay (2018), in a study exploring the involvement of older people, identified that constructions of older people as inherently vulnerable reduced their opportunities to be engaged, removing their agency within professionals' responses to safeguarding concerns. Some SARs have concluded that MSP has been misinterpreted, placing undue emphasis on the individual's stated wishes (often about service refusal) to the exclusion of a fuller consideration of risk and ongoing monitoring and evaluation of options (Braye et al., 2015a; Preston-Shoot, 2017b; Braye and Preston-Shoot, 2017b). The focus on the person's wishes and goals must not result in the exclusion of discussion about risk; practice must comprise questioning and the respectful challenging of choices. An emphasis on autonomy should not automatically result in case closure. Instead a fine-tuned risk-appraisal process is called for, balancing often competing imperatives – skilled work for which skilled supervision is necessary (a point emphasised by statutory guidance; see DHSC, 2018a).

Clearly close observance of the principles of the Mental Capacity Act 2005 and recognition of the need for mental capacity assessment is crucial in such circumstances; SARs have provided evidence of capacity to decline services being assumed rather than tested, with practitioners missing warning signs that could indicate impaired decision-making ability. Lennard (2016) emphasises the importance of challenging the presumption of capacity in order to distinguish unwise decisions made without capacity from those made with capacity, with the threshold at which a capacity assessment should take place, and the nature of that assessment, both being crucial to determine.

The role of advocacy in s.42 enquiries

The Care Act (s.68) provides a duty to involve an independent advocate for a person who is the subject of a safeguarding enquiry, if without one they would have substantial difficulty understanding, retaining and using or weighing relevant information or communicating their views, wishes and feelings, and where they have no appropriate person to represent and support them. Advocates must have suitable experience, appropriate training, competence, good character, work independently (from the local authority) and engage in regular supervision (DHSC, 2018a).

Cooper and Bruin (2017) note that advocacy organisations have refocused their activity to meet these new requirements, but that advocacy involvement is taking time to embed in practice and more needs to be done to ensure that appropriate consideration is given to whether safeguarding advocacy is required. This mirrors evidence to suggest that the parallel Care Act requirement for advocacy in relation to care and support assessments (s.67) has been slow to gain traction, with Dixon et al. (2018) noting that levels of commissioning are less than might be expected and that professionals lack awareness about advocacy rights, are confused about different forms of statutory advocacy,[1] and have mixed attitudes towards it. While Newbigging et al. (2016), reviewing advocacy commissioning practice, identified more encouraging evidence, they found that a reliance on single, larger providers was limiting diversity in provision. Again frontline staff lacked understanding of their referral duties, reflecting similar findings from Scotland where late referrals compromise advocates' potential contribution (Sherwood-Johnson, 2016). Lonbay and Brandon (2017) nonetheless show the benefits of advocacy in supporting older people through safeguarding, while also identifying factors that inhibit advocates' involvement: the tight timeframes for safeguarding decisions and professionals' understanding of advocates' role. They consider strategic representation of advocacy organisations on SABs to be an important way of building the necessary interagency relationships.

The scale of safeguarding activity

Local authorities are required to report to NHS Digital on s.42 enquiries. A robust statistical picture is beginning to emerge (NHS Digital, 2017b; 2018). Comparing 2016/2017 (the first year in which reporting was mandatory) and 2017/2018, there was an increase of 8.2% between the two reporting years, tipping the number of concerns raised to just over 1,000 per day. In 2017/2018, 38% of concerns resulted in safeguarding enquiries; the number of section 42 enquiries started decreased by 1.1% but those categorised as 'Other'[2] rose by 1.8%. The 'conversion rate' of concerns to section 42 enquiries declined from 41% to 38% and equates currently to 245 individuals per 100,000 population. There was, however, considerable variation between authorities and between age categories, with people over 85 in particular much more likely to be involved in a safeguarding enquiry. Some caution about variations in the conversion rate of concerns to enquiries is necessary, given differences between local authorities in demography, demand, definitions and recording (for example, local authority IT systems used to record concerns and enquiries do not always differentiate between s.42 and 'Other' categories).

Among s.42 enquiries that concluded within the year, neglect and acts of omission accounted for one-third of the risks identified, followed with declining frequency by physical, financial and material, psychological/emotional, sexual, organisational, self-neglect, domestic, discriminatory, sexual exploitation and modern slavery. The adult's home was the most frequently involved location, followed by residential and nursing care homes. Service providers were the largest source of risk for the categories of neglect and acts of commission and organisational abuse. Over the two reporting cycles the percentage of adults involved who had mental capacity in relation to safeguarding decisions[3] decreased slightly, with a corresponding small rise in those lacking capacity (27% to 31%) and those who were supported by an advocate, family or friend (73% to 79%). Figures for mental capacity either not known or not recorded have fallen to 18% but there was considerable regional variation in this figure. In terms of outcomes in 2017/2018, in 69% of enquiries a risk was identified and some form of action taken.[4] In 63% of those cases the risk was reduced, in 27% it was removed, and in 10% it remained.

Safeguarding service models

Local authorities have complete discretion over the organisational arrangements they make for responding to adult safeguarding concerns. A study undertaken prior to implementation of the Care Act (Graham et al., 2016, 2017; Norrie et al., 2017) provided insight into the diverse organisational models that had developed. The picture is diverse, and the model can impact on what is considered a safeguarding concern and influence the response (Graham et al., 2017). Key features were whether safeguarding duties were located with generic or specialised staff, and whether they were dispersed across locality teams or centralised. The evidence pointed to specialist arrangements being associated with improved prioritisation of safeguarding cases, consistency across cases and better knowledge, but balanced by reduced continuity of involvement due to cases being reallocated at key points in the care pathway and de-skilling of non-specialist teams. This diversity still exists, although new evidence reliably updating the picture post-Care Act is not yet available.

Section 43 – duty to establish Safeguarding Adults Boards

The Law Commission (2011), in its proposals to Parliament on the reform of adult social care law, considered that certain features of SABs – lead responsibility, function and core membership – were of such importance that they should be the subject of primary legislation, not merely of regulations. Section 43 is the result. While SABs had developed over some years in response to No Secrets guidance on multiagency collaboration (Department of Health, 2000), local authorities now under the Care Act have a statutory duty to establish Safeguarding Adults Boards (SABs), whose members must also include Clinical Commissioning Groups and the police as statutory partners and may be extended to include other statutory and independent agencies. The objective of the SAB is defined as being to help and protect adults in its area in cases of abuse and neglect (s.43(2)) by coordinating and ensuring the effectiveness of what each of its partners does (s.43(3)). It can do anything necessary or desirable in order to achieve this objective (s.43(4)), including the publication of guidance on procedures for referral and response pathways, the provision of training and the commissioning of SARs (s.44). Thus it has an important leadership, development, coordination and quality assurance role in relation to interagency adult safeguarding arrangements, focusing on how partner organisations work both individually and collectively to prevent abuse and neglect and to support and safeguard adults at risk. Education, support and challenge are all important parts of this role.

All Board partners are subject to the duties of co-operation (sections 6 and 7) that apply to all local authority functions, and more specifically have to provide information (section 45, Care Act 2014) to assist the Board to fulfil its statutory functions. Schedule 2 of the Act provides further detail on membership and chairing, funding of the SAB by its partners, and requirements to work to a strategic plan and publish an annual report. Statutory guidance (DHSC, 2018a) further elaborates expectations of SAB activities, which must be underpinned by six key principles – empowerment, prevention, proportionality, protection, partnership and accountability.

The Act permits local authorities to merge their Boards, and a number have done so, creating bodies that oversee safeguarding across a range of smaller local authorities, often unitary authorities in urban areas.

Most SABs employ an Independent Chair (in line with statutory guidance (DHSC, 2018a), which encourages such appointments), who is responsible for ensuring that all organisations contribute effectively to the work of the Board. The Chair, accountable to the Chief Executive of the local authority, also provides accountability for the Board's work by way of reports to relevant strategic committees and wider partnerships such as Health & Wellbeing Boards and Community Safety Partnerships. The statutory guidance emphasises the importance of the Chair being up to date with and being able to promote good practice, case law, research findings and other sources of learning and development.

There is little systematic evidence as yet on governance developments since implementation of the new statutory Board arrangements. Prior to the Care Act, and to inform its development, the Department of Health commissioned research (Braye et al., 2011) into the role and function of the non-statutory Boards that had developed under the previous guidance, providing an evidence base for understanding how Boards operated. Since then, Cooper and Bruin (2017) found that SABs have undertaken significant work to ensure their structures, systems and governance are fit for purpose under the new requirements, although some structural elements, such as securing user involvement in Boards and forging links with Health and Wellbeing Boards, Quality Surveillance Groups, Community Safety Partnerships and the CQC, remained a challenge. A survey of SABs to assess the impact of SABs becoming statutory partnerships (Templeton, 2017) similarly found there was a need to clarify and build more consistent relationships with other strategic partnerships. SABs also found their broadened remit across new forms of abuse and neglect a challenge, as too was securing funding and ensuring consistency of MSP implementation across the partnership.

Thus SABs' governance mandate is not without its challenges. As has also been observed in relation to Local Safeguarding Children Boards (LSCBs) (Preston-Shoot and Pratt, 2014), the mandate was not accompanied by new funding and the provision in the statutory guidance for agencies to contribute resources is weak. SABs can request resources from partner agencies but cannot command them and the level of funding between Boards varies considerably. In an age of financial austerity, relationships between partners may prove insufficiently persuasive in terms of budgetary contributions, with problematic implications for Boards in relation to resourcing multi-agency audits, training and analysis of performance data.

This is one example of the impact of grafting the requirement for partnership working onto single agency structures, with each individual organisation having its own financial imperatives and strategic priorities. SABs cannot impose strategic direction or operational practices upon partner agencies, and they cannot compel members to participate, for example in the collection and analysis of performance data or multi-agency audits. A Board's effectiveness will depend on the stability, seniority and authority of its members, and the quality of the relationships between them. The statutory guidance is silent on how to seek to engage the disengaged, or those who do not collaborate.

Similarly, effectiveness will be dependent on the leadership that Board members provide. For instance, effective accountability, monitoring of effectiveness, and generating and embedding learning depend on openness and transparency within and between agencies regarding the collection and analysis of performance data, referrals of cases for consideration as SARs and then co-operation in any review process. However, the picture here is variable, which may result in an SAB overlooking the importance of particular issues. An associated concern relates to the independence of the Board. The vast majority of members will be representatives of organisations whom the Board is seeking to hold accountable for their effectiveness in preventing and safeguarding people from abuse and neglect, and the Board thus relies to a large extent on agencies' willingness and ability for self-regulation.

Finally, there is the challenge of the breadth of scope of adult safeguarding. This spans preventive activities such as community awareness raising and educational or risk management initiatives through to reactive responses, such as specific initiatives to address identified harm to individuals or groups (Braye et al., 2012). Boards are not the only bodies with an interest and role in these fields. To be negotiated here too are linkages with Local Safeguarding Children Boards,[5] Health and Wellbeing Boards, Safer Community Partnerships and Multi-Agency Risk Assessment Conference arrangements, for example, with respect to types of abuse and neglect such as sexual exploitation, modern slavery and domestic abuse with which these groupings are also concerned.

An important question is how SABs are held to account. SAB decision-making is open to judicial review and investigations by the Local Government Ombudsman, hence the importance of legal literacy, including adherence to statutory guidance and the principles of administrative law, transparency of decision-making and the careful management of record keeping. SABs are not, however, listed as public authorities within Schedule 1 of the Freedom of Information Act 2000 (nor have they been added to that list by any order of the Secretary of State (s.4, FOIA 2000)) and are therefore not subject to freedom of information requests, the significance of which is explored further below in relation to SARs.

Section 44 – Safeguarding Adults Reviews

The SAB has a duty to commission an SAR where an adult with care and support needs has died as a result of abuse or neglect (or remains alive but has experienced serious abuse and neglect) and there is cause for concern about how agencies have worked together (s.44(1)).

The statutory purpose (s.44(5)) is to identify the lessons to be learnt and apply that learning to other cases. SABs also have power to commission SARs in other circumstances (s.44(4)), including where there are lessons to be learnt from good practice. This distinction between cases where reviews are mandatory or discretionary has led to talk of statutory and non-statutory reviews. In fact all reviews are 'statutory', as the review mandate, whether a duty or a power, resides in primary legislation. A more accurate terminology is mandatory reviews where the SAB is under a *duty* to commission an SAR and discretionary reviews where there is a *power* to do so.

In relation to national monitoring of SAR activity (NHS Digital, 2018), since 2015–16 local authorities have been required to submit data on mandatory SARs completed,[6] thus three years of data are available. In year 2 (2016–17) there was a 22% increase in the number of mandatory SARs compared to year 1, from 90 to 110, the figure then remaining stable in 2017–18, with 110 SARs again conducted (involving 140 individuals, 61% of whom had died, with 39% having suffered serious harm). The number of SABs undertaking SARs rose from 60 in year 1 to 75 in year 2, dropping back to 70 in 2017–18. Variations between the nine regions are also apparent. In 2017–18 London and Yorkshire & Humber had the highest number of SARs, each with 25, with the latter showing a very significant increase compared to each of the previous two years. London and the North West, having seen a large increase in SAR activity in year 2, in 2017–18 completed fewer than previously, as did the South-West and East of England. While the West Midlands, East Midlands and North East regions have remained the same across all three years, the South East has risen steadily to its 2017–18 level of 20.

These figures resonate with other evidence of variability in the frequency with which SABs are commissioning SARs (Braye and Preston-Shoot, 2017a; Preston-Shoot, 2017a), raising questions about how thresholds within the criteria of serious abuse and neglect and/or concerns about multi-agency working are being interpreted. It also seems likely that some SABs have yet to complete an SAR.

Some aspects of this statutory mandate are also problematic. Statutory guidance (DHSC, 2018a) advises that reviews should be completed within a six-month period but few reviews appear to be completed within this timeframe because of the complexities involved (Braye and Preston-Shoot, 2017a; Preston-Shoot, 2017a). Parallel processes represent a further challenge. The purpose of SARs is to uncover and implement lessons to improve policy and practice standards, yet they may run alongside Coroner inquests and investigations by regulatory authorities, such as the Care Quality Commission, Health and Care Professions Council or the Independent Office of Police Complaints. Some cases may involve criminal investigation leading to prosecution. Certain types of death will already have triggered processes such as Fire Investigation Reports by the Fire Service and Sudden Death Reports by the police. Those involving people with learning disabilities will fall under the Learning Disabilities Mortalities Review programme; an SAR in a case of death resulting from domestic abuse may run parallel with a Domestic Homicide Review; a case involving a family with children may trigger a Serious Case Review.[7]

The potential for review processes to duplicate and in some circumstances compromise each other requires SARs to be carefully timed. SABs must resolve locally how these interfaces will be managed, and in practice SABs have considerable flexibility to determine the approach that is taken to a SAR, which may assist its interface with other review processes.

The SAR learning process can itself be challenging. Holding individual professionals and agencies accountable may generate defensiveness if openness about lessons learnt is feared to compromise the individual or agency in some parallel process or to create vulnerability to future civil claims for damages. There have been examples where agencies have declined to co-operate with a review, despite the s.45 duty to share information (Braye and Preston-Shoot, 2017a), and it is unclear what powers SABs then have.

SABs must follow statutory guidance (DHSC, 2018a) in commissioning and carrying out an SAR. The requirements, however, do not prescribe the method. Families must be involved where possible, but otherwise the SAB's primary concern is to choose a review method that will best promote effective learning and improvement action (DHSC, 2018a). The principles of administrative law apply here too. The Local Government Ombudsman, investigating an SAB's decision not to undertake a review, found that the Board's definition of abuse was inconsistent with statutory guidance (LGO and Wiltshire County Council). In another case (LGO and Nottinghamshire County Council (2016)), a complaint about whether lessons had been learnt from an SAR was not upheld by the Ombudsman since reasonable steps had been taken by agencies to implement the review's recommendations, with clear timeframes for completion and allocated individuals responsible for overseeing implementation of each recommendation. SABs must also be clear whether documents, such as case chronologies and reports submitted by participating agencies as part of an SAR process, belong to the SAB or to the submitting agency. Material held by a public authority (for example a report prepared by a local authority and submitted to the SAB as part of an SAR) may be subject to a request by a third party for disclosure under the Freedom of Information Act 2000. If the council holds the material not for its own purposes but on behalf of the SAB, it may be exempt from disclosure; if the material is held for the council's own purposes, it could be subject to disclosure. Information Commissioner decisions on ownership have varied. A 2016 Tribunal decision, *McClatchey v The Information Commissioner and South Gloucestershire District Council* (2016), questioned how SAR material held by the local authority could be deemed to belong to the SAB when the local authority was the lead member of the SAB; this has influenced a recent Information Commissioner decision relating to the disclosure of SAR meeting notes (ICO (2018) West Sussex County Council).

Until mid-2018 the absence of a national repository for SARs restricted the ability of individual SABs and SAR authors to learn from findings elsewhere. While SABs may choose to publish SARs, and many do – either a full report or a summary – there is no requirement for them to do so, and published SARs reside in individual Boards' websites, requiring extensive searching. The exception has been the repository of reviews (including SCRs and SARs) relating to people with learning disabilities, developed through the Learning Disabilities Mortality Review Programme (www.bristol.ac.uk/sps/leder/repository/) and collation work carried out by regional groups, for example the West and East Midlands and Hampshire (www.hampshiresab.org.uk/learning-from-experience-database/serious-case-reviews/). Access to learning should become easier as the national repository, launched in 2018, becomes established (www.scie.org.uk/safeguarding/adults/reviews/library/project).

A small number of thematic reviews of SARs have been published. These often also include serious case reviews conducted prior to the Care Act 2014, and cover either a range of abuse and neglect categories (Manthorpe and Martineau, 2011; Hull Safeguarding Adults Partnership Board, 2014; Manson, 2017) or specific topics: self-neglect (Braye et al., 2015a; Preston-Shoot, 2017b); dementia (Manthorpe and Martineau, 2016); housing (Parry, 2014); pressure ulcer care in care homes (Manthorpe and Martineau, 2017); older residents of care homes (Manthorpe and Martineau, 2017). In addition, two studies focus on SARs commissioned in particular regions since implementation of the Care Act across all categories of abuse and neglect: London (Braye and Preston-Shoot, 2017a) and the South-West (Preston-Shoot, 2017a).

What is clear is that the learning from SARs commonly casts light on features of the *whole* adult safeguarding system. Scrutinising the direct work and decision-making often reveals flaws in organisational structures and systems that influence how practitioners carry out their work. Workflow expectations and timescales, supervision, levels of management scrutiny, IT systems, guidance (or its absence) and training are all commonly implicated. Between agencies and professions there are information-sharing barriers. Equally, reviews may identify gaps in SABs' approach to multiagency governance.

SARs often result in recommendations to the commissioning SAB to lead changes in how agencies work under local safeguarding procedures or in how the SAB exercises its governance role. SABs therefore commonly produce and monitor action plans going forward – indeed their annual report must include details of what they have done during that year to implement the findings of reviews they have carried out (Care Act 2014, Sch.2, para 4). There is little evidence as yet, however, on how best to embed learning that requires organisational change, and how changes to policy and procedures influence practice and its outcomes. While SABs are taking innovative approaches to disseminating learning broadly through their networks, tracking the impact of policy and practice development is less developed (Preston-Shoot, 2018).

Some findings that emerge from SARs, however, are beyond the power of individual SABs to address.[8] The thematic review of London SARs (Braye and Preston-Shoot, 2017a) concludes: *'there are systemic structural, legal, financial and policy challenges that affect practitioners and managers across all agencies'*. These include the impact of ongoing financial austerity on statutory and voluntary agency services, including care home provision and specialist mental health facilities, and ongoing misunderstandings as a result of legislative drafting of how mental capacity is to be assessed or where the law permits information-sharing about adults at risk of abuse and neglect. Other national issues emerging include the effectiveness of the Care Quality Commission in identifying and following through on concerns about regulated service providers, the utility of national guidance on health and safety regulation in registered provision, and the sharing of placement information by commissioners and contract managers across CCGs and local authorities.

Work has been done on evaluating the quality of SARs. The overview of London SARs (Braye and Preston-Shoot, 2017a) identified a number of features that could be deemed markers of a good quality review. The SCIE/RiPfA SARs repository project has since produced a SAR quality markers checklist, with the intention that these should be used to inform the SAR process as it unfolds, as well as to evaluate the process and identify improvements for future SARs.

Section 45 – information-sharing

SABs have the power (s.45(1)) to request information they need from others, who have a duty to comply provided the request is to enable or assist the SAB in carrying out its functions, that it is made to someone likely to have information relevant to that purpose, and that it relates to a relevant activity they carry out or to information supplied to another person subject to an SAB request (s.45(2) –(5)). Some SARs have reported difficulties securing information during SAR processes (Braye and Preston-Shoot, 2017a), despite requests to agencies being made under s.45. Delays in information from agencies are a common reason for extended SAR time-scales, as well as the need for repeated requests for clarification of poor-quality information.

Very limited options, however, are available to Boards in the event of an agency failing to comply with an s.45 information-sharing request. If the person or agency is providing a regulated service, then that breach of duty could be reported to their regulator. Seeking a judicial review would be an option but would be time-consuming, expensive and ultimately a blunt instrument in terms of improving local relationships.

Section 46 – repeal of power to remove individuals

The Care Act repealed the National Assistance Act 1948 power (section 47) to remove people from their homes in certain circumstances. This was widely anticipated because of concerns about its compatibility with human rights. No new powers to protect adults from abuse and neglect were included in the Care Act, the Law Commission (2011) having left it to government to determine whether new powers were needed. In two critical respects a comparative perspective from Scotland and Wales is informative here.

There is provision for a power of entry in order to speak with an adult who may be experiencing abuse and neglect in Scotland (Adult Support and Protection (Scotland) Act 2007) and Wales (Social Services and Well-being (Wales) Act 2014). However, no such power was enacted in England. The government was not persuaded that powers existing in the Mental Health Act 1983 (section 135), the Police and Criminal Evidence Act 1984 (section 17), the Crime and

Security Act 2010 (domestic violence protection notices and orders) and the Mental Capacity Act 2005 (sections 5, 6 and 44) were insufficient to safeguard adults where family members might be preventing access. Evidence from Scotland regarding the limited but effective use of a power of entry (Preston-Shoot and Cornish, 2014) was discounted.

SARs (Preston-Shoot, 2017b) and research studies (Stevens et al., 2017a) provide instances where a third party has obstructed access. While such cases might not be numerous and the majority are resolved by practitioners (Manthorpe et al., 2017; Norrie et al., 2018), they do illustrate the potential limitations of existing legislation. For instance, concern for welfare would probably be insufficient to trigger the power of entry available in the Police and Criminal Evidence Act 1984 (FitzGerald and Ruck Keene, 2014). Stevens et al. (2018b) found support among social workers and managers for increased powers for social workers; while some expressed reservations, a power of entry as a last resort would, it was thought, strengthen the legal basis of safeguarding and provide legitimacy for social workers to act.

The Adult Support and Protection (Scotland) Act 2007 also enacts three protection orders relating to assessment, removal and barring. Prior to that Act receiving royal assent, concerns were expressed about compatibility with human rights and whether paternalistic practice would result. In the event, research has found that the provisions are used sparingly, that human rights concerns have not surfaced, perhaps because of the way the provisions are codified in the legal rules, and service users have expressed positive comments about their effectiveness in safeguarding people (Preston-Shoot and Cornish, 2014). Again this evidence was ultimately discounted in the new arrangements in England.

Concluding discussion

Adult safeguarding, despite its use of a common legislative structure, is a broad and diverse field, ranging from prevention to remedial action, engaging both individuals and communities, and involving people with widely varying needs. It is also a changing field, as forms of abuse become more widely recognised. Recent research is beginning to cast light on how certain groups fare within the new safeguarding framework. Examples include evidence on financial scams by people unknown to them (Fenge and Lee, 2018); mass marketing fraud (Olivier et al., 2016); financial abuse people with learning disability (Dalley et al., 2017); self-neglect, where early intervention has proved effective (Anka et al., 2017); modern slavery, requiring a focus on broader, international, structural factors alongside responses to individuals (Kidd and Manthorpe, 2017); the use of family group conferences in reframing responses to abuse of older people (Parkinson et al., 2018).

In a study of the impact of personal budgets on safeguarding, Stevens et al. (2018a) explore approaches to managing risks in supporting people to use direct payments safely. They identify within the accounts of social work practitioners a strong theme of balancing risk and choice – the need to balance the likelihood of positive benefits of self-determination against the likelihood and severity of harm. Their view that this involves reconciling competing policy objectives – a new form of the familiar balance between care and control, autonomy and duty of care – is illustrative of how safeguarding more generally and consistently raises complex and challenging dilemmas, requiring resolutions that are driven both by policy imperatives and moral responsibilities. Practitioners must negotiate a tightrope between the competing imperatives of autonomy and protection (Braye et al., 2017). This is not surprising, as Penhale et al. (2017: 171) have noted: 'the Care Act 2014 was a compromise ... there is nothing inevitable about the legal rules that were developed, and ... they are the result of how competing perspectives, and arguably interests, are ultimately in some form reconciled'. As such, decision-making in safeguarding must draw on structured and careful approaches to risk appraisal that seek to balance those competing mandates within a nuanced appraisal:

> The emphasis must be on sensible risk appraisal, not striving to avoid all risk, whatever the price, but instead seeking a proper balance and being willing to tolerate manageable or acceptable risks as the price appropriately to be paid in order to achieve some other good – in particular to achieve the vital good of the elderly or vulnerable person's happiness. (MM (An Adult) [2007])

This implies that knowing the person, their hopes, fears, motivations and aspirations, is central to making good safeguarding decisions, in order to achieve which relationship-based practice is essential.

But it also signals the need to question and move beyond restrictive notions of vulnerability. Pritchard-Jones (2018) recognises the very real strides forward in safeguarding made by the Act, but also suggests that the shift of terminology from 'vulnerable adult' to 'adult at risk' does not change the Act's reliance on a status-based understanding of vulnerability rather than one that reflects the multiple social and contextual sources of an individual's experience. Safeguarding duties are engaged when the individual's own care and support needs prevent them from protecting themselves. She argues that a more nuanced perspective is better suited to the complex nature of decision-making for those experiencing abuse. This is in the context of judicial decision-making, but the argument is more broadly applicable; indeed Stevens et al. (2017b), writing about powers of entry, report that evidence from a review of the literature on conceptualisations of vulnerability, autonomy and privacy suggests that more socially-mediated understandings of these concepts allow for more nuanced approaches to social work practice.

It is important to remember also that the Care Act, in creating an organisational governance framework for safeguarding and providing a duty to enquire and determine what needs to be done to protect an adult at risk, stops short of providing further powers and duties of intervention. Thus it does not put in place a comprehensive statutory safeguarding scheme (Pritchard-Jones, 2016a) but requires practitioners to find other avenues for action. One such avenue is the inherent jurisdiction of the High Court, which may be relevant where an abusive or coercive personal relationship (rather than a lack of mental capacity) is affecting an individual's ability to make self-protective choices. Equally, it has been argued (Ruck-Keene et al., 2015) that the role of the Court of Protection needs to be better understood where an individual is known or suspected to lack the capacity to make relevant decisions.

The statutory guidance (DHSC, 2018a) is clear that adult safeguarding is a key domain for social work practice under the Care Act: '*It is likely that many enquiries will require the input and supervision of a social worker, particularly the more complex situations and to support the adult to realise the outcomes they want and to reach a resolution or recovery. For example, where abuse or neglect is suspected within a family or informal relationship it is likely that a social worker will be the most appropriate lead*' (para.14.81). To support this, the guidance also calls on local authorities to ensure that principal social workers lead on ensuring the quality and consistency of social work practice in fulfilling its safeguarding responsibilities and recognises the importance of both legal literacy and the professional evidence base for practice: '*In particular they should have extensive knowledge of the legal and social work response options to specific cases and in general*' (para.1.31). Thus while social work figures less prominently in other roles and responsibilities under the Care Act, safeguarding remains an area in which social work knowledge and expertise make the most vital contribution. It is to be hoped that, as further research evidence unfolds on implementation of the new framework, social work can be shown to be living up to this promise.

Case study: Barbara

In Chapter 3 (Implementing the Care Act: assessing need and providing care and support) and Chapter 5 (Carers and the Care Act) you met Barbara, who was receiving care and support, and her son Robert, who lives with her. This case study continues their story.

Barbara has complex health needs and is a heavy drinker and smoker. She receives a daily care and support visit for personal care each morning. Her son Robert, who lives with her, received a carer's assessment, following which he was given information about a carers' support group (although he has not engaged with this support). It has now become apparent that Barbara is increasingly neglecting her personal care and her diet, and that her living accommodation is dirty and bleak, bare of comforts of any kind. She spends her days and often nights too smoking and drinking in an armchair, surrounded by the magazines that are her main interest. It appears that Robert no longer provides any practical support for her. Barbara continues to receive a daily care worker visit, but often declines the personal care offered. On these occasions the only care and support she will agree to is for the care workers to provide food for her; she refuses everything else. She promises to eat the food that has been prepared, but doesn't. Occasionally she will agree to change her clothes, which are always very dirty due to her incontinence, but she doesn't carry this through. She is losing weight and now appears quite severely malnourished. It is also some time since the community nurses have visited to manage her leg dressings. Her son has told them that his mother does not want them to visit any more as she can apply the emollient cream herself and that she doesn't want their help. Barbara herself has told the care workers that she is now rather frightened of her son; she knows he has financial problems and for this reason she lets him collect and keep her benefits. The care agency's concerns about the situation lead to them raise a safeguarding referral with the local authority's safeguarding team.

Commentary

On receipt of the care agency's concerns, the local authority must determine whether a safeguarding enquiry should be carried out (section 42, Care Act 2014). If Barbara appears to be in need of care and support, and is experiencing (or likely to experience) abuse and neglect, including self-neglect, and as a result of her care and support needs is unable to protect herself from that abuse and neglect, then the criteria for a safeguarding enquiry will be met and the local authority has a duty to conduct one. The procedures to be followed will be those set out by the local Safeguarding Adults Board.

Neither Barbara's nor Robert's consent is required for either the referral from the care agency or the decision to conduct an enquiry. In line with the duty to cooperate (sections 6 and 7), adult safeguarding practitioners have the power to request information from other agencies, for example healthcare practitioners, who must cooperate if what is requested from them relates to their roles and responsibilities. The Data Protection Act 2018 also permits information-sharing where this is necessary to safeguarding and promoting the welfare of an adult at risk.

In line with the principle of making safeguarding personal, the enquiry should be person-led and outcome-focused, designed to enhance Barbara's choice and control, and to improve her quality of life, safety and wellbeing. Once again, advocacy (section 68) should be considered if this would facilitate her involvement in the enquiry. Responsibility for the safeguarding enquiry may be delegated to another agency but the local authority remains responsible for determining what action, if any, should be taken, by whom and when.

Barbara may be reluctant to engage with an enquiry, and provided she has mental capacity to make this decision, practitioners will be mindful of promoting her autonomy and self-determination. However, before closing down any enquiry, practitioners must attempt to explore the risks in Barbara's situation. They should also seek to understand the nature of the historic and current relationship between Barbara and Robert. This will involve skills of questioning 'lifestyle choice' and of respectful challenge. The aim is not to remove all risk but to explore different options as part of exercising a duty of care.

The outcome of the enquiry should be shared with the care agency and with other agencies known to be involved. It may be appropriate to review Barbara's care and support plan, and indeed her son's support plan, as part of the enquiry. Good practice also involves bringing all the practitioners involved together in a multi-agency risk management meeting. The purpose here is to share information, discuss the risks involved in the situation, and to agree a risk mitigation plan. On the basis of the information already available, members of the primary care team (GP and community nurses), the Department of Work and Pensions, the police and the Fire and Rescue Service may have important contributions to make alongside the local authority's adult social care team. Legal advice should be available at such meetings to ensure that all available legal options are considered. Decision-making should be recorded clearly.

Further Reading

Brammer, A. and Pritchard-Jones, L. (2019) *Safeguarding Adults* (2nd edn). Basingstoke: Palgrave Macmillan.

Braye, S. and Preston-Shoot, M. (2016) *Practising Social Work Law* (4th edn). Basingstoke: Palgrave Macmillan.

Cooper, A. and White, E. (2017) (eds) *Safeguarding Adults under the Care Act 2014*. London: Jessica Kingsley.

Notes

1. In addition to Care Act 2014 requirements, the Mental Health Act 1983 (amended 2007) and the Mental Capacity Act 2005 both require advocacy in certain circumstances.

2. Other enquiries are those in which the adult did not meet all of the s.42 criteria but the local authority considered a safeguarding enquiry was necessary and proportionate.

3. Mental capacity here is defined as being able to contribute to decisions about their protection, including participation in safeguarding, and capacity at the time of the incident causing concern.

4. Although overall action was taken in 77% of enquiries, implying that an enquiry might result in action even in the absence of an identified risk.

5. Following implementation of the Children and Social Work Act 2017, LSCBs will be replaced with new local arrangements for safeguarding children. SABs will have to engage with these new arrangements.

6. Submission of data on discretionary reviews is voluntary and the NHS Digital figures therefore under-represent the review and learning activity being carried out by Boards.

7. Also with the new arrangements being introduced by the Children and Social Work Act 2017.

8. This point is explored further in Chapter 13 by Flynn and Citarella.

8 The Care Act 2014 and the Mental Capacity Act 2005: learning lessons for the future?

Laura Pritchard-Jones

Introduction

Both the Care Act 2014 and the Mental Capacity Act 2005 attempted to fill 'legal vacuum[s]' (Manthorpe et al., 2013: 369): the Mental Capacity Act by providing explicit legal frameworks for capacity and best interests assessments, and the Care Act by comprehensively codifying the rights of people with needs for care and support for assessment and provision, providing the same rights for carers, and placing adult safeguarding obligations on a statutory footing. More importantly, they arguably represent a paradigm shift in the ethics behind social welfare work with people with care and support needs: a shift whereby the voice of the person with needs is foregrounded in any decision-making or assessment process, whether that be an assessment of needs for care and support, or preparing a care plan under the Care Act, or the capacity assessment and best interests decision-making processes under the Mental Capacity Act (Boyle, 2008; Donnelly, 2009a; Manthorpe et al., 2008).

Given these similarities between the two Acts, and more than ten years on from implementation of the Mental Capacity Act, this chapter provides an opportunity to consider the evidence as to how the Act has been applied in practice for people with needs for care and support. It provides an opportunity to see what lessons can be learned from the Mental Capacity Act and its implementation that can be transferred to the Care Act. In effect, what can evidence surrounding the Mental Capacity Act teach us about how best to effectively implement the Care Act? The chapter proceeds in two sections. The first asks in more depth why it is important to consider the two Acts in this way; why is it important to learn from the implementation of the Mental Capacity Act, and transpose these lessons over to the Care Act? The second then considers in more detail the trends that have emerged in the literature on the Mental Capacity Act. What concerns – or, indeed, evidence of good practice – have emerged in understanding and applying the Mental Capacity Act, and how can we use those findings to understand what is happening with emergent literature on the implementation of the Care Act?

Why consider the two Acts together?

There is, first and foremost, a practical element to this question, in that the two Acts operate in tandem. Many people who have needs for care and support and come into contact with the assessment, care provision and safeguarding mechanisms available under the Care Act may lack mental capacity in relation to particular decisions and therefore also fall under the remit of the Mental Capacity Act. Practitioners undertaking anything mandated by the Care Act must always bear in mind the question of whether the individual has the capacity to make any decisions they are being invited to make. For example, might they lack the capacity to make decisions as to their needs assessment; or to accept or decline a care and support package; to decide how a personal budget is to be spent or manage any direct payments if these are proposed; or to participate in a safeguarding enquiry? In effect, the Mental Capacity Act must always be a factor for consideration in anything that practitioners seek to do under the Care Act.

More specifically, however, and perhaps evidence of the above point, is that there are precise points of overlap where the two Acts meet. Under the Care Act, for example, section 67 requires advocacy to be provided where a failure to do so means that the individual would experience substantial difficulty in understanding, retaining, or using and weighing information, or communicating their wishes in relation to assessments undertaken under the Act.[1] Similar provisions exist in relation to advocacy for participating in safeguarding enquiries and reviews under section 68. The wording used in sections 67 and 68 is similar to the functional assessment of capacity under section 3(1) of the Mental Capacity Act; the person is unable to use, weigh, or retain information, or communicate their decision. This, along with the requirement in section 2(1) of the Mental Capacity Act – that the lack of capacity is because of an impairment or disturbance in the functioning of the mind or brain – forms the legal standard for assessing whether someone lacks the capacity to make a particular decision. While both Acts are similar in this regard, even within the provisions in section 67 and 68 of the Care Act there are some differences however. First, the ability to communicate requirement is different between the Acts. Under the Care Act, the substantial difficulty must be to communicate their *views, wishes, and feelings*, whereas in the Mental Capacity Act the inability must be to communicate their *decision*. Second, under section 67(4), the Care Act only requires *substantial difficulty*, not being *unable* to understand, weigh, retain, or communicate as is required by section 3(1) of the Mental Capacity Act. The advocacy provisions in the Care Act therefore only seemingly take effect when an individual has substantial difficulty; they do not necessarily need to lack capacity under the Mental Capacity Act. Moreover, under sections 67(6) and 68(5), where the local authority is satisfied that there is an appropriate person to represent the individual concerned – thereby negating the obligation to appoint an advocate found in sections 67(2) and 68(2) – *and* the individual also has capacity, they must consent to the appointment of that appropriate person. If they lack capacity, the local authority must be satisfied that the appointment of the appropriate person is in the individual's best interests, ostensibly using the approach to best interests found in section 4 of the Mental Capacity Act.

The Mental Capacity Act also plays other roles in the Care Act, however. Section 11(2)(a) of the Care Act, for example, allows individuals to refuse needs assessment unless, as stipulated in section 11(2)(a), the person lacks the capacity to refuse,[2] and it would be in their best interests to undertake the assessment. While neither the Act nor its accompanying Statutory Guidance (DHSC, 2018a) specifies that lacking the capacity to refuse an assessment, or best interests in appointing an appropriate person where the individual lacks the capacity to consent to their appointment, rely on the tests for capacity and best interests contained in the Mental Capacity Act, it is to be expected that this is the case.

Beyond the obvious statutory overlap between the two pieces of legislation, it is also arguable that they both represent ethical shifts in how professionals should engage with persons with needs for care and support in care assessment and planning, and in assessing mental capacity. Much has been written on the problems in social welfare and the law regulating decision-making of people with mental illnesses or cognitive impairments prior to the enactment of the Mental Capacity Act or the Care Act (Dunn et al., 2008; Keywood and Flynn, 2010; Pritchard-Jones, 2016b). These criticisms are specifically focused on the lack of participation of individuals with needs for care and support or with mental impairments in care assessment and decision-making, and the paternalism inherent in the law and its implementation on the ground. As the Law Commission noted in its consultation on adult social care prior to the drafting of the Care Act:

> *A further objective of the proposals put forward in this paper is to bring adult social care law into line with modern understandings of disability by eradicating the use of discriminatory and stigmatising concepts and developing legislation that is more consistent with human rights considerations.* (Law Commission, 2010: para 2.4)

Both Acts, in various ways, make great strides forward in this respect. Both effectively create a legal requirement to place the person at the centre of social work practice. Section 1 of the Care Act gives fundamental primacy to promoting a person's wellbeing, but moreover, assumes that the person themselves is best placed to determine their own wellbeing (s.1(3)(a)). Moreover, there is a *duty* on anybody exercising a function under the Act to have regard to the individual's views, wishes, feelings, and beliefs (s.1(3)(b)), and the individual should also be fully involved in any assessments or decisions (s.9(5)(a), and regulation 3(1)(b) of the Care and Support (Assessment) Regulations 2014. Likewise, the Mental Capacity Act states that someone is not to be taken to be unable to make a decision simply because they make an unwise one (s.1(4)), and all practicable steps should be taken to ensure a person is supported to make the decision for themselves in the first instance (s.1(3)). Where a person lacks capacity, their voice should be given great weight in deciding what is in their best interests, and all practicable steps should be taken to ascertain their wishes (s.4(6)(a)). As Jackson J notes in *Wye Valley NHS Trust v B* [2015], 'that a person lacks decision-making capacity is not an "off switch" for his rights and freedoms' (para. 11).

More importantly for the rest of this chapter, both Acts share a fundamental similarity in their purpose and function. Unlike much legislation, they are not simply there to *regulate* the provision of social welfare; they are more than simply a body of rules dictating which individuals get which services, although this is a core feature of both Acts. They go beyond regulation and are, in fact, designed to be implemented in social work practice; in effect, they dictate how and when social care practice is to be done, and how such decisions are to be made. First, they both involve assessments. The Care Act and the accompanying Care and Support (Eligibility Criteria) Regulations 2015 (DoH, 2015b) place a legal obligation on local authorities to undertake an assessment for needs for care and support and make a decision as to whether someone meets the eligibility criteria in respect of those needs, as well as providing specific detail as to how those assessments are to be conducted and who is to be involved. Likewise, the Mental Capacity Act places an obligation on professionals to conduct assessments of whether someone lacks the capacity to make a particular decision and provides rules as to how a capacity assessment is to be conducted, and principles that must be adhered to. Moreover, both Acts also involve similar processes in deciding what to do if and when someone falls above or below the thresholds set by those assessments. The Mental Capacity Act requires a best interests decision, and provides clear rules as to exactly what considerations must be taken into account when making a decision in someone's best interests. The Care Act involves assessments as to if, and what, services are necessary to meet the person's needs for care and support and, again, provides clear rules on what factors professionals must consider when deciding upon the provision of services.

Both Acts therefore require professionals to make difficult decisions in what are often very 'messy' situations, and both Acts tell professionals the processes that must go into making those decisions. But neither Act can – nor should – tell professionals *what* decision to make in any given set of circumstances. It is unsurprising then that both Acts present social care professionals with ethical dilemmas between the principles of autonomy and protection in relation to what decisions they ultimately make. Implementing the provisions of both Acts requires social work professionals to understand and navigate this perceived binary between these two principles (Keywood, 2010), whilst still maintaining the letter of the law, and as Braye, Orr and Preston-Shoot note, '[h]ow practitioners understand the legal framework within which they work has a powerful influence on professional judgement' (2017: 326).Considering the lessons learned from more than ten years' worth of literature on the Mental Capacity Act can therefore highlight deeper issues within social care practice, and how best to navigate the perceived binary between autonomy and protection in implementing the Care Act. In effect, identifying and scrutinising trends in implementation of the earlier Act may shed light on trends emerging in relation to the later Act.

Learning lessons for the future of the Care Act

More than ten years since the implementation of the Mental Capacity Act and three years on from the Care Act, it is unsurprising that the literature is beginning to move beyond the doctrinal – the substance of the provisions contained therein – to the empirical, as to how the two Acts are being implemented in practice. Over the past ten years, legal literacy – or the lack thereof – has been a dominant theme in the literature on the Mental Capacity Act, not least in Serious Case Reviews, now called Safeguarding Adults Reviews (Preston-Shoot, 2017a; Braye et al., 2015b). This section focuses on two particular problems in legal literacy that emerged from the Mental Capacity Act – failures in understanding and implementation of assessment processes – and considers to what extent the same trends may be emerging in relation to processes under the Care Act.

Since its implementation in 2007, the literature on the Mental Capacity Act has been peppered with examples of difficulties in implementing the assessment processes contained therein. A particular example of this is a failure to conduct capacity assessments where there may be doubts as to an individual's capacity, or poorly or inappropriately conducted capacity or best interests assessments. The first of these is particularly noticeable in relation to safeguarding adults. Evidence from adult safeguarding literature highlights that 'capacity is key' (Manthorpe et al., 2013) to safeguarding adults at risk from abuse. Understanding whether adults at risk may lack mental capacity in relation to certain decisions is crucial to proper and effective safeguarding, not least because the Mental Capacity Act opened up a raft of measures that otherwise would not be available. Yet the findings of many Safeguarding Adults Reviews show that the Mental Capacity Act is often unexplored in relation to adults perceived to be at risk, and capacity assessments are frequently not undertaken, or properly recorded. In a study of 40 Serious Case Reviews concerning failings in relation to adults who had self-neglected, mental capacity was identified as a crucial issue in 14 reviews, whether this was in relation to '... levels of knowledge of legislation ... and procedures, or the thoroughness with which assessments are completed and reviewed' (Braye et al., 2015b:14), and subsequent evidence shows that mental capacity remains a dominant theme in such reviews (Preston-Shoot, 2017b), as well as other reviews concerning other forms of abuse and neglect (Braye and Preston-Shoot, 2017a; Preston-Shoot, 2017a). Such issues led the House of Lords Select Committee (2014) to suggest that the presumption of capacity in section 1(2) of the Act:

> ... is widely misunderstood by those involved in care. It is sometimes used to support non-intervention or poor care, leaving vulnerable adults exposed to risk of harm. In some cases this is because professionals struggle to understand how to apply the principle in practice. In other cases, the evidence suggests the principle has been deliberately misappropriated to avoid taking responsibility for a vulnerable adult. (para. 105)

A recent Safeguarding Adults Review (SAR) into the death of Lee Irving (Newcastle Safeguarding Adults Board, 2017) exemplifies the intricacies and extent of these failures in relation to mental capacity assessments. Lee Irving was a 24-year-old man with a learning disability, who was killed as a result of beatings sustained over a number of weeks by a group of individuals he had been involved with for some years, with a relationship described as one of 'subservience with Lee beholden to the primary perpetrator for drugs and shelter and where Lee looked up to the primary perpetrator and, desperate to fit in, tolerated continued violence and abuse' (Newcastle Safeguarding Adults Board, 2017: para. 1.2.5). There was a history of concerns for Lee's welfare between 2008–2013 during which time he engaged in petty crime, failed to return home on numerous occasions, failed to attend appointments with various services, and had what is described as a chaotic lifestyle and association with the group of 'friends' who exploited him. Moreover, there was evidence dating back several years that he had difficulty understanding and managing risk, but with capacity assessments only being undertaken in relation to risk in 2010 and 2015. It is noted that his 'capacity was often disguised by his seeming ability and determination to make decisions albeit unwise ones' (Newcastle Safeguarding Adults Board, 2017: para. 2.1.6), therefore masking the extent of his true decision-making ability. Like the 2010 assessment, the 2015 capacity assessment again found he did not have capacity to keep himself safe when alone in the community, and resulted in considering options of supported living, which were underway at the time of Lee's death (Newcastle Safeguarding Adults Board, 2017: para. 2.1.9). Despite these two assessments, the SAR notes that many agencies dealing with Lee did not identify concerns around his mental capacity or undertake capacity assessments. Given the Act is time and decision specific, 'had all agencies assessed Lee Irving's capacity at the time of their involvement in adherence with the [Mental Capacity Act] the response of these agencies may well have been different' (Newcastle Safeguarding Adults Board, 2017: para. 4.6.4). As a result, various options available under the Mental Capacity Act were not pursued throughout the time Lee was in contact with the various agencies until just before his death when supported living arrangements *were* being considered, albeit too late.

The SAR findings not only show failures in actually implementing available processes – in this case, conducting capacity assessments – but also highlight how this can result in failing to explore all potential remedies or mechanisms for intervention. In this regard, the Care and Support Statutory Guidance (DHSC, 2018a) reminder that mental capacity assessments form a crucial part of adult safeguarding is to be welcomed:

> ... *Of course, where the adult may lack capacity to make decisions about arrangements for enquiries or managing any abusive situation, then their capacity must always be assessed and any decision made in their best interests ... In order to make sound decisions, the adult's emotional, physical, intellectual and mental capacity in relation to self-determination and consent and any intimidation, misuse of authority or undue influence will have to be assessed.* (para.14.108–14.109).

Given that this only appears in the Statutory Guidance, it is arguable that the Care Act could have gone further in incorporating the Mental Capacity Act into adult safeguarding in order to address some of the concerns identified through SARs. This, for example, may have been through a provision that *requires* capacity assessments to be undertaken where organisations reasonably suspect there is cause for concern regarding an individual's capacity, and the extent to which this may impact their ability to protect themselves from the risk of abuse or neglect to be considered. In this regard there may have been a missed opportunity for developing the interface between the two Acts further.

Notwithstanding this, there is evidence of good practice through the implementation of more coherent and consistent national and regional guidance to practitioners on the importance of capacity assessments in adult safeguarding— not least, as noted above, a much greater focus on capacity in the safeguarding chapter of the Care and Support Statutory Guidance. More locally, regional adult safeguarding guidance has also seen a greater emphasis on the relevance of mental capacity assessments. The West Midlands Adult Safeguarding Policy and Procedure (West Midlands Adult Safeguarding Editorial Group, 2016), for example, in its *procedural* guidance, reminds practitioners that:

> ...{i}t is important that an individual's mental capacity is considered at each stage of the adult safeguarding process (para 7.5) ... {a}t the concern stage, the most common capacity & consent issues to consider will usually be ... whether the adult has the mental capacity to understand & make decisions about the abuse or neglect related risks, & any immediate safety actions necessary ... {i}t is important to establish whether the adult has the mental capacity to make decisions. (para. 8.5.7.3)

This increasing practical emphasis on the role of the Mental Capacity Act – and particularly the role of capacity assessments – in adult safeguarding *procedure*, as opposed to just in policy, is to be welcomed.

Moreover, even where capacity assessments or best interests assessments *have* taken place, the literature also evidences concerns around the adequacy of the assessments themselves, and whether they adhere to the principles and provisions of the Mental Capacity Act. A key component of the Act is the involvement of family and carers, particularly in making best interests decisions. Section 4(6)(a)–(b) requires decision makers to consider the individual's past and present wishes and feelings, and the beliefs and values that would be likely to influence their decision if they had the capacity. Although the precise weight to be given to these depends on the particular circumstances of the case (*ITW v Z* [2009]), in recent years there has been increasing acknowledgement that 'the wishes and feelings, beliefs and values of people with a mental disability are as important to them as they are to anyone else, and may even be more important. It would therefore be wrong in principle to apply any *automatic* discount to their point of view' (*Wye Valley NHS Trust v B* [2015], para.11, emphasis added). Likewise, section 4(7)(a) –(b) places an obligation on those making best interests decisions to take into account the views of anyone engaged in caring for the person who lacks capacity, or who has an interest in their welfare, or anyone named by them as to be consulted. Indeed, failing to do so where it would have been practicable to have done so is not only a breach the Act itself, but may also be a violation of the right to private and family life contained in Article 8 of the European Convention on Human Rights (*Winspear v City Hospitals Sunderland NHS Foundation Trust* [2015]).

Yet since implementation of the Mental Capacity Act in 2007, the literature shows only patchy adherence to these provisions. One of the central concerns outlined by the House of Lords Select Committee in their Post-Legislative Scrutiny of the Mental Capacity Act (House of Lords Select Committee, 2014) was a regular lack of involvement in capacity assessments and best interests decision-making by both the individual concerned and their family or carers. More recently, such concerns have been evidenced in the latest annual report of the National Mental Capacity Forum:

> *Despite the process laid out in the {Mental Capacity Act} for taking a best interests decision on behalf of the person, the way meetings are sometimes conducted can leave the family overwhelmed and intimidated, feeling inadequate weight has been given to their expression of the views and values of the person they love.* (HM Government, 2018:19)

This trend is replicated in the broader empirical literature. Emmett et al., (2014) found that families' involvement in best interests decision-making regarding the discharge of a family member with dementia from hospital into long-term care was hampered by a number of factors. These included a lack of involvement in the decision-making process by either the person who may have lacked capacity and/or their family, a lack of effective information provision for either the individual or for the family, and inequalities of power between the family and the professionals or other family members. Further research identifies that these particular problems are not uncommon (Cox, 2015; Emmett et al., 2013; Williams et al., 2012; Williamson et al., 2012). In addition, other failings in assessment such as a 'concertina effect' – 'whereby ... the best interests decision had effectively already been made, and it appeared the assessment of (in)capacity was then carried out to provide the basis for that decision' (Williamson et al., 2012:189) – have also been identified (see also Murrell and McCalla, 2016; Williams et al., 2012). This is in spite of the Mental Capacity Act stating that a person must not be deemed unable to make a decision merely because they make an unwise decision (s.1(4)).

An example of this can be found in the report of a Local Government Ombudsman into the treatment of an older couple, Mr and Mrs N (LGO and Cambridgeshire County Council (2015)). The local authority in question moved Mr N, who had dementia, to a care home fourteen miles away from his home and his wife, against both their wishes without conducting proper capacity assessments or best interests decisions, and without providing either Mr or Mrs N with proper information regarding the availability of suitable care home options, or the deprivation of liberty process, or the opportunity to challenge the decisions made. Moreover, one aspect of the relevant paperwork completed by the local authority states that '*the purpose of the {capacity} assessment is to determine whether (Mr N) is able to retain and weigh basic information to enable him to make informed decisions about the most appropriate accommodation for his safety'* (para.46, emphasis in original). In effect, rather than assessing Mr N's capacity to decide where to live, the issue as the local authority saw it was whether Mr N was able to appreciate that the safest place for him was in a care home; the decision that it would be in Mr N's best interests to move him, as it was the safest place for him to live, had been made prior to the capacity assessment being undertaken.

In summary, the literature on the implementation of the Mental Capacity Act shows how the potential capacity assessment and best interests decision-making processes have not always been realised, either through failures in implementing the proper assessments, or through inappropriately conducted assessments. Early emergent evidence in relation to the Care Act betrays many similar features – failures in legal literacy in implementing the assessment or reassessment processes in the Act. Two recent decisions by the Local Government Ombudsman (LGSCO and Bromley LBC (2018); LGSCO and Wiltshire County Council (2018)) in particular point towards such problems. The first concerned a young man, Mr N, whose care plan was cut without adequate reassessment under the Care Act. Mr N was placed in a residential college, and his care package had been in place since 2013. He had been assessed in 2013 as needing, among other things, 28.5 hours of one-to-one support, and three days a week at a specialist centre. Yet from October 2015, the local authority reduced the amount paid to Mr N in relation to this one-to-one support from 28.5 hours to 25 hours, and failed to put in alternative arrangements, or funding, following the closure of Mr N's specialist day centre. This latter failure was not in accordance with the *original* needs assessment identified in 2013, but neither had the reduction in care from 28.5 to 25 hours been done in accordance with a proper reassessment under the Care Act. The Ombudsman noted that the local authority *'should have carried out a review a year after July 2013 to establish whether Mr N's needs had changed. Its failure to do so is fault ... {it} should ensure it reviews care plans at least annually, in accordance with guidance and legislation'* (para. 27).

The second decision concerns Mr P, who has severe learning difficulties and epilepsy and needs constant care, which in the main is provided by his parents, Mr and Mrs N. Mr N had recently become disabled and Mrs N took up caring for both her husband *and* her son. Since leaving school, Mr P had attended a daycare facility on week days, and for a number of years the transport to and from this centre had been provided by the local authority. Following a house move by Mr and Mrs N in 2016, the local authority in question notified Mrs N that it had decided to cut Mr P's transport funding by two days a week, leaving Mrs N to undertake the transport herself or to pay the local authority to continue to provide the transport on those two days. In upholding her complaint (LGSCO and Wiltshire County Council (2018), para.74), the Ombudsman found that this removal of transport was not based on an assessment of need of either Mr P or Mrs N, and moreover did not sufficiently accord with the Care Act in that it did not take into consideration her own wellbeing as his carer, nor her obligations in caring for her husband (para. 75-79), which they are statutorily obliged to under section 1, and section 10 and section 3 of the Care and Support (Eligibility Criteria) Regulations 2015 (DoH, 2015b).

The failures evidenced from these two LGO reports are not standalone, and emergent empirical evidence reflects the fact that such failures to conduct assessment processes may be more widespread, especially in relation to carers' assessments. In 2016 the Carers Trust (Carers Trust, 2016a) published an initial survey of 844 individuals – 438 of whom were carers – into how well the Care Act 2014 had begun to embed into practice: 65% of carers surveyed had not had an assessment under the Act,[3] and of those that had, 37% had not received a support plan following their assessment (2016a:13). Moreover, many respondents highlighted an emerging trend that the local authority only offered carers support if a service to meet their needs was available, otherwise there was a tendency to find the carer ineligible rather than sourcing other services (p.16), and there was also evidence that practitioners were not always clear that the carers' eligibility for services is standalone: that is, it does not depend on the person they are caring for meeting the eligibility criteria or whether they are in receipt of services (p.14).

Perhaps more crucially, there is also evidence that such failures in implementation of assessments under the Care Act could result in decisions that are open to challenge by means of judicial review. *R (JF) v London Borough of Merton* involved JF, a 24-year-old man with autism and severe learning difficulties. He had a longstanding placement at a residential college but by June 2016 he and his parents had been informed that this placement was to end. An alternative placement had been identified with Sussex Health Care, which – based on a report by Sussex Health Care produced in July 2016 – the local authority said could meet JF's multiple and complex needs. No care and support plan detailing these changes was prepared until April 2017. JF sought a judicial review of the decision by the local authority to terminate his existing placement based on the fact that the report produced by Sussex Health Care was deficient. It did not properly quantify or address JF's speech and language therapy and occupational therapy needs; it did not express any view on JF's need for an on-site multi-disciplinary team, which JF had enjoyed for many years; nor did it identify the importance of continuity and familiarity in JF's residential placement. Second, it was contended on behalf of JF that either way, the decision to terminate his original placement was unlawful because it did not result from a properly conducted needs assessment, and the defendant had therefore failed to comply with the wellbeing principle in section 1 of the Care Act, and the requirement for a full and proper needs assessment under section 9.

The Court held that while the report prepared by Sussex Health Care was deficient in many respects, the most prominent of these was that it failed to identify and explore JF's needs for an on-site multi-disciplinary team. As a result, in failing to consider this particular matter, the local authority had failed to comply with its assessment duties under section 9 of the Care Act and its duties in relation to JF's wellbeing under section 1. In effect, '[a]ny re-assessment of JF's needs must be based on his current situation and not conducted ... from the position that his placement is no longer available to him' (para. 55). Much as the concertina effect in relation to the Mental Capacity Act has been criticised for conflating the best interests assessment with the capacity assessment, the judge's findings of the local authority in *R(JF) v London Borough of Merton* [2017] represent an attack on a similar concertina effect between care provision and needs assessment under the Care Act that occurred here, and arguably in the cases scrutinised by the Local Government Ombudsman noted above. In effect, as the judge goes on to conclude in JF's case:

> ... {t}he decision to terminate JF's placement cannot be said to be rational. On one persuasive view, it was made before JF's needs had been conclusively assessed under the Act. On any view, it was made before the preparation of the Care and Support Plan. In those circumstances, it is difficult to see how the decision can have been in compliance with the statutory duties contained in section 1 and 9(4) of the {Care} Act... (para. 61)

There is, in addition, further evidence that failures to provide independent advocates under section 67 of the Care Act will also render care assessments unlawful. *R(SG) v London Borough of Haringey* [2015] involved the refusal of a local authority to provide accommodation under section 21 of the National Assistance Act 1948, and thereafter under the Care Act 2014. The claimant (SG) was an Afghan asylum seeker who had been the victim of torture, rape and physical abuse, and who suffered from severe mental health problems including post-traumatic stress disorder, insomnia, depression and anxiety, did not speak English, and was illiterate (para.7). She had been provided with accommodation under section 95 of the Immigration and Asylum Act 1999, but it was also contended that she should have been provided with accommodation by the local authority by virtue of her needs for care and support. It was also argued that the review of her needs conducted by the local authority on 20 May 2015 under the Care Act – which found no need for accommodation arising – was unlawful based on the fact that the authority had not arranged an independent advocate for SG under section 67: 'this appears to me the paradigm case where such an advocate was required, as in the absence of one the claimant was in no position to influence matters' (para.40).

If the apparent concertina effect and the failures in assessment processes are two key similarities that emerge from the literature on the implementation of both the Mental Capacity Act and the Care Act, this raises questions as to *why* these common themes are emerging in the implementation of both Acts. As both Donnelly (2009b) and Skowron (2018) note, the Mental Capacity Act requires complicated legal provisions to be understood, applied, and delivered by non-legally trained professionals, often in very difficult, messy, and complex situations. Skowron argues that, '[i]n reality, capacity assessments face a variety of legal uncertainties, tangles, and paradoxes. Most people applying the Act are not legally trained, so it seems optimistic to expect them to successfully navigate these intricacies' (Skowron, 2018: 25). In its post-legislative scrutiny of the Mental Capacity Act, the House of Lords Select Committee (2014) concluded that legislation should be clearly drafted, to ensure that duties incumbent on professionals are clearly understood and implemented. Indeed, uncertainties as to legal obligations was one of the core reasons for placing adult safeguarding on a statutory footing (Commission for Social Care Inspection, 2008b: para. 2.1) and has also been evidenced in relation to other legislation (Perkins et al., 2007), particularly around uncertainties in relation to information sharing (Pinkney et al., 2008). Yet evidence also suggests that the Act *can* be used effectively and practitioner confidence in using the provisions can be increased where appropriate training, supervision and knowledge transfer mechanisms are put in place (Samsi et al., 2012; Manthorpe et al., 2014), and this is also frequently a key recommendation of SARs (Braye et al., 2015b). The same problems of interpretation perhaps arise in the Care Act because that Act, too, requires complex legal provisions on how and when assessments are to be conducted and when eligibility criteria for services are met to be understood, applied, and delivered by non-legally trained professionals. If, as noted above, evidence suggests that the Mental Capacity Act depends on the strength of training, it would seem to be common sense that the same is also true of the provisions of the Care Act. Perhaps more crucially, it is also the case that social work and social welfare have been hit by the effects of austerity, which may also have impacted on the ability to deliver the 'personalisation' agenda that has effectively become statutorily enshrined in both Acts (Pinkney et al., 2008; Lymbery, 2012). With these two factors being particularly prominent, it is perhaps unsurprising that we have seen legal literacy problems emerging in translating the vision of both the Mental Capacity Act and the Care Acts into practice.

Conclusion

Without rigorous empirical data, it is impossible to make any definitive claims as to what exactly is happening on a wider scale in terms of implementing the Care Act. Yet the evidence presented here, from an analysis of the current information available, suggests we are beginning to see similar trends emerging as those that have characterised the implementation of the Mental Capacity Act over the past ten years. Moving forward, the waters between the two Acts may become further muddied given that it remains unclear how the proposals in the Mental Capacity (Amendment) Bill to reform the Deprivation of Liberty Safeguards will develop, and where best interests will sit within the care planning process. It is true that both Acts are unique in some respects in that although they are pieces of law, their proper application and implementation rest with practitioners on the front line. As one of the participants in Murrell and McCalla's (2016) research points out, '[A] capacity assessment is only as good as the person who's doing it' (Murrell and McCalla, 2016: 27). Much the same could be said for needs assessments under the Care Act. Yet while it is important to remember that neither Act *makes* difficult decisions for practitioners – they operate as frameworks within which practitioners must operate – a failure to learn from the literature on the Mental Capacity Act may mean we run the risk of repeating the same trends in implementing the Care Act. Legal literacy is, and indeed *should* be, a major concern for those implementing both pieces of legislation.

Case study: Barbara

In Chapters 3 (Assessment) and 5 (Carers) you met Barbara, who was receiving care and support, and her son Robert. In Chapter 7 (Safeguarding) we discussed a safeguarding enquiry that took place as a result of concerns about self-neglect, neglect and financial abuse. This case study continues discussion of their situation by considering Barbara's mental capacity.

Barbara has complex health needs and is a heavy drinker and smoker. She lives with her son Robert, who has received a carer's assessment but who no longer provides any care or support to her. Although receiving a daily care and support visit Barbara refuses much of the care offered and her self-neglect has resulted in a severe decline in both her personal care and the conditions in her home, which are dirty and bleak. The only care and support she will agree to is for the care workers to provide food for her; she refuses everything else. She promises to eat the food that has been prepared, but doesn't. Occasionally she will agree to change her clothes, which are always very dirty due to her incontinence, but she doesn't carry this through. She is losing weight and now appears quite severely malnourished. It is also some time since the community nurses have visited to manage her leg dressings as her son cancelled their visits. Barbara has said that she is frightened of Robert, who takes her money. A safeguarding enquiry is taking place to identify the nature of the risks in this situation, and as part of this there are concerns to identify whether Barbara has the mental capacity to make decisions in relation to her living conditions, care and support and relationship with Robert.

Commentary

In assessing whether Barbara has the mental capacity to make decisions, there are important principles to consider. Firstly, mental capacity is decision-specific: assessors must be clear about the decision for which they are assessing capacity. Self-neglect typically arises from difficulties in making a series of different decisions over time. Secondly, mental capacity is time-specific: assessors must be clear about the timing of the decision for which they are assessing capacity, but may need to take account of a pattern of decisions over time.

Under the Mental Capacity Act 2005 Barbara will lack capacity if she has an impairment or disturbance of the mind or brain (sometimes called the diagnostic test) as a result of which she is unable to understand, retain, or use and weigh relevant information, or to communicate her decision (sometimes called the functional test). This assessment involves assessors:

a) being clear about what is relevant information and this will depend on:
   i. what decision they are assessing Barbara's capacity for;
   ii. why the decision is important: the consequences of making (or not making) it;
   iii. understanding of risks: the level of understanding required may vary depending on the level or risk;
b) discussing with Barbara a range of relevant information, including the reason the decision needs to be made, the risks relating to the situation in which it arises, the pros, cons and consequences of deciding one way or another;

→

c) being clear about what they are looking for in relation to her 'retention' of relevant information, testing that Barbara can recall the relevant information at different points in the discussion;

d) being clear about what they are looking for in 'using and weighing' information: ensuring Barbara can tell them why she makes the decision she makes and exploring how her decision shows that she has taken account of the relevant information;

e) considering executive brain function: frontal lobe impairment can affect the ability to retain, use and weigh relevant information *when it is time to act* (rather than in the abstract) and can pose difficulties in carrying through a decision. Barbara's failure to eat despite her assurance to the care workers that she will do so may indicate a need to use an 'articulate and demonstrate' model of assessment – observing Barbara at the time and in the context where her decisions (such as eating, drinking) are being made.

Because mental capacity assessment may need to be conducted over time and at different times, establishing a relationship will facilitate better engagement and better information from Barbara. Assessors must ensure that they allow for fluctuating capacity (for example, where alcohol is involved, or where the time of day affects her ability to reason). Considering the impact of physical factors such as malnutrition, dehydration or infection on her mental capacity will also be important.

Assessors must consider what or who could assist Barbara to make a decision. This may involve family and friends, the provision of information or advocacy, discussion of options and time to reflect. Assessors should also consider the need for multi-disciplinary involvement. This may assist assessors in determining whether Barbara has an impairment or disturbance in the functioning of the mind or brain. Medical involvement may facilitate consideration of frontal lobe dysfunction. Mental health services may help to identify symptoms of any mental disorder. An occupational therapist can assess Barbara's ability to perform activities of daily living. All the detail of the assessment process and its outcome must be recorded and then shared with the other agencies involved.

For Barbara, the outcome will be significant. If she does not have the capacity for any specific decision, her best interests in relation to that matter must be determined and necessary decisions made on her behalf to achieve them. Before deciding or taking action, the decision maker must have regard for whether alternatives that are less restrictive of her basic rights and freedoms could achieve her best interests.

If Barbara has mental capacity, this is not the end of the story. Practitioners should not walk away but should consider whether and when to reassess (for example after elapse of time/ development of relationship/ health decline/event triggers). Patterns over time can be important to establish in self-neglect, and the MCA Code of Practice (DCA, 2007: para 2.11) is clear that repeated unwise decisions that entail significant risk of harm may indicate a need for further investigation. Where her capacity is confirmed through assessment but the risks of harm are

→

significant and likely, other legal options should be considered. For example, is there evidence of a medical condition that is affecting Barbara's capacity to make particular decisions? Is she influenced by undue pressure and/or coercive and controlling behaviour from someone else? Answers here may prompt application to the High Court for use of its inherent jurisdiction.

Further Reading

Feldon, P. (2017) *The Social Worker's Guide to the Care Act 2014.* St Albans: Critical Publishing.

House of Lords Select Committee on the Mental Capacity Act 2005 Report of Session 2013–14 (2014) *Mental Capacity Act 2005 Post Legislative Scrutiny.* London: HMSO.

Kong, C. and Ruck Keene, A. (2018) *Overcoming Challenges in the Mental Capacity Act 2005: Practical Guidance for Working with Complex Issues.* London: Jessica Kingsley.

Notes

1. A failure to do so will render an assessment under the Act unlawful: *R(SG) v London Borough of Haringey* [2015] EWHC 2579.

2. Under section 11(2)(b) an assessment must also be carried out regardless of the fact that the person may be refusing if they are, or are at risk of, experiencing abuse or neglect.

3. Braye and Preston-Shoot's (2017a) review of SARs across London also echoes this finding.

9 Navigating practice at the interface between mental health and social care law

Simon Abbott

Introduction

This chapter considers best practice on how mental health legislation can support adult social care provision. It further highlights opportunities for social care legislation to support the provision of mental health social care. A person with mental health problems could fall under the provisions of the Care Act 2014 (hereafter CA) without ever being subject to the provisions of the Mental Health Act 1983 (hereafter MHA). Their care and support needs, whether arising from a mental health condition or other circumstances, would require assessment and decisions in the usual way. However, a person subject to the MHA, notably guardianship (s7 MHA), community treatment (S25A MHA), leave (s17 MHA) and discharge from hospital, will necessarily also fall under certain provisions of the CA. This chapter focuses on the latter category where both adult social care and mental health legislation apply alongside each other.

The interface between the MHA and CA is explored by comparing the two Acts. This comparison identifies tensions and how the principles of the MHA (s118) and CA duties of wellbeing (s1) and prevention (s2) also support their complementarity. Thereafter, the chapter considers the CA concepts of wellbeing and prevention as an organising framework to consider mental health aftercare (s117 MHA). Evidence of practice at the interface of the two Acts is explored to highlight the challenges and achievements of the CA, drawing on research, case law and cases involving the Local Government Ombudsman. Finally, best practice guidance is outlined, focusing on legal literacy incorporating recovery-orientated practice approaches to realise the potential of the CA key concepts of wellbeing and prevention at the interface with the MHA.

Comparing and contrasting the two Acts

The MHA provides a legal framework for the assessment and treatment of people who have a mental disorder. Mental disorder is defined widely as 'any disorder or disability of the mind' (s1(2)). There are exclusions within this definition, for example dependence on drugs or alcohol is not considered to be a disorder or disability of the mind (s1(3)). The CA provides a legal framework for care and support to adults, including those with mental health problems, underpinned by the duty to promote wellbeing (s1 CA).

The contrast between the two pieces of legislation resides in their competing imperatives. The MHA provides legally mandated coercion (Campbell, 2010), either in the form of detention in a psychiatric hospital (s2, s3, s4, s37, s38, s45A, s47, s48), supervised treatment in the community (s25A, s41) or guardianship (s7, s37). The MHA also provides rights to free aftercare in certain circumstances when a person is discharged from hospital (s117). Discharge from detention in hospital, however, will not always end the dynamic of coercion. Campbell and Davidson (2009) identify the challenges of maintaining a commitment to emancipatory and recovery-oriented approaches in the context of resource constraints that limit effective community support options for people experiencing acute mental distress. Equally they remind us (Davidson and Campbell, 2007) that coercion is not always legally mandated; it can also occur without a legal mandate during interactions between mental health services and service users. For instance, many 'voluntary' interventions between mental health service users and professionals occur within what Fennell (2010) refers to as compliance in the shadow of compulsion. In contrast, the cornerstones of the CA are personalisation, independence, choice and control of the individual in achieving the outcomes they personally value (Braye and Preston-Shoot, 2016). The interface between the CA and MHA therefore engages important issues concerning individual liberty that have profound implications in relation to the power of the state to intervene in the lives of citizens, where competing imperatives of coercion and care often sit in tension.

This tension is dynamic and shifting, eluding neat delineation between the concepts of coercion and care. Their relationship is complex (Davidson and Campbell, 2007; Campbell and Davidson, 2009; McSherry and Freckelton, 2015; Braye et al., 2017). For instance, detaining a person in hospital under the MHA could lead to improvements in their mental wellbeing and prevent further deterioration in their mental health. In this context, coercion under the MHA is closely related to care and wellbeing. A person discharged from psychiatric hospital under supervised community treatment (s25A), guardianship (s7) or leave (s17) may be obliged to receive care and support services under the CA, rather than choosing to present for them. In this context, the wellbeing principle underpinning the CA becomes closely linked to coercion. This dynamic relationship is evident in the term 'coercive care' (McSherry and Freckelton, 2015), coined to describe the use of mental health law to provide compulsory mental health care. Acknowledging this shifting tension between coercion and care at the interface of the two Acts supports the argument for 'more nuanced and less dichotomous interpretations of the moral imperatives for autonomy and protection' (Braye et al., 2017: 9). For instance, Courtney and Moulding (2014) suggest that there are indeed spaces for creative approaches to involuntary mental health treatment that are consistent with social work values and ethics and with aspects of a recovery orientation. This literature highlights that in compulsory admission to psychiatric hospital, coercion and care can be positioned as complementary concepts (Courtney and Moulding, 2014; Davidson et al., 2016; Duffy et al., 2016), as opposed to permanently sitting in opposition. Indeed, as Hood et al. (2019) point out, it is in their relationships with service users that social workers are obliged to confront the familiar paradoxes of their profession. This adds further understanding on the shifting dynamic tension between coercion and care when both Acts are in play and highlights the important role of practice in the law/practice relationship. This is because the law is enacted in the interactions between professionals, service users, family members and carers, privileging practice in determining how the law is used (Abbott, 2018).

The Code of Practice: Mental Health Act 1983 (Department of Health, 2015c) (hereafter the Code) highlights discharge from hospital as an important interface with the CA, but it is necessary first to explain how admission under the MHA occurs. Most patients detained in psychiatric hospital are subject to 'civil sections' (MHA Part II): under section 2 (admission for assessment or assessment followed by treatment) detention lasts up to 28 days and cannot be renewed; under section 3 (admission for treatment) detention lasts up to 6 months and can be renewed for a further 6 months and yearly thereafter. A smaller group of patients are concerned in criminal proceedings or under sentence (MHA Part III. Although it is possible to be admitted as a voluntary patient (s131 MHA), increasing numbers of such patients are subsequently detained under s2 or s3 (NHS Digital, 2018). The number of patients made subject to s3 following admission under s2 is also increasing (NHS Digital, 2018).

The interface between the two Acts is acknowledged in the Code (Department of Health, 2015c), placing an emphasis on the CA as a vehicle for local authorities, NHS commissioners and providers, and housing services to work together to provide person-centred care and support.

The Care and Support Statutory Guidance issued under the Care Act 2014 (DHSC, 2018a) (hereafter the Guidance) also highlights key areas of interface between the CA and the MHA. The first involves an integrated approach to assessment, which may also include putting processes in place to ensure that the person is referred for other assessments such as an assessment for aftercare needs under the MHA. Where there are concerns about capacity to make a specific decision about care and support, then a capacity assessment will be needed under the Mental Capacity Act 2005 (DHSC, 2018a). The Guidance emphasises that where a person has both health care needs and care and support needs, local authorities and the NHS should work together effectively to deliver a high quality, coordinated assessment. A multi-agency approach is advocated when following the Care Programme Approach (CPA) for people with a severe mental disorder who need multi-agency support or intensive intervention, under the direction of a named care coordinator (Department of Health, 2015c).

Wellbeing

Whilst distinct in purpose, the MHA and CA are also closely related, linked by principles with common features. The MHA, following amendments in 2007, emphasises five over-arching principles: least restrictive option and maximising independence; empowerment and involvement; respect and dignity; purpose and effectiveness; efficiency and equity. These principles are required to be reflected in the Code (Department of Health, 2015c) to inform decision-making on care, support or treatment provided under the MHA (s118 MHA). The first three principles share complementary features with the duty to promote individual wellbeing (s1 CA) and prevention (s2 CA). The principle of least restrictive option and maximising independence provides that wherever possible independence should be encouraged and supported, with a focus on promoting recovery. Empowerment and involvement requires that the person is fully involved in decisions about care, support and treatment. This includes considering the views of families, carers and others, if appropriate. Respect and dignity require that the person, their family and carers are treated respectfully and their dignity maintained. Within this context, both Acts are concerned with the needs of people with mental health problems, their families and carers.

The relevance of social care legislation to mental health is brought into focus by a social perspective towards responding to mental health needs (Tew, 2005, 2011; Hatfield, 2008; Webber et al., 2016). Positioned within a bio-psycho-social understanding of mental health (Engel, 1977), in preference to the bio-reductionism of the medical model (Pilgrim, 2002), a social perspective can draw on the CA duties of promoting wellbeing (s1) and prevention (s2) in work with people who fall under the provisions of both pieces of legislation.

Wellbeing is described (CA, s1(2)) as relating to the following: personal dignity (including treatment with respect); physical and mental health and emotional well-being; protection from abuse and neglect; control over day-to-day life; participation in work, education, training or recreation; social and economic well-being; domestic, family and personal relationships; suitability of living accommodation; the individual's contribution to society. The relevance of the wellbeing principle, applied to a person subject to the provisions of the MHA (or at risk of becoming so), lies in recognising the impact that mental health problems could have on their wellbeing. Guidance from Public Health England suggests that the life expectancy with a serious mental health problem such as bipolar disorder or schizophrenia is 15 to 20 years less than in the general population (Public Health England, 2016). The associated risks to wellbeing also include wider social determinants such as unemployment, unstable housing, stigma, discrimination and social exclusion (Hatfield, 2008; Thornicroft, 2006; Public Health England, 2016). The CA wellbeing principle provides potential for social interventions that focus on improving access to social capital, which can positively impact on mental health and wellbeing (Tew, 2011; Tew et al., 2012; WHO, 2014; Webber et al., 2016; Public Health England, 2016). Social interventions can be mobilised by the CA, driven by the wellbeing duty (s1), enabling key social recovery processes. Identified by Tew et al. (2012), these include: empowerment and reclaiming control over one's life; rebuilding positive personal and social identities (including dealing with the impact of stigma and discrimination); connectedness (including both personal and family relationships, and wider aspects of social inclusion).

Prevention

Prevention (s2 CA) implies prevention of mental health crisis, which in turn raises opportunities for prevention of resort to the MHA through the provision of adequate social care under the CA. Care Quality Commission data suggest that increasing numbers of people are detained on more than one occasion in a calendar year (CQC, 2018d), raising questions about the adequacy of social care for people who are discharged from a psychiatric hospital. Being re-admitted to psychiatric hospital under the provisions of the MHA within a calendar year suggests that care and support in the community may not have been adequate on initial discharge. Conceptualising the CA as preventing detention under the MHA is an approach cognisant of the message to social workers provided by the sociologist and ex-social worker Stanley Cohen: 'As long as you do nothing about original causes, you will continually just be pulling out bodies, mopping up the casualties' (Cohen, 1984: 236).

CA contribution to prevention of mental health crisis is further underpinned by the UK's international law obligations. In 2009 the UK ratified the United Nations Convention on the Rights of Persons with Disabilities (UN, 2007) (hereafter CRPD). Whilst not integrated into UK law the CRPD nevertheless occupies an influential position, quoted in judicial decisions and by government. It requires states to provide adequate community provisions to avoid the use of coercion under mental health legislation. In a climate of austerity, 'systems failure' (Siddique, 2015) in mental health services, including concerns about a lack of community provision, undermines these obligations. The CRPD has further implications for best practice at the interface between the MHA and CA, specifically in the requirements to support people to make their own decisions about their care, treatment and support (Davidson et al., 2016). The MHA Code reinforces this, together with the importance of a social perspective, requiring professionals to "consider the principles that the Care Act introduces about the centrality of the patient and a holistic approach to care and support. These are in line with the guiding principles proposed in this Code".

Aftercare

Discharge from psychiatric hospital is a key area of interface between the MHA and CA. The MHA Code provides that, in addition to the requirements of the MHA, professionals involved in discharging or treating patients in the community should also consider the general responsibilities on local authorities provided in the CA (Department of Health, 2015c).

For those who have been detained under the provisions of longer-term sections 3, 37, 45A or 48 s117 (MHA), aftercare is the organising framework in which the CA is applied. Under section 117, local authorities and clinical commissioning groups have a joint duty to arrange the provision of mental health aftercare services for people who have been detained in hospital for treatment under those sections. The local authority must not charge for services provided under s117 (*R v Manchester City Council ex parte Stennett* [2002]).

The CA (s75) defines aftercare services for the first time, amending section 117 MHA. They must have the purposes of 'meeting a need arising from or related to the person's mental disorder' and 'reducing the risk of a deterioration of the person's mental condition and, accordingly, reducing the risk of the person requiring admission to a hospital again for treatment for mental disorder' (MHA s117(6)). The range of possible services is broad (Department of Health, 2015c), encompassing healthcare, social care and employment services, supported accommodation and services to meet wider social, cultural and spiritual needs, and to promote recovery and participation in society, provided these services meet a need that arises directly from or is related to the patient's mental disorder and help to reduce the risk of a deterioration in their mental condition (Department of Health, 2015c). It would not include boarding for pets, storage of personal belongings, general needs/ordinary accommodation (*R (Afework) v LB Camden* [2013]).

Section 117 applies regardless of a person's immigration status; aftercare is available to a person who otherwise has no recourse to public funds. It applies to people of all ages, including children and young people, and must be provided free even where a person is awarded damages for future care costs. In *Tinsley v Manchester City Council & Ors* [2017] the local authority's argument that it was not under a duty to provide s117 aftercare in such circumstances was dismissed on appeal, the court ruling that personal injury awards cannot excuse the authority from providing s117 provision without charges. A person may decline to accept aftercare. Any decision to decline them should be fully informed, and unwillingness to accept services does not mean they are not needed (Department of Health, 2015c).

The Code (Department of Health, 2015c) highlights the ultimate aim of aftercare services: to maintain patients in the community, with as few restrictions as are necessary, wherever possible (para 33.3). Aftercare should provide support in regaining or enhancing skills, or learning new skills, in order to cope with life outside hospital. The duty to provide aftercare begins when the person is discharged from hospital and lasts for as long as the person needs the services. It also applies during leave of absence. For those on community treatment orders, aftercare must be provided for the duration of the order, although this may not end at the same time as the order.

Aftercare planning

Planning aftercare should begin when a person is detained in hospital. The CPA should be used (Department of Health, 2015c) and the local authority should undertake an assessment of need in line with section 9 CA (ADASS, 2018b). The CA assessment must address the individual's social care related needs in their own right while also considering any social care services required to contribute to section 117 aftercare (ADASS, 2018b).

Direct payments

A person who has their care and support needs met by a local authority must receive a personal budget as part of their care and support plan, setting out the money allocated to meet their eligible needs. Agreeing on how best to meet those needs might involve direct payment, or local-authority arranged care and support, or a mixture of both (DHSC, 2018a). Direct payments present both challenges and opportunities in the interface between the two Acts. When considering a request for direct payment the local authority must consider whether it is an appropriate way to meet the needs in question. At the interface with the MHA the question is whether direct payments are an appropriate way for the local authority to discharge its s117 aftercare duty (DHSC, 2018a). The statutory guidance to the CA recognises that, in the interface with the MHA, there may be instances where a person is required to receive services as a condition of mental health legislation (s25A; s7; s17). In these cases, although receiving services may be an obligation rather than a choice, it might still be appropriate to give the person responsibility of meeting their needs via direct payment. However, the guidance also recognises that there may be cases where direct payment is not appropriate to meet needs. Direct payments would cease once the clinical commissioning group and local authority are satisfied that the person is no longer in need of aftercare services (DHSC, 2018a).

Hamilton et al. (2016) conducted an empirical study of mental health service user engagement with personal budgets, and the impact of this on their empowerment and relationships with mental health professionals. They highlight a need for a shift of culture and expectations around power relations between mental health service users and mental health services if personal budgets are to benefit the majority of people with mental health problems who are eligible for local authority social care. Their evidence shows that many practitioners either were not committed to increasing choice and control or were not managing to do so with all those they supported. It suggests that generic local authority systems for processing personal budgets were not always suited to people with mental health difficulties, who may have fluctuating levels of need and mental capacity. These bureaucratic systems may also have discouraged initiative and imagination on the part of service users and practitioners, thus undermining the potential for personal budgets as a tool in enabling a recovery approach. The most important message for social workers, arising from the research findings, is recognising the importance of the relationship with the service user to achieve the exercise of meaningful choice. The key message in relation to relationships was the value of longer-term involvement where mutual trust could be developed.

Independent advocacy

A further important point of interface involves CA duties to provide independent advocacy in the assessment of need. Under the MHA, 'qualifying patients' are entitled to support from an Independent Mental Health Advocate (IMHA): those detained under the MHA; those liable to be detained, even if not actually detained, including those on leave of absence from hospital, or absent without leave, or those for whom an application or court order for admission has been completed; conditionally discharged restricted patients; those subject to guardianship; those subject to a community treatment order (Department of Health, 2015c). Those whose care and support needs are being assessed, planned or reviewed as part of s117 aftercare planning, but who do not retain a right to an IMHA, should be considered for an advocate under the CA (s67), if they have substantial difficulty in being involved and if there is no appropriate person to support their involvement (DHSC, 2018a). A person who qualifies for advocacy under the CA could also qualify for advocacy under the Mental Capacity Act 2005. In this case, the same advocate could provide both CA and MCA advocacy (DHSC, 2018a).

In *R (SG) v Haringey LBC* [2015] the individual, a victim of torture, physical and emotional abuse, arrived in the UK from Afghanistan in 2013 seeking asylum. One of her eight children had died and she did not know the whereabouts of her husband and seven surviving children. As a result, she suffered from severe mental health problems. She did not speak English and could not read or write. The local authority's decision that this person was not entitled to accommodation under the CA was deemed to be defective and quashed, in part because no independent advocate was provided to support her during the assessment process.

Cooper and Bruin (2017) highlight a practice gap in the requirement for advocacy to be embedded in practice, suggesting that more needs to be done by professionals to ensure that consideration is given to whether advocacy is needed. An independent national review of Independent Mental Health Advocacy focused on the experience and impact of IMHA provision across eight study sites. The study (Newbigging et al., 2015) involved 289 participants, 75 focus group participants and 214 individual participant interviews. Participants included 90 people eligible for IMHA services, as well as advocates, hospital and community-based mental health professionals, and commissioners. The findings indicate a clear need for IMHA services based on participants' experience of the disempowering nature of compulsion under the MHA. Access to advocacy was found to be variable and problematic for people with specific needs relating to ethnicity, age and disability. Uptake of advocacy was influenced by available resources and attitude and understanding of mental health professionals. Service user satisfaction with IMHA provision was associated more closely with positive experiences of the process of advocacy as opposed to tangible impacts on care and treatment under the MHA. The authors propose increasing access to advocacy by a system of opt-out as opposed to opt-in, and a shift from a narrow conception of statutory advocacy as safeguarding rights to one emphasising self-determination and participation in decision-making.

Ordinarily resident

The duty to commission or provide mental health aftercare rests with the local authority for the area in which the person was ordinarily resident immediately before they were detained under the MHA, even if the person becomes ordinarily resident in another area after leaving hospital (DHSC, 2018a). The concept of ordinary residence is not always straightforward to determine. Ordinary residence in the case of an adult who has the capacity to make a decision where to live will need to consider the guidance provided in *Shah v London Borough of Barnet* [1983]: ordinary residence is the place the person has voluntarily adopted for a settled purpose, whether for a short or long duration. However, a person who lacks capacity may not have voluntarily adopted to be in the place they reside in. In this case, *R (on the application of Cornwall Council) v Secretary of State for Health* [2015] has clarified that the essential criterion is the residence of the person and the nature of that residence, and therefore, local authorities should follow the approach of *Shah v London Borough of Barnet* [1983] (DHSC, 2018a).

Ending s117 aftercare

The duty to provide aftercare exists until both the CCG and the local authority are satisfied that the person no longer requires it (Department of Health, 2015c).[1] The Code does not expressly require that the person themselves, or their carers, must be satisfied that the services are no longer required, an omission at odds with the emphasis on holistic, person-centred care outlined in the Code and the Guidance (DHSC, 2018a). However, the Code does highlight that fully involving the patient and (if indicated) their carer and/or advocate in the decision-making process will play an important part in the successful ending of aftercare. The circumstances in which ending section 117 aftercare is appropriate will vary according to the nature of the services being provided (Department of Health, 2015c). The Code suggests that the most clear-cut circumstance is where the person's mental health improved to a point where they no longer needed services to meet needs arising from or related to their mental disorder. If these services included, for example, care in a specialist residential setting, arrangements for their move to more appropriate accommodation would need to be in place before support under section 117 was withdrawn (Department of Health, 2015c). In this case, a clear interface emerges with the CA, which would replace s117 as the appropriate framework for care and support provision. Aftercare services may be reinstated if it becomes obvious that they have been withdrawn prematurely (Department of Health, 2015c). ADASS guidance suggests that a decision to bring s117 to an end should only be taken after a multi-disciplinary reassessment of the person's needs (ADASS, 2018b). However, some elements of the aftercare package may be discharged sooner than others if a specific need has been successfully met, e.g. resettlement support may stop after a relatively short period of time, though continuing mental health care may be required for a longer period. Any changes to the support plan and care and support package, including a recommendation to discharge some or all of the services, must be formally recorded and authorised by a service manager or the relevant resource panel (ADASS, 2018b).

Even when the person is settled in the community, they may continue to need aftercare to prevent a relapse or further deterioration in their condition (Department of Health, 2015c). The interface with the CA's emphasis on prevention (s2) arises here as a rationale for continuing to provide s117 aftercare for a person who is rebuilding their life in the community. ADASS suggests that discharge from s117 aftercare should be considered if care/support/treatment related to mental disorder is no longer needed to minimise the risk of deterioration and/or readmission. This is highlighted as a measure of recovery and increasing independence (ADASS, 2018b). On the face of it, this measure, originating in s75 CA, seems to privilege the notion of clinical recovery, potentially overshadowing a more holistic recovery approach. However, it can entail a recovery approach to practice that uses strengths-based assessment and a person-centred approach to care planning (Slade, 2009). This more nuanced approach might also acknowledge continuation of s117 aftercare services in the context of supporting a person to get on with what they personally value in their life, despite experiencing ongoing mental distress, as an equal measure of recovery and independence.

Evidence of practice at the interface between mental health and social care law

Consideration of best practice at the interface between mental health and adult social care legislation needs to acknowledge the wider practice and organisational context where this takes place (Hamilton et al., 2016). Indeed, Lymbery (2014) highlights a difficult practice terrain of austerity, positing that local authority budget reductions limit opportunities for social workers to practise within the context of personalisation. Spicker (2013) also argues that personalisation falls short of the policy rhetoric underpinning the 'personalisation agenda', which emphasises placing the service user in greater control with increased choice regarding their needs and support. As Hamilton et al. (2016) point out, there is concern that the concepts of choice and control may be largely illusory in the context of austerity.

The potential of the CA to impact on mental health legislation also requires consideration of the practice context of mental health social work. Karban (2017) highlights that social work in mental health is practised against a backdrop of conflicting pressures and imperatives, pointing out that on the one hand the policy rhetoric emphasises personalisation, recovery, user involvement and community care, while in reality pharmacology is the primary mode of intervention, supported by psychological therapies. This provides further rationale for a social perspective on mental health to underpin best practice at the interface between the two Acts and brings to light the dynamic tension experienced by professionals: reconciling the reality of the challenges faced in practice with idealised notions of their professional role (Lipsky, 1980).

Evidence on implementation at the interface between the MHA and CA is available in reports by the Local Government Ombudsman who, as the final stage of complaint on adult social care, has considered complaints about the interface of s117 MHA and s9 and s10 CA in several cases. In LGSCO and Northumberland, Tyne & Wear NHS Foundation Trust (2018), Miss B complained about the care and support provided by the Council and the Trust under the provisions of s117 MHA, saying she did not get extra support to attend hospital appointments. It was found that the council should have considered this request for extra support under the provisions of s9 and s10 CA and had failed to do so.

In LGSCO and NHS Sheffield Clinical Commissioning Group (2018), the complainant, Mr D, suffered significant injustice when the CCG and Council failed to provide adequate support under s117 MHA and s9 and 10 CA after his care provider terminated its contract and there was no contingency plan in place. The new provider did not meet all of Mr D's needs and his mental health deteriorated because of the lack of support, culminating in him being admitted to hospital. Following his discharge he had to live with his parents for five weeks during which time they had little formal support and no carer assessment was carried out. This impacted adversely on Mr D's wellbeing and that of his parents.

In LGSCO and Enfield LBC (2018), the complainant's son, Mr F, was caused significant injustice when the CCG and the council failed to take responsibility for his care and support arrangements after the CCG placed him in a care home. Mr F remained in an inappropriate placement that struggled to meet his needs for longer than he should have. This impacted adversely on his wellbeing and caused the complainant distress. When Mr F was subsequently detained under the MHA, a dispute between the authorities resulted in Mr F remaining in hospital for more than 12 months after he was fit for discharge.

In LGSCO and Hillingdon Clinical Commissioning Group (2018), an injustice was found in relation to not following the provisions of s117 MHA and s9 CA. Poor recordkeeping about s117 and charging a service user for aftercare services provided under s117 were combined with a flawed social care needs assessment under s9, which resulted in nine hours of care per week being withdrawn.

In LGO and Milton Keynes Council (2016), the Trust and the Council failed to consider and provide formal aftercare services under s117 MHA to the complainants' daughter, Miss C, after she was discharged from hospital. This led to poor responses to changes in Miss C's health, social care and accommodation needs. The Trust and the Council also failed to consider and provide formal support to meet the complainants' needs as carers (s10 CA).

Case law also provides evidence of the CA and MHA interface in practice. In R (JF) v Merton LBC [2017] a young man was deemed by his family to be at risk of being detained under the MHA in the absence of the social care provisions that he should have been receiving. The young man involved had complex needs and lived in a residential college for many years. He required 1-1 supervision at all times and 2-1 when in the community. His multi-disciplinary team support included psychiatric input. The local authority decided he should move to an alternative placement, based on a pre-admission assessment undertaken by the proposed placement. The decision of the local authority was quashed as it was deemed unlawful because it was not rational, the local authority neglecting to undertake a lawful assessment under the provisions of the CA. The case is important because it clearly establishes the prominence of the wellbeing principle (s1 CA) as a central element of decisions on care and support. The ruling set out the statutory framework in the following summary:

The central elements of the framework are 1) the well-being principle 2) the assessment of needs 3) making the arrangements to meet those needs 4) in certain cases, identifying the adult's personal budget. There is a clear statutory theme placing the individual at the heart and centre of the process so that he or she is fully involved in decision making. This is emphasised by the duty to have regard to the wishes and preferences of the individual.

The ruling underlines that in assessing need under the CA, a local authority has a duty to promote the wellbeing of the person being assessed and must have regard for all dimensions of wellbeing set out in s1.

An interesting interface with the MHA was raised in this case, through applying the CA principles of wellbeing (s1) and prevention (s2) in the context of arguing that the provision of adult social care prevented the claimant from being detained under the MHA. The argument, felt strongly by family members, was that removing the accommodation would subsequently place JF at risk of being detained in hospital under the MHA. Whilst this argument did not form part of the final ruling, it raises the potential of prevention (s2 CA) forming the basis of future arguments on adequate social care provision serving to prevent a person becoming liable to detention under the MHA.

Good practice

Braye and Preston-Shoot (2016) highlight and challenge the myth that the law provides clarity and distinct boundaries. They demonstrate, with reference to s117 MHA, that the law in fact provides no such clarity for practice. Indeed Bourdieu (1987) considered the law as an area of socially patterned activity or practice. Notwithstanding acceptance of the rule of law, he asserts that social practices, whilst not explicitly recognised, are deterministic of how the law really functions.

Good practice therefore involves an acknowledgement that the law is not enough on its own (Braye and Preston-Shoot, 2016). In practice, law is enacted in the relationships between professionals and service users and carers. Indeed, the importance of such relationships has been identified in the use of the CA (Braye et al., 2014, 2017; Hamilton et al., 2016). As Hood et al. (2019) point out, the implementation of policies should take into account relationship-based work, but also that relationships themselves may prove resistant to codification. Bourdieu is useful here in thinking about the nature of the relationship between law and practice, whereby human action is defined as habitus, which he refers to as patterned and structured without being rational or calculative (Bourdieu, 1990).

Achieving best practice needs to draw on professional values, knowledge and skills to enhance the potential of the CA and MHA in practice. The concept of legal literacy (Braye and Preston-Shoot, 2006; Braye et al., 2011; Preston-Shoot and McKimm, 2012; Braye and Preston-Shoot, 2016) provides a useful conceptualisation of the law/social work relationship. Three imperatives are highlighted here: doing things right, referring to the need for knowledgeable use of legal rules; doing right things, referring to the law's interface with values; and rights thinking, referring to action by reference to human rights. In the context of the interface between the CA and MHA this will involve the integration of all three components when using the law.

Good practice should consider the CA 'upstream' to prevent mental health crisis 'downstream'. This acknowledges the relationship between wellbeing and prevention by providing adequate social care to strengthen access to social capital to prevent, as far as possible, a deterioration in mental health and thereby possibly preventing use of the MHA as a response to a mental health crisis. This approach recognises mental distress from a bio-psycho-social perspective whilst privileging social responses to mental distress. The CA can be used as a tool to identify and provide care and support that draws in holistic, social approaches to promoting mental health.

Finally, good practice needs to carefully consider the concepts of wellbeing (s1 CA) and prevention (s2 CA) alongside the s117 MHA aim of 'maintaining' a person in the community with the purpose of promoting recovery. It is important for professionals to take a person-centred approach, which fully involves service users in how these concepts are understood and promoted. They need to be brought into sharp focus, particularly when reviewing s117 MHA care plans. This process does not need to equate a person functioning well with a rationale to remove care and support. It is the aim of s117 MHA to maintain a person in the community. When a person achieves this level of functioning it should not necessarily mean that the support is no longer required; the opposite may be the case. This approach is consistent with strengths-based and recovery approaches to mental health practice that are focused on personal recovery, in contrast to notions of clinical recovery. This involves the person rebuilding their life by reclaiming valued social roles and a positive self-identity despite having mental health problems (Slade, 2009; Tew et al., 2012; Duffy et al., 2016). The principles of wellbeing and prevention, along with the expressly stated purpose of s117 MHA in preventing re-admission, provide a strong rationale for caution in ending s117 MHA aftercare.

Considering best practice at the interface between the Acts needs to acknowledge the limits of legislation in addressing some of the social determinants of mental health problems. There is convincing evidence that in societies with high levels of inequality, such as that of the UK, there are also high levels of mental distress (Wilkinson and Pickett, 2009). This is relevant when considering prevention. The interface between inequality in society and mental distress has been described as the causes of the causes, requiring political will to address (Wilkinson and Pickett, 2009).

Conclusion

Using the law in practice is a nuanced and complex undertaking (Braye and Preston-Shoot, 1990; 2005; Braye et al., 2011; Brophy and McDermott, 2013; Courtney and Moulding, 2014; Davidson et al., 2016). Applying social care and mental health law

(Continued)

(Continued)

involves participation in the process of constructing legality (Ewick and Sibley, 1998; Sibley, 2005). This participation involves talk, interaction and meaning making. Translating the CA duties of wellbeing (s1) and prevention (s2) into practice is framed by an environment of austerity in local government that creates a challenging terrain, where idealised notions of both law and professional roles are challenged and brought into question. The role of practice in its relationship with law therefore requires further scrutiny. One way of doing this is to take a legal literacy approach to practice. This concept should not be misapplied to denote that strict adherence to legal rules is all that is required. Rather, it is useful precisely because it acknowledges that the law is not enough on its own to realise wellbeing (s1) and prevention (s2). This complements an approach to practice that draws on person-centred and personal recovery approaches at the interface between the two Acts to realise their combined potential.

Case study: Barbara

In Chapters 3 (Assessment) and 5 (Carers) you met Barbara, who was receiving care and support, and her son Robert. In Chapter 7 (Safeguarding) we discussed a safeguarding enquiry that took place as a result of concerns about self-neglect, neglect and financial abuse. Assessment of Barbara's mental capacity in these circumstances was discussed in Chapter 8 (Mental capacity). This case study continues the discussion by considering Barbara's mental health.

Barbara has complex health needs and is a heavy drinker and smoker. She lives with her son, Robert, who has received a carer's assessment but who no longer provides any care or support to her. Although receiving a daily care and support visit Barbara declines much of the care offered and her self-neglect has resulted in a severe decline in both her personal care and the conditions in her home, which are dirty and bleak. The only care and support she will agree to is for the care workers to provide food for her; she refuses everything else. She promises to eat the food that has been prepared, but doesn't. Occasionally she will agree to change her clothes, which are always very dirty due to her incontinence, but she doesn't carry this through. She is losing weight and it is some time since the community nurses have visited to manage her leg dressings as her son cancelled their visits. Barbara has said that she is frightened of Robert and that he takes her money. A safeguarding enquiry has taken place to identify the nature of the risks in this situation and Barbara's mental capacity to make decisions in relation to her situation has been assessed. There are concerns about her mental health and a referral has been made to the community mental health team.

$\longrightarrow$

Commentary

The first question to be answered here is whether the referral is for a mental health assessment or a Mental Health Act 1983 assessment. Any appropriately qualified mental health professional can conduct a mental health assessment. However, Mental Health Act 1983 assessments must involve an approved section 12 (Mental Health Act 1983) doctor, a medical practitioner who knows Barbara, and an Approved Mental Health Professional.

Whatever type of assessment has been requested, it should be characterised by several principles, including Barbara's past and present feelings and wishes, her involvement in care planning and, unless contraindicated, the views of her son Robert. The aim should be to maximise her wellbeing and safety. Intervention in cases of self-neglect should be based on an understanding of Barbara's lived experience, which may involve loss and trauma, mental distress and a negative self-image. Depending on how her self-neglect comes to be understood, counselling, motivational interviewing, cognitive behavioural therapy and peer support groups may be indicated.

A Mental Health Act assessment will involve consideration of whether she has a mental disorder of a nature or degree that warrants admission to hospital, and whether in the interests of her own health or safety or for the protection of others she should be admitted. Dependence on alcohol is not itself a mental disorder although disorders may arise from or be associated with dependence, and it is clear that Barbara may have other mental health needs also. An AMHP must interview Barbara 'in a suitable manner' (section 13, Mental Health Act 1983) and decide whether in all the circumstances of her case admission is the most appropriate way of providing the care and treatment Barbara needs. It would appear likely that Barbara's nearest relative is her son. Given what is known about their relationship, and informed by Barbara's views, consideration should be given as to whether it is reasonable and practicable to consult him, and whether he should be displaced as the nearest relative.

The assessment will involve consideration of the need for Barbara's admission into a psychiatric ward, either voluntarily (section 131) or compulsorily (sections 2 or 3), or alternatively into guardianship (section 7). The outcome should be characterised by the choice of the least restrictive alternative, and an approach that demonstrates respect, promotes her dignity and maximises her involvement, independence and empowerment (Department of Health, 2015c).

Risk assessment will be key to determining the least restrictive alternative. This will involve consideration of the chronicity and prognosis of her presentation, jeopardy to her own health and safety, and that of others, her own views and those of others who know her, her own skills in managing her situation, and the potential advantages and disadvantages of different approaches to managing the risks involved. The mental health assessment should also be combined with a review of Barbara's care and support plan since enhancement of this provision may obviate the need for more restrictive interventions.

Further Reading

Braye, S. and Preston-Shoot, M. (2016) *Practising Social Work Law* (4th edn). London: Palgrave.

Davidson, G., Brophy, L. and Campbell, J. (2016) Risk, recovery and capacity: competing or complementary approaches to mental health social work, *Australian Social Work*, 69 (2): 158–68.

Tew, J. (2011) *Social Approaches to Mental Distress*. Basingstoke: Palgrave Macmillan.

Note

1. An exception to this is where a person is subsequently once more detained in hospital under section 3, 37, 47, 48, or 45A MHA 1983. In these circumstances, any existing after care duty owed to that person ceases, but a new entitlement would start when discharged from hospital following the new period of detention (ADASS, 2018b).

10 Hidden in plain sight: social work, Acquired Brain Injury and missed opportunities for change

Mark Holloway

Introduction

It was as recently as the 1980s that disabled people's movements in the UK, inspired and underpinned by a social model of disability, began winning the battle for self-determination and autonomy in relation to how care and support services were provided (Evans, 2003; Oliver, 1990). This caused a significant shift in policy, leading to the development of the Independent Living Fund in 1988, and to the implementation (in 1997) of the Community Care (Direct Payments) Act (1996), which allowed local authorities to make cash payments to meet eligible needs instead of services, thereby increasing autonomy over how those needs were to be met. The battle to end the enforced segregation of people with disabilities also led to a change in social work practice; no longer would there be an automatic assumption that severely disabled working age adults' needs could first and foremost be met through the provision of residential care (Glasby, 2005).

Personalisation and notions of self-directed care and budget-holding by the user of the services have increasingly become the norm, and shifts in the power relationship between people with disabilities and care staff have been reported (Leece and Leece, 2011). Running concurrently with these changes has been a move within adult social care away from relationship-based work towards care management, the social worker/care manager acting to broker packages of self-directed care for the autonomous person with a disability (Dustin, 2007; Leece and Leece, 2011; Lymbery, 2012; Postle, 2001; Carey, 2014). Such trends are also embedded within the Care Act 2014.

Criticisms of the increased drive towards personalisation have tended to focus upon its uneven uptake or bias towards middle-class service users (Leece and Leece, 2006; Priestley et al., 2006), on the negative impact it may have upon support staff (Leece and Peace, 2010) and upon the impact inadequate funding has during times of austerity (Roulstone and Morgan, 2009; Lymbery, 2012). It is notable that criticisms are not based on the underpinning principles of autonomy or self-determination, nor the application of a social model of disability. Personalisation, well applied and funded, would appear to be in line with the United Nations Convention on the Rights of Persons with Disabilities of which the UK is a signatory.

In this environment therefore social work may prove to be emancipatory, providing opportunities for participation that had previously been not existed (Adams, 2008). The assessment process, at its most basic, is a conversation between the potential service user (would-be budget holder) and the social worker/care manager (broker). Eligibility criteria and financial assessment for contribution notwithstanding, this is a duologue to identify need and ascertain the financial package required to meet it. The Care Act 2014 makes local authorities duty bound, under certain circumstances, to provide an independent advocate (s67) to facilitate assessment and to involve 'any carer' that the assessed person has (s9.5). The local authority must also involve:

> *Any person whom the adult asks the authority to involve or, where the adult lacks capacity to ask the authority to do that, any person who appears to the authority to be interested in the adult's welfare.* (S9.5.c)

This is the environment within which adults with an acquired brain injury (ABI) in the UK may encounter social workers and it will be argued that there are particular difficulties and challenges faced (and presented) by this highly heterogeneous group in the context of assessment (whether of care and support needs or of mental capacity) and planning for provision to meet their needs (Holloway and Fyson, 2016). These difficulties are, in part, based upon social workers' lack of knowledge of ABI, a lack of understanding of the process of neuro-rehabilitation and an assessment process that is contra-indicated in the context of a naively applied model of social disability.

In this chapter the complex nature of acquired brain injury is outlined and the failure of practice caused by uni-disciplinary, ill-informed and facile assessment is highlighted. By utilising more effectively the duties the Care Act creates to work with partners from other disciplines and to apply more intellectual rigour to the process, a social worker is identified as being better able to support families affected by ABI.

Acquired Brain Injury

Whilst the causes of acquired brain injury (ABI) may differ, the sudden onset of the condition and its very uncertain outcomes provide a significant challenge to individuals, families, communities and of course for health and social services.

Advances in understanding abound. Neurosurgical interventions continue to be updated in response to this understanding (Giacino et al., 2014; Schramm, 2016) as do the quality and efficacy of nursing and other interventions for those who require them (Adam and Osborne, 2016; Golisz, 2015). Data collected in the UK suggest that, on average, 445 people are admitted to hospital with a head injury every day (Headway, 2015). Road traffic accidents, assaults, falls and sporting injuries can cause traumatic injuries to the brain; diseases such as encephalitis and meningitis similarly cause damage, as do incidents of anoxia, haemorrhage and the idiopathic consequences of neurosurgery for tumour or cyst removal, aneurysm clipping or invasive treatment for severe infection.

Five hundred and sixty-six people per 100,000 of the population were admitted to UK hospitals in 2013–2014 for reasons of ABI and admissions are noted to have increased by 10% since 2005–2006 (Headway, 2015). Survival rates have increased as a consequence of improvements to paramedicine, neurosurgery, neuro-imaging and intensive care treatment; the development of artificial ventilating systems has had a direct impact upon mortality rates (Fins, 2015; Klemen and Grmec, 2006; Powell, 1997). Despite these improvements ABI is still noted to be the commonest cause of death or disability in those aged 1–40 years. The vast majority (95%) of admissions to hospital present with a normal or relatively unaltered state of consciousness: 0.2% of admissions will result in death during the acute phase of admission (NICE, 2014).

Whilst the majority of people reporting to UK hospitals with what is defined as a mild ABI will make a good recovery (Wilson et al., 1998), it is estimated that between 10 and 15% do not, with long-standing symptoms that affect a range of issues including balance, cognition, fatigue, executive impairment, and mood and affective disorders (Iverson, 2005; Marshall et al., 2015; McMillan et al., 2012). Those who suffer more severe injuries are noted to experience a high incidence of sometimes very severe sequelae that affect all aspects of life. Difficulties with behavioural management, with cognition, executive skills, mood, emotion and physical and sensory impairments impact upon an individual's ability to live independently in the community, on their ability to work and on their interpersonal relationships (Anderson et al., 2011; Dikmen et al., 2009; Fleminger and Ponsford, 2005; Tate et al., 1989). These difficulties regularly occur in the absence of any obvious physical impairment (Department of Health, 1996). Their impact can therefore be exacerbated by this 'invisibility' and compounded by the brain-injured person's regularly reported lack of insight (Prigatano, 2005; Bach and David, 2006). Frequently the individual, their family and the wider community also lack knowledge and understanding of why changes to affect and functional abilities occur following injury (Holloway, 2014; Linden and Boylan, 2010; Ownsworth et al., 2010; Stuss, 1991).

Further complicating assessment of need and of mental capacity still is the potential for the brain-injured person to demonstrate an intellectual awareness of their difficulties in an extrinsically governed and managed process of assessment but not to be able to apply this outside of this setting (Manchester et al., 2004). This has been particularly observed in instances where the frontal lobes of the brain have been damaged. This 'frontal paradox' (Walsh, 1985) is a considerable challenge for social workers or others who base their care and support needs assessments or mental capacity assessments on the verbal output of the person they are talking to rather than assess actual functioning over time (Acquired Brain Injury and Mental Capacity Act Interest Group, 2014; Owen et al., 2017), resulting in an individual perhaps being 'good in theory, poor in practice'. The nature of ABI-related executive impairment is such that the assessment process itself may become the compensatory strategy required for an individual to describe their difficulties and needs (accurately) but only to do this for the duration of the assessment; this knowledge and, importantly, its application, do not take place outside of the assessment (George and Gilbert, 2018; Lennard, 2016). The ability to 'use and weigh' relevant information in the moment – when actually required – (rather than in the abstract as part of the structured/guided conversation of a capacity assessment) is not adequately assessed in this manner. Actual executive capacity, how one functions in real world settings, requires real world assessment, an issue recognised in the parliamentary debate on mental capacity (Hansard HL Deb., 22 October 2018) and in recent NICE Guidelines regarding decision-making:

> *Practitioners should be aware that it may be more difficult to assess capacity in people with executive dysfunction – for example people with traumatic brain injury. Structured assessments of capacity for individuals in this group (for example, by way of interview) may therefore need to be supplemented by real-world observation of the person's functioning and decision-making ability in order to provide the assessor with a complete picture of an individual's decision-making ability.* (NICE, 2018)

Put more simply, by structuring the conversation, by generating the ideas, maintaining an agenda and 'organising' the thinking within a meeting, a social worker (or other) can create the set of circumstances necessary to create 'competence' or capacity in the individual they are talking to but only for the duration of the assessment. This is a function of the condition and is why more accurate assessment is a process, informed by evidence of actual functioning and knowledgeable third parties, either family/friends and/or ABI specialist professionals (Clark-Wilson et al., 2014). Assessment, whether of care and support needs or of mental capacity, to be accurate, must be underpinned by knowledge both of actual functioning (not intended actions or inaccurate self-report) and of the drivers behind changes in functioning that ABI brings (Priestley et al., 2013). Such an approach would appear to run entirely contrary to a social model of disability that presupposes expertise about one's needs and gives this primacy in assessment. A rigid and dogmatic adherence to such a model limits the social worker's potential for accurate assessment and meaningful intervention and has been criticised accordingly for lacking theoretical rigour (Shakespeare, 2014).

Despite evidence of the effectiveness of rehabilitation for people with ABI (Oddy and Da Silva Ramos, 2013; Turner-Stokes, 2008), a lack of adequate provision is regularly reported (Clark-Wilson and Holloway, 2015; Gridley, 2013; Mantell, 2010). The National Institute for Clinical Excellence notes that there is a lack of capacity in the UK to provide specialist neurorehabilitation (NICE, 2014).

Research clearly points to the difficulties experienced by family, often as roles change from equals to providers of care/support and the impact of changes in personality, behaviour and community integration is faced (Anderson et al., 2012; Bishop et al., 2006; Blake, 2014; Degeneffe, 2001; Nabors et al., 2002). As a long-term condition this impact is felt over many years, potentially as a lifetime chronic and enduring condition, and not a one-off event (Masel and DeWitt, 2010). For some, psychosocial functioning does not improve but deteriorates over time (Fleminger, 2012; McMillan et al., 2012; Olver et al., 1996; Whitnall et al., 2006). Suicide rates are noted to be significantly higher than in the non-brain-injured population (Fleminger et al., 2003; Simpson and Tate, 2007). For others the brain injury is the start of a prolonged (potentially lifelong) period of severely disordered consciousness, a state that challenges our understanding of what it means to be alive (Kitzinger and Kitzinger, 2014, 2015).

Such varied, potentially severe and most usually life-altering changes may occur to an individual but the roles that an individual plays are also affected, as well as their place within family, work and wider society (Wilson et al., 2014, 2015). ABI is therefore an area where one may expect social work to play a part, in line with an international definition of the profession as a 'practice based and academic discipline that promotes social change and development, social cohesion, and the empowerment and liberation of people' (International Federation of Social Workers, 2014). UK-based social workers therefore, as well as having statutory duties to safeguard, are bound by culture and professional expectation to use, create and apply knowledge in situations and settings where such application meets aims of empowerment and facilitates change when challenges are encountered by individuals, communities and families. Yet the evidence base that informs the practice of UK social workers in relation to ABI is scant (Mantell et al., 2012; Mantell et al., 2017), albeit that the potential for contact with people with ABI is significant and not uncommon (Holloway, 2014).

Damage to the brain changes individuals but does so in a way that is neither static nor straightforward to understand (Lövdén et al., 2013; Thomas et al., 2014). Functional changes to activity or performance, that which is observed or experienced, can manifest as a consequence of a range of differing, complex and interrelated issues (Giles et al., 2018). Understanding what it is that underpins these changes to activity, identifying the drivers behind (usually) negative changes to behaviour and ability, is what informs the response to such changes (Clark-Wilson et al., 2014).

The outcome for individuals who experience such injuries is, understandably, very variable (and varies temporally for an individual) and this variation is in part dependent upon the site and severity of the injury but also on pre-morbid, co-morbid and environmental factors (Ponsford, 2013). Extensive research has been undertaken to identify the main drivers behind outcome from ABI. Injury-related measures and factors such as neuroimaging findings, lowest Glasgow Coma Scale rating (a scale used to rate the severity of coma/altered consciousness at the time of injury), duration of post-traumatic amnesia, presence of other injuries, cognitive and behavioural impairments, demographic factors (including age, gender, genetic status, education, pre-injury

IQ and employment status), and social factors including family and other social support, are all found to be implicated in outcomes (Ponsford, 2013). In this sense the condition is one that may be considered to be 'bio-psycho-social', where the outcome is intricately linked to a range of interlinked biological, psychological and social factors. Credit for popularising this model is usually accorded to Engel (1977), whose primary concern was to humanise medicine through a greater appreciation of the equal relevance of the psychological and social dimensions of illness. In the context of brain injury, attempts to isolate neurological damage from the context in which it occurs negate the reality of life post-ABI and are described as reductionist and flawed (Engel, 1980). A bio-psycho-social approach, one that does not seek to pathologise or separate the injured party from the dynamics of their condition, their personal situation, their environment and their society, is recognised as providing a more holistic and realistic base from which to provide rehabilitative and support services (Ownsworth et al., 2006; Williams and Evans, 2003; Yeates et al., 2008). Such an approach integrates developing knowledge of neural development/neuroplasticity with recognition of the personal, cultural and social factors that influence decision-making, functioning and opportunities (Garland and Howard, 2009; Zittel et al., 2002). Whilst some caution of the risks of the potential for dominance of the medicalising 'bio' aspects of the approach, a balanced critical engagement and understanding of this dimension is noted to potentially strengthen holistic and ethical practice (Healy, 2015). Certainly, it is hard to see how professional practice that is inadequately informed by an appreciation of the neurological, alongside the psychological and social, can effectively benefit individuals and their families.

The risks of failing to assess adequately and support appropriately

There is an increasing body of UK and worldwide evidence relating to outcomes for people with an ABI (Holloway, 2014). Rates of ABI amongst homeless people are reported to be nearly 50%, with 90% of those surveyed noting that their ABI pre-dated their loss of accommodation (Oddy et al., 2012). Mortality amongst homeless people with an ABI is considerably higher than for non-brain injured homeless people (McMillan et al., 2015). Prevalence of ABI amongst UK male prisoners is noted to be around 50–60% (Shiroma et al., 2012; Williams et al., 2010) and suicide is noted to be around three times more than community norms (Simpson and Tate, 2007). Parenting ability post-ABI is noted to be deleteriously affected (Holloway and Tyrrell, 2016; Kieffer-Kristensen and Johansen, 2013) and rates of return to work are low (van Velzen et al., 2009). Significant longer-term mental health risks are associated with mild brain injury in childhood (Sariaslan et al., 2016) as are rates of incarceration for violent crimes and the likelihood of substance misuse difficulties (McKinlay et al., 2014).

Professionals' failure to engage with complicated people with an acquired brain injury, particularly those with co-morbid difficulties, has been reported to lead to death (Norman, 2016). The Serious

Case Review that followed the death of 'Tom' identified significant failings in social work and other agencies' approach, mistakenly relying upon Tom's self-reporting of his needs/actions (Flynn, 2016). Tom had extensive executive difficulties and this was not taken into account by those who assessed him or provided him with services/housing. It was reported that:

> ... *the assessment processes experienced by Tom were not integrated and had no impact on inter-professional working.* (Flynn, 2016: 24)

The highly critical report noted that staff did not perceive Tom as having impaired executive functioning but rather they viewed his behaviour as a reaction to various life events. There was an absence of risk assessment:

> *It does not appear that the risks of not eating, living in unhygienic conditions, self-neglecting, of tolerating discarded needles in his home, of combining prescribed and street drugs, of being with exploitative peers, and of suicide, for example, were considered individually or collectively.* (Flynn, 2016: 25)

Tom was noted to have a long history of being exploited by others and had no intrinsic ability to resist this or promote his own safety and wellbeing as a direct consequence of his brain injury. The executive skills one requires to self-preserve, organise, plan and carry out meaningful activities were significantly compromised. There was also a lengthy history of agencies failing to engage with Tom and of him not meeting the eligibility criteria for services. The assessments that informed these decisions were deeply flawed, failing to take account of the very condition that had caused his vulnerability. Tom's family attempted to advocate on his behalf for many years but their experience and knowledge of him were not taken into account. After his death it was noted:

> *It would appear that degree of agency and freedom of choice that Tom had after his brain injury was more severely compromised than professionals ... had appreciated.* (Flynn, 2016: 28)

The Serious Case Review recommended:

> *The fact of a person's traumatic brain injury and mental capacity (should be) fore-grounded in all professional assessments and referrals and ... family involvement ... prioritized ...* (Flynn, 2016: 29)

In Tom's case this was too late; he committed suicide, as he warned he would, by tying an electric cord to his wheelchair and hanging himself (Norman, 2016).

A lack of professional curiosity and lack of knowledge of ABI by social workers and its impact upon functioning are noted to be at the root of such failures (Morgan, 2017). Similarly, a failure to integrate knowledge about an individual's violent post-ABI behaviour has led to significant harm to children. A man with an ABI, who was uncontrollably aggressive and regularly violent, injured his child and partner. Practitioners were reported to show a lack of understanding of the risks he presented to his family; again staff relied upon what was said by the brain injured man in assessments and not what he did in reality (Summerfield, 2011). Whilst a social worker's lack of knowledge is clearly a limiting factor in the creation of adequate assessments, it is *the lack of awareness* of this lack of knowledge that prevents appropriate engagement with colleagues from other disciplines. This lack of knowledge may lead to questions of whether some social work practice is in breach of Health and Care Professions Council Standards of Proficiency for Social Workers, in particular standard 1.1 which states that social workers must:

> ...*know the limits of their practice and when to seek advice or refer to another professional.* (HCPC, 2017)

This lack of knowledge and awareness of the condition places social workers in conflict with paragraph 6.3 of the Care Act Statutory Guidance. This specifically identifies that those undertaking Care Act assessments must have the *"right skills and knowledge"* to perform this role, and paragraph 6.4 notes that assessment may require the input of a number of professionals (DHSC, 2018a). Paragraph 6.28 of the same statutory guidance places a duty on local authorities to ensure that those undertaking Care Act assessments *"have the skills, knowledge and competence to carry out the assessment in question"* (DHSC, 2018a). People with an acquired brain injury and their families are regularly clients of social workers, be that in children's or adults' services. That the condition is not identified or necessarily responded to may be the greatest challenge facing social work today. In a national survey of the relatives of people with an acquired brain injury, social work was rated the lowest of all of the many services encountered (Holloway, 2017).

Such a complex and heterogeneous condition as ABI leads clearly to the potential for input from a number of disciplines and/or authorities and organisations when assessments are being undertaken. The Care Act specifically makes a local authority duty bound to co-operate with relevant partners, including NHS bodies (sections 6 and 7). Such a duty underpins the rationale for interdisciplinary working and the assessment of eligibility for Continuing Health Care funding. Paragraph 126 of the National Framework for NHS Continuing Healthcare and NHS-funded Nursing Care guidance (DHSC, 2018c) states with regard to assessments:

> *It is important that those contributing to this process have the relevant skills and knowledge. It is best practice that where the individual concerned has, for example a learning disability, or a brain injury, someone with specialist knowledge of this client group is involved in the assessment process.*

It is notable that the multidisciplinary team and holistic approach recommended in the guidance carries significant weight and such a team's recommendations must only *not* be carried out in exceptional circumstances (paragraph 153). Social workers are able to play a vital and co-ordinating role with colleagues from other disciplines in such processes.

Social work and acquired brain injury in practice

To support the identification of the difficulties social workers face when endeavouring to utilise the Care Act, Table 10.1 dichotomises the possible differences that may present at assessment. Column 1 describes a previously unimpaired, autonomous, employed and independent adult who suffers a serious orthopaedic injury following a road traffic accident but has no damage to the brain, for example a spinal cord injury. Column 2 describes the same individual but where instead the road traffic accident causes severe injury to the brain, with no identifiable loss of IQ and no physical impairment but results in a complex constellation of executive, behavioural, cognitive and emotional sequelae in the context of loss of insight. The statements are general and are not intended to stand as a universal description of either possible scenario, but instead to highlight the potential differences between the outcomes.

Table 10.1   Differences that may present at assessment

Column 1: Physical impairment only	Column 2: Acquired brain injury
Knowledgeable about own needs and how these needs may be met; able to learn about changed circumstances by understanding, retaining, internalising and integrating environmental feedback; able to apply this learning.	Lacking insight into needs, does not agree that needs exist or, if these are agreed, struggles to maintain agreement; great difficulty in learning about changed circumstances, maintaining that learning and applying it in situ.
Requests support and/or assessment, recognises the role support, aids or adaptations may have in promoting independence and improved quality of life.	Does not request support or assessment; does not recognise the role support, aids, adaptations or compensatory strategies may have in promoting independence and improved quality of life.
Needs static or change slowly over time; potential for deterioration/increased level of need; likely to recognise change in needs and respond appropriately.	Needs vary over time depending upon environment and access to rehabilitation; improvements to autonomy and independence are possible as is deterioration and poorer psycho-social functioning; highly unlikely to recognise change in needs and respond appropriately.
'Care' needs mostly physical and practical in nature; needs directly relate to impairment and are easily defined and responded to.	Needs may relate to cognitive, behavioural, emotional and, importantly, executive difficulties (idea generation, problem solving, planning, reasoning etc.); needs are therefore more complex to define, are interrelated and environmentally affected.
The majority of needs can be met by the provision of a personal assistant or support work staff; service user guides staff activity and defines their role and all of their actions.	Support work staff needs may be extensive (or not), may be rejected and the role of staff may be to prompt activity, manage behaviour and pre-empt difficulties; staff activity may be defined, guided, managed and monitored by specialist therapy and case management services.
Likely understanding and accepting of the concept of a family 'carer' as an unpaid person who undertakes tasks on one's behalf owing to impairment or disabilities (socially constructed or otherwise).	Likely not to recognise or acknowledge the role others play in managing behaviour, forward planning, predicting and avoiding difficulties.

(Continued)

Table 10.1   (Continued)

Column 1: Physical impairment only	Column 2: Acquired brain injury
May have or develop an identity as a person with a disability; may use peer support organisations accordingly.	Does not identify as a disabled person; does not therefore see the need to seek peer support or an identity.
Likely to recognise the benefit of outside support and advocacy and be able to name individuals who are able to provide support during assessment processes.	Does not recognise difficulties and therefore does not see the need for outside support and advocacy; may not see the need for assessment at all.
Likely to be able to understand the benefit of engaging in a process of assessment.	Likely to be difficult to engage within a process of assessment, requiring skilled communication to do so.
Has mental capacity and ability to manage financial affairs; recognises and understands the role and responsibilities of being an employer of support staff.	May lack the mental capacity to manage financial affairs; may not recognise, in the moment, how actions/behaviour are contrary to roles and responsibilities of an employer of support staff.
Can learn from experience and apply this learning across settings and time to self-support autonomously; can internalise learning and generalise knowledge and experience.	Learning from experience and applying across time and settings is dependent upon intact insight and is therefore absent; is not able to internalise learning or generalise knowledge or experience.

Good practice for social workers

Given the relatively recent implementation of the Care Act and the absence of any extensive literature on social work with ABI, there is little evidence as yet on how the new legal rules may be influencing practice, but there are clear pointers to the opportunities they provide. Achieving practice that is compliant with the Care Act 2014 and the Mental Capacity Act 2005 when working with people who have ABI requires practitioners to use insights derived from ABI research to shape their implementation of the legal rules. This has implications for how assessment is conducted, when and by whom, for the scope of family engagement and for interdisciplinary and interagency practice. It also requires strong connections to be forged with sources of specialist advice.

Assessment

Owing to the nature of acquired brain injury the process of assessment required is more likely iterative, will benefit from the involvement of individuals who know the injured person pre- and post-ABI, and will be informed by professionals from other disciplines. Whilst the definition may be somewhat contested, this is a 'case management' approach (Lukersmith et al., 2016; Sullivan and Floyd, 2012). The social worker, rather than simply brokering a package to meet the needs identified by the potential service user, engages in a process of identifying needs and integrating any health or social care service that is required to meet them. This is a proactive model of working to support engagement by individuals who may not see the need for intervention and has been recognised in research examining good practice (Gridley, 2013). Case management has been identified as improving discharge planning

(Hammond et al., 2012) and in supporting parents with a brain injury (Holloway and Tyrrell, 2016). Brain injury case managers are identified as using skilled and nuanced approaches to support decision-making by individuals who have significant difficulties with executive impairment and demonstrate difficult to manage behaviour (Harding and Tascioglu, 2017). Levels of case management use are noted as not related to degree of physical impairment but instead are dependent on lack of insight and executive impairment (Clark-Wilson et al., 2016). The lifetime nature of the condition and its complexity has led to notions of 'Life-Care Planning', potentially predicated on a long-term therapeutic relationship (Clark-Wilson and Holloway, 2015; Moxley, 1996). The Care Act statutory guidance paragraph 6.43 specifically identifies the benefit of using specialised tools to support assessment:

> *The Brain Injury Rehabilitation Trust has produced the Brain Injury Needs Indicator, which is a tool that can be used as part of the assessment to help identify deficits of people with a suspected or diagnosed acquired brain injury.* (DHSC, 2018a).

Think family

Brain injury has long been recognised as a 'family condition'; the injury may occur to one person but the impact is felt by those around them (Romano, 1974). The unclear nature of the condition and its invisibility has led to the grief felt by family to be considered unending, and losses are noted to be 'ambiguous' (Boss, 2006; Kreutzer et al., 2016). Learning to love (or even tolerate) a person who has changed significantly, who may lack empathy, be aggressive and lack insight into how they have changed, is noted to be emotionally very draining (Petersen and Sanders, 2015; Yeates et al., 2008). Brain injury case management focuses upon the family rather than an individual and was the highest-rated service by relatives in a national survey (Holloway, 2017), in stark contrast with social work, which was ranked the lowest. The Care Act section 10 specifically identifies a duty to assess carers' needs, and section 20 identifies the duties and powers to meet those needs. To do so a social worker will need to understand the impact an ABI has upon an individual and the secondary impact this has upon family members who may or may not identify as carers. Prompting, structuring activity, planning, organising, reducing potential conflict and managing complex behaviours are frequently roles that family members play (Knox et al., 2015). A social worker's understanding of the impact of executive impairment will affect their capacity to conceptualise the 'carer' role and respond to it adequately.

Interdisciplinarity

Social workers have long played a role within interdisciplinary teams (Bronstein, 2003) and have been noted to hold some of the potentially more challenging conversations (Black, 2005). Individuals with an ABI will potentially encounter a range of professionals from a number of disciplines, employed by various organisations. Co-ordinating the input of the team required is a case manager's task, integrating the knowledge and input of each party to generate a more cogent response to a complex and often changing picture (Parker, 2006).

Perhaps one of the more significant challenges for social workers is that of involvement in the process of neurorehabilitation. Services provided to people with an ABI have the potential to reduce dependency over time, reintegrate people into the community and increase participation and wellbeing. Support therefore is not solely to facilitate engagement and participation but to possibly enable the brain-injured party to relearn skills and tasks and develop habits, strategies and routines that compensate for their difficulties (Giles, 2001). An individual's ability to benefit from rehabilitation varies; the skills required to learn are the very ones often damaged by the ABI (Bajo and Fleminger, 2002). For individuals with executive dysfunction a 'neurofunctional' approach is more likely indicated (Clark-Wilson et al., 2014). However the rehabilitation is undertaken, in the community or in a specialist unit, a goal-based approach is recommended (Jackson et al., 2014). This tends to be a relatively intensive multi-disciplinary endeavour and require skilled support staff to rehearse and practise agreed protocols and procedures over time (Jackson and Manchester, 2001). Notwithstanding the somewhat medicalised jargon that may come hand-in-hand with neurorehabilitation and its practitioners, it is ultimately a social task. The aim of the process is for individuals to gain more autonomy, re-establish former or new roles and adapt to changed circumstances. The Care Act, with its intention of promoting individual wellbeing, promoting the integration of care and support with health services and the duty to assess and involve others in the assessment, is wholly aligned with a specialist case management approach to working with individuals affected by brain injury.

Similarly, in the case of assessments of mental capacity, expertise from other disciplines can be vital in understanding the reasoning behind the behaviour or concerns that led to capacity being questioned. Notwithstanding the usefulness of such a multi-disciplinary approach to informing and improving assessments, social workers have been identified as failing to take account of the knowledge of others and indeed actively and intentionally dismissing and ignoring specialists (Acquired Brain Injury and Mental Capacity Act Interest Group, 2014; George and Gilbert, 2018); this is in direct contravention of section 4.51 of the Mental Capacity Act Code of Practice.

Sources of specialist advice

Whilst the academic basis for social work with people with an ABI is very underdeveloped, particularly in the UK (Mantell et al., 2017), there are increasing numbers of resources developed by charities and from the independent sector (BISWG and BASW, 2016). The Brain Injury Rehabilitation Trust has developed a 'Brain Injury Needs Indicator' (available free on the Trust's website) to support social workers to undertake assessments, highlighting potentially hidden aspects of the condition and recommending that all information obtained is checked against actual functioning. At the time of writing, the British Association of Brain Injury Case Managers, formed in 1996, has nearly 600 practising members of which 7.5% are social workers (BABICM, 2019). The organisation provides peer support and training for professionals providing specialist brain injury case management. The Brain Injury Social Work Group (BISWG) similarly provides training and advice for social workers and others and the national brain injury charity Headway provides free information and advice for individuals, families and professionals.

Conclusion

As can be seen from the above analysis, individuals with acquired brain injury do not easily fit into a model of assessment and service provision that runs contrary to the underlying impairments and needs that are present. The social model of disability and the struggle for emancipation, control and autonomy undertaken by people with disabilities is not inherently in conflict with the needs of people with an ABI. The absence of knowledge of the condition by professional staff, who labour in structures and with practices that do not adequately engage with ABI, and who apply notions of personalisation naively and without integrating an understanding of how ABI manifests, are perhaps of much more concern. Acquired brain injury is a bio-psycho-social condition and knowledge of each of its aspects and how they interact is required. Assessments and interventions need to be undertaken by social workers with adequate knowledge and with the support of colleagues from other disciplines. Unless this is done the model applied serves to oppress not empower people with an ABI, human potential will remain diminished and lives will be harmed by the very services that are intended to help. A model of service provision that can work extremely well for people with a physical impairment, noting the role society plays in creating and maintaining disability, is not best suited to many people with an ABI. Such individuals' needs are ignored if the 'client as expert' dogma is rigidly adhered to and assessments are based upon verbal output and not actual functioning. This is not an inevitability; relevant knowledge, information, training and good practice do exist. Effective partnerships are made by social workers with brain-injured people, their families and the services they utilise and need. Our professional curiosity, our willingness to learn from and engage with others, and our ability to be flexible and work alongside people as they face possibly the biggest challenge of their lives are what define the difference. It is up to social workers to decide if they wish to be part of the problem or part of the solution.

Case study: Joshua

Prior to having a severe brain injury in a bicycle accident, Joshua was a 23-year-old graduate who had returned to live with his parents and was working hard to save money to go travelling. Following four months as an inpatient in hospital he was transferred to a third sector specialist neuro-rehabilitation setting to relearn activities of daily living. After nine months the unit refers to social services in Joshua's home area, asking for an assessment and a package of support and community rehabilitation to be put in place. The referring neuropsychologist expresses concerns that Joshua lacks complete insight into his condition and perceives he will need no support, but that his mother, conversely, believes he needs to remain as an inpatient until he is functioning as he was pre-injury. Joshua's father attended the first MDT meeting at the unit only; he did not contribute and was angry and abusive towards staff. His views about the future are unknown. A weekend trial home-visit reportedly went very poorly; Joshua became lost in his home town and cannot account for several hours of time nor where his money went. The neuropsychologist states that Joshua needs the opportunity to rehearse the routines and compensatory strategies he uses in the unit in his home, to re-establish links with friends, family, work and meaningful activity. Joshua has no physical impairment.

Commentary

None of this is untypical; a situation exists where different people have different views and there are many unknowns. At one extreme there are risks that Joshua's human rights are abused owing to risk aversion; at the other there are potentially significant safeguarding risks owing to the impact his cognitive and executive difficulties may have in the unstructured environment of the community. The social worker's role is broad and, initially at least, is one of information collection – gathering views, knowledge and ideas from all parties. Developing an understanding of Joshua's condition and of his and his family's expectations and pre-injury life, and learning how he has re-learnt skills/routines is key. Understanding what it is that supports Joshua within the unit is important – what prompts, structures and environmental 'scaffolding' exist there that do not automatically exist in the community? To do this effectively a skilled social worker uses their ability to form relationships in very difficult circumstances; all voices need to be heard, all plans need to be explicit. This is not always a comfortable process, but it is an essential one. The bespoke and well-informed assessment that is drawn from this process will require liaison and engagement with health services; an element of the support is rehabilitative and this needs to be integrated (backwards) with the rehabilitation unit and (forwards) with support and community services.

There is no right answer here, there is simply a process of trial and error, of plans that develop iteratively and that are reviewed as the evidence develops. No package of support implemented at time of discharge from the unit will remain static. The social worker's role is ongoing, relies upon information, knowledge and support from colleagues from other disciplines and is integrative. Asking questions about what needs to be done, who needs to do it, how

→

will we know it has been done, and what does this look like if it has worked/not worked, is vital. Maintaining open and honest lines of communication with every party ensures relationships are clear and able to be built upon. An effective social worker needs time to make this work, the confidence to ask 'how will this work?', to recognise their own learning needs/ knowledge limitations, and to view this as a process. A good social worker also needs a good supervisor; the ambiguous losses and ongoing grief and trauma of family members are hard to bear witness to. We are not unaffected when we offer to stand alongside other people and 'gaze into the glare' of their grief to 'help minimise its terrible isolation'. (Adapted from Charon, R. (2012) At the membranes of care: stories in narrative medicine, *Academic Medicine*, 87 (342–47): 346)

Further Reading

Boss, P. (2006) *Loss, Trauma, and Resilience: Therapeutic Work with Ambiguous Loss.* New York, London: Norton.

Newby, G., Coetzer, R., Daisley, A. and Weatherhead, S. (2013) *Practical Neuropsychological Rehabilitation in Acquired Brain Injury: A Guide for Working Clinicians.* London: Karnac.

Powell, T. J. (2004) *Head Injury: A Practical Guide.* Bicester: Speechmark.

11 The interface between the Care Act 2014 and asylum law: exclusions and innovations

Forough Ramezankhah and Alison Brammer

Introduction

Since its implementation the Care Act 2014 claims to have transformed adult social care, superseding a patchwork of legislation on care and support dating back to the creation of the Welfare State in 1948. The Act provides a revised and reformed legal framework for current practice. This chapter provides a prior and post perspective in respect of the gaps that the Act attempts to close and provisions it promises to deliver. It has been claimed that the Act supplies a consolidated legal framework for adult social care but it is debatable whether this can be expanded to asylum seekers as a category of vulnerable adults. The chapter, adopting a practitioners' perspective, considers the Act in light of the support it provides to, and/or withholds from, asylum seekers. Once asylum seekers are granted refugee status they fall under mainstream provisions in respect of care and support offered to citizens. The Act does not distinguish between a citizen and a refugee. It is asylum seekers who have a precarious status in terms of rights and access to provision and from whom support can legally be withheld.

This chapter draws partly on empirical data gathered from conducting biographical interviews with asylum seekers. It consists of three sections. The first section argues that asylum seekers inherently ought to be considered vulnerable based on case studies and case law. The next section provides an overview of the challenges and uncertainties encountered by asylum seekers prior to the Act. Finally, the last section considers the case law since implementation of the Act and concludes that the restrictive measures put in place by the Act provide safeguards only by the process of trial and error.

The Care Act 2014 and asylum seekers

Asylum seekers who are the focus of this chapter are subject to restrictions under many different statutes. Their legal position is very complex, since they are simultaneously subject to numerous legal rules, including those relating to immigration, local authorities, the Department for Work and Pensions, the NHS and the police, as well as education, housing, adult social care, and children and young people's social care. From a practitioner's perspective, working with asylum seekers is a particularly challenging task, since not all the rules and regulations in respect of asylum seekers are contained in one single piece of legislation. As a result social workers, healthcare providers and other frontline practitioners in direct contact with asylum seekers find themselves to be quasi lawyers, educators, police officers, housing officers and counsellors amongst others.

An asylum seeker is defined under the Immigration and Asylum Act 1999, section 94 (1) as, 'a person who is not under 18 and has made a claim for asylum which has been recorded by the Secretary of State but which has not been determined'. The same section also clarifies that a claim for asylum means 'a claim that it would be contrary to the United Kingdom's obligations under the Refugee Convention or under Article 3 of the Human Rights Convention, for the claimant to be removed from, or required to leave, the United Kingdom'. The Home Office provides support to asylum seekers and their dependants who would otherwise be destitute under the powers set out in section 95 of the Immigration and Asylum Act 1999. Support is usually provided in the form of furnished accommodation (rent and utilities free), plus a weekly cash allowance to enable the persons to meet other 'essential living needs'. Pursuant to the Immigration and Asylum Act 1999, the Asylum Support Regulation 2000 (Statutory Instrument, 2000 No. 704) created the national mechanism to deliver this support, formally known as National Asylum Support Service.

Contrary to the widely reported myth that asylum seekers are drawn to the UK because of its generous benefits system, the support provided is actually very limited. The Asylum Support (Amendment) Regulations 2018 (Statutory Instrument 2018 No. 30) revised regulation 10(2) of the Asylum Support Regulations 2000 (S.I. 2000/704) to provide that the weekly cash payment that may be made by the Secretary of State in respect of the essential living needs of persons to whom the Secretary of State has decided to provide asylum support, was increased from £36.95 to £37.75. This is the first rise in eighteen years.

The general rule is that asylum seekers awaiting a decision are supported by the Home Office. Failed asylum seekers may still be supported by the Home Office under section 4(2) of the Immigration and Asylum Act 1999 if they meet certain eligibility criteria. If asylum seekers are subject to immigration control and outside of the Home Office support then they may fall under the local authority's support mechanism (Farmer, 2017). In *R (Westminster City Council) v National Asylum Support Service* [2002], the House of Lords decided that the role of asylum support under Part 6 of the Immigration and Asylum Act 1999 was residual and that, when assessing whether or not a person subject to immigration control required care and attention for the purposes of section 21 of the National Assistance Act 1948, it was necessary to disregard the potential availability of support under Part 6 of the 1999 Act. In *R (M) v Slough Borough Council* [2008], the House of Lords decided that a person needed 'care and attention', for the purposes of section 21, if he needed looking after, in the sense of needing something doing for him that he could not, or could not be expected to, do for himself. The Care Act 2014, s.21, restates the stance of the previous law to exclude asylum seekers from any entitlement to care and support that has arisen solely from destitution.

Refugee law and the vulnerability of asylum seekers

Although the law and policy guidelines do not view adult asylum seekers generally as a vulnerable group per se, this chapter takes the stance that adult asylum seekers in general ought to be treated as such until and unless information suggests otherwise. The laws governing refugee status are humanitarian in theory but it can be argued that they are policy and politic driven in practice. This area of law has been governed by complex and ever evolving international law, EU and domestic legislation. The 1951 Refugee Convention in the aftermath of World War II is the most instrumental. International Refugee Law, the EU Asylum Law and Policy play a crucial role in managing, regulating and determining the veracity of asylum claims. In order to determine and be granted refugee status, asylum seekers need to present and then convince the Home Office, with the standard of proof being the reasonable degree of likelihood that if returned they will be persecuted in their country of origin.

The UN High Commissioner for Refugees states that:

> It should be recalled that an applicant for refugee status is normally in a particularly vulnerable situation. He finds himself in an alien environment and may experience serious difficulties, technical and psychological, in submitting his case to the authorities of a foreign country, often in a language not his own. His application should therefore be examined within the framework of specially established procedures by qualified personnel having the necessary knowledge and experience, and an understanding of an applicant's particular difficulties and needs. (UNHCR Handbook, para. 190)

The UNHCR highlights the many challenges faced by asylum seekers, in doing so recommending that decision makers are to consider these challenges and the vulnerabilities that all asylum seekers experience to varying degrees. It can be argued that the language of the paragraph suggests that asylum seekers are normally in a particularly vulnerable situation. In fact they are inherently vulnerable since all asylum seekers do indeed experience some if not all of the challenges listed above.

The vulnerable situations in which asylum seekers find themselves are multifaceted. In an adversarial court setting, a judge and/or legal representative can help to safeguard individuals against leading and/or trick questions. Equally, the hypothesis formed in the mind of the opposing legal representative is revealed to witnesses and the defendant's legal representative. However, in the asylum process, the examiner simultaneously assumes the roles of adversary, inquisitor, and judge of the claim. Given the different levels of ability in the testimonial styles and presentational skills of asylum applicants, it is reasonable to expect that an interview as significant as a substantive asylum interview conducted by the Home Office would involve some level of prior familiarisation and training for the asylum seeker (Ramezankhah, 2017). This lack of familiarity with the process and procedures can add yet another layer of vulnerability to asylum seekers and exacerbate the challenges that they experience during the process of seeking asylum and determination of refugee status.

In *Kaja (Political asylum: standard of proof) (Zaire)* [1994] the judge held that:

> In assessing whether or not the appellant's account is a true account of historical facts, I see no reason why, on a common sense basis or in law, the burden of proof should be any lower than the normal civil standard of balance of probabilities. The appellant is simply required to tell the truth, and that should be no more difficult in an asylum appeal than in any other type of appeal. (Para 41)

This clearly highlights the ignorance of the judiciary to the vulnerability experienced by asylum seekers in presenting their claim, which is fundamental to them gaining refugee status and the enjoyment of the rights and privileges thereafter. The viewpoint that the asylum seeker 'is simply required to tell the truth' rejects any hidden personal data such as learning difficulties, lacking a basic education, substance misuse, depression, post-traumatic stress and potentially being a victim of torture and/or rape in addition to the 'particular vulnerable situation' and the 'serious difficulties' that the UNHCR Handbook recalls.

The case study presented below is part of a series of qualitative interviews and sheds light on the standpoint presented above in respect of vulnerabilities faced by asylum seekers. The data presented here were generated in the course of doctoral research conducted by one of the authors (Ramezankhah, 2013). The method of data generation is free association narrative interview with a psychosocial approach to data interpretation (Hollway and Jefferson, 2013).

At the time of Ali's interview he was an Iranian asylum seeker awaiting the Home Office decision on his application for refugee status in the UK. Reference to the revolution is the Iranian revolution of 1979 and the war refers to the Iran-Iraq War (1980–88). Ali recollects his childhood in Iran:

> When one keeps revisiting the past memories, one keeps remembering it – all the time. Yes, I was seven when the revolution happened {pause}, yes {long pause} for instance at the

> *time of the war, those images that I had at night, suddenly the red alert {air-raid siren}*
> *was heard and we had to run down the stairs and then BANG BANG BANG, the*
> *noise of the anti-aircraft guns, all of these are in front of my eyes and continuously goes*
> *round and round in my head...*

Ali, the child of the Iranian revolution, at the age of seven is habituated to resentment, defiance and retaliation, with enemies far and near, with the war inside and outside of him. In the related context of World War II, research shows that psychoanalysts demonstrated 'a link between a real "war outside" and an emotional "war inside", they [psychoanalysts] contributed to an increase in state responsibility for citizens' mental health' (Shapiro, 2008). This was especially evident in respect of the children; the war caused them to be 'anxious, aggressive subjects'.

It is argued that all asylum seekers are inherently vulnerable unless and until proven otherwise. The list of vulnerabilities referred to in the **UNHCR** Handbook above can be expanded by others such as mental health and learning disability as well as depression and substance misuse. In the above excerpt Ali shows signs of persistent and chronic stress if not post-traumatic stress disorder, a vulnerability that may be unknown to him and hidden from the authorities.

In this excerpt, Ali is a teenager (16 years old) awaiting immediate execution of his sentence for having a girlfriend:

Ali: *When you enter the room you see a bed and all around the room on the walls there are different kinds*
       of whips {smile} in variety of sizes {smile} with many different ranges of width and thickness and
       made from different materials, you could choose the one you wanted. {sarcastic hysterical laughter}

Ali: *Yes, it's very interesting; he {the executer} would choose one {whip} and would look at it and wave*
       it in the air to see whether he is happy with its likely performance on the body. He said to me, "Let
       me see if this whip has a nice touch." {hysterical laughter}

FR: *I am really sorry. {laughing ...}*

Ali: *{while laughing and trying to convince the interviewer} No, it is the truth. He asked me, "What did*
       you do?" I said, "Brother, nothing, swear to God. I went to the house of this girl to get some notes
       for the exam." He said, "So you had gone to get class notes? Lie down."
       The sentence of 50 lashes was executed ...
       Then Ali said, "I felt that I lost my dignity, I lost my pride. It affected me by causing resentment
       in me."

It seems likely that we are all a product of a complex mix of social, economic, cultural and unconscious factors, and there is widespread evidence that those involved in particularly violent and horrific crimes habitually have a history of emotional deprivation and abuse in childhood. In the majority of cases of violence against others and self-destructive behaviour, whose most extreme form is suicide, it is generally recognised that experience of physical or sexual abuse in childhood, often in combination with social deprivation, frequently plays a crucial role (Minsky,

1998: 153–54). Ali suffered from depression and substance misuse, vulnerabilities that he was unaware of, as he was of their importance, as were the authorities in charge of determining his application for asylum. The aim of highlighting his story is to display its importance in establishing the vulnerability of asylum seekers and how oblivious to its extent those making asylum decisions may be.

Such individual cases exist in a cultural context and there are potentially many other intersecting factors that may increase the vulnerability of an asylum seeker. As an example, according to Taherkhani et al. (2017) in their consideration of Iranian women and domestic violence, cultural norms and sociocultural factors including 'fear of negative consequences of help-seeking' may present as further barriers exacerbating vulnerability.

Challenges prior to the Care Act 2014

This section provides an overview of the challenges and uncertainties encountered by asylum seekers prior to the Act. It highlights a paucity of knowledge followed by presentation of innovative and strategic solutions to combat shortcomings of the support system. By means of a mother and child's case, the role of the local authority, advocacy and interagency collaboration in respect of asylum seekers are examined, questioning how effectively asylum seekers' need for care and support was met prior to the 2014 Act.

This was a CLOCK assisted case (The Community Legal Outreach Collaboration Keele (CLOCK), a legal/educational initiative).[1] The case highlights the multiple issues concerning a 34-year-old (at the time of assistance) Syrian mother and her 4-year-old daughter. Haya's husband was killed in Syria during the civil war. She had five children but initially only one child of 4-years-old travelled with her to the UK. The summary of their route consisted of escaping Syria and fleeing to Turkey, then travelling from Turkey to Bulgaria. Whilst being granted refugee status in Bulgaria, the situation became unbearable. Finally, Haya and her youngest daughter left Bulgaria for the UK and sought asylum once again, contrary to the Dublin Regulation III (Regulation (EU) No.604/2013).

In October 2014, CLOCK received a referral in respect of Haya. In order to investigate further and provide a fresh consideration as a last resort and possible signposting, Haya's case was assigned to one of the authors of this chapter (Forough Ramezankhah). At the time she was fighting imminent deportation under the Dublin Regulation. In other words, since Haya was granted refugee status in Bulgaria, it would have not been permissible for her to submit a claim for asylum in the UK too. This is to prevent asylum shopping within the EU. An extract of Haya's witness statement reads as follows:

> We left with the agent and we went to Turkey. We were in Turkey for around a month or so. The agent then took us to another country where we were fingerprinted. This was when I knew I was in Bulgaria. We were released after nine days and on our release the agent

was outside and I do not know how he knew we were released, but I was glad as I thought I was safe and with the agent. The agent took us to a house and he spoke to me in a room separate to the children. The agent said that he needed more money from me to get us to a safe country like Germany or Sweden, or the UK. It would cost me a further 5,000 Euros for each of us which is 30,000 Euros; money I did not have. I said I did not have that much money and I begged him to help me. (para 10)

Since Haya sought asylum in the UK with her young daughter, she was known to her local authority social services. It was established by her legal advisers that under the Dublin Regulation, the Home Office had made the correct and legal decision to return Haya and her young daughter to Bulgaria. However, on a careful consideration of Haya's witness statement, it became apparent that she might have been a victim of trafficking:

He said that there was another way I could pay for the journey and that he could help me get a job that would pay for all of us within a year. I asked him what job this was, and he said that it involved going out on dates with different men and meeting their needs whatever they were. I was shocked as he basically wanted me to be a prostitute. I said that I could not do that. He said that it was not really an option and that he had already arranged for my new employers to meet me tomorrow. He said that they had already agreed the transaction and committed money to the agreement (that they had paid for my journey and I had to work it off). He then took me back to the room with the children and looked {sic} the door. Before locking the door, he said we should not try and escape as people were watching the house and in {the} event his friends were gangsters/Mafia {and} would find me anyway. (para 10)

Firstly, it was established that despite the firm belief by the Home Office, Bulgaria may not be a safe country to return the mother and child to. At the time warnings were expressed by a number of non-governmental organisations that returns to Bulgaria should be halted until the dignified treatment of asylum seekers and refugees could be ensured.

Despite some improvements in the material conditions in the camps, there are many new problems for refugees stemming from the speeding-up of the procedure to grant legal status and the increased number of granted legal statuses (only to Syrian citizens). The lack of coherent institutional frameworks for integration, together with the general economic conditions in Bulgaria, most often leave the holders of refugee and subsidiary statuses under the aegis of homelessness, unemployment, poverty, and social isolation. (Hristova et al., 2014: 4)

Secondly, by examining Haya's witness statement, it was found that she may be a victim of trafficking. The author, having identified the National Referral Mechanism (NRM) for Potential Victims of Trafficking, referred the matter to the designated First Responders.[2] and it is here that the main challenge presented. From the long list of nominated First Responders, the author made contact with the Home Office, local authority and finally the Salvation Army. The Home Office caseworker had no knowledge of the NRM in general or more specifically in respect of asylum seekers who may have been victims of trafficking. The local authority also displayed a paucity of knowledge, although they are amongst the First Responders. Once the Salvation Army was contacted as the First Responder, upon a telephone interview with the potential victims (Haya and her daughter), they placed a halt on the Home Office deportation/return process to Bulgaria.

Since Haya was an asylum seeker and subject to immigration control, the First Responder, the Salvation Army, referred the case to the Home Office as one of the two competent authorities that makes the definitive decision based on a two-stage procedure. Stage one is the reasonable grounds and Stage two is the conclusive decision. The Salvation Army initiated Stage one (reasonable grounds). The NRM team has a target date of five working days from receipt of referral in which to decide whether there are reasonable grounds to believe the individual is a potential victim of human trafficking or modern slavery. Consequently, the mother and child were taken to a safe house. Subsequently, Stage two (conclusive decision) is triggered, whereby during the 45-day reflection and recovery period the competent authority (Home Office, UKVI) gathers further information relating to the referral from the First Responder and other agencies. The Home Office found Haya and her daughter to be victims of trafficking and granted them discretionary leave to remain in the UK.

From a practitioner perspective, the Home Office caseworker's and local authority's lack of knowledge in respect of NRM and failure of these two First Responders to conduct a needs assessment showed a real risk in relation to care and support afforded to the mother and child. Practitioners from many different agencies, coming into contact with asylum seekers and having to conduct assessments and reach decisions, face a real challenge in that these frontline practitioners, who ought to provide support and care to asylum seekers, need a consolidated legal framework and preferably one piece of legislation that has under its ambit all the relevant asylum and immigration laws. The two First Responders (UKBA at the time, now UKVI, and the local authority) that were approached initially were completely oblivious to the fact that an asylum-seeking mother and her child can also be victims of trafficking and as a result in need of support of the local authority, at the very least in terms of their knowledge of the matter.

This paucity of knowledge in the case of Haya and her daughter displayed the lack of interagency collaboration at both strategic and operational levels. It also highlighted many shortcomings in the local authority's functions in terms of knowledge, advocacy and need assessment. The asylum seekers in this case were granted discretionary leave to remain mainly because the potentiality of trafficking was identified by one of the authors, a legal academic.

In respect of Haya and her young daughter's referral as potential victims of trafficking, additional considerations were required, even after a negative reasonable grounds or conclusive grounds decision, since children may still have safeguarding needs, especially if they are unaccompanied and seeking asylum. Consequently frontline practitioners should ensure that a negative NRM decision does not have an adverse impact on children's care and does not override the statutory duty placed on local authorities by the Children Act 1989.

It is notable that in the expanded definition of abuse and neglect in the Care Act 2014 Statutory Guidance (DHSC, 2018a) a new category of modern slavery is included, incorporating human trafficking. This marks a policy change in that prior to the Act trafficking was clearly conceptualised as a criminal justice matter. The inclusion of modern slavery in the statutory guidance as a form of abuse means that it is now included in the remit of adult safeguarding in England (Kidd and Manthorpe, 2017), where it presents a new challenge to safeguarding practitioners due to the often organised rather than individual nature of the abuse.

SL v Westminster City Council [2013] is another case decided before the Care Act 2014. It concerns the scope of the obligation of local authorities under s.21(1)(a) of the National Assistance Act 1948 to provide accommodation to individuals who, by reason of age, illness, disability or any other circumstance, are in need of care and attention that is not otherwise available to them. According to s.21 (1A) of that Act, accommodation may not be provided to persons subject to immigration control if their need for care and attention has arisen solely because they are destitute or because of the physical effects, or anticipated physical effects, of destitution:

> *The need has to be for care and attention which is not available otherwise than through the provision of such accommodation. As any guidance given on this point in this judgment is strictly obiter, it would be unwise to elaborate, but the care and attention obviously has to be accommodation-related. This means that it has at least to be care and attention of a sort which is normally provided in the home (whether ordinary or specialised) or will be effectively useless if the claimant has no home.* (para. 48, emphasis added)

The Supreme Court draws a distinction between the care and support to which accommodation is a 'critical part' and that to which accommodation is 'essential', in which the provision of care and attention will be 'effectively useless' in the absence of accommodation. The Supreme Court ruled that in SL's case the provision of accommodation was a critical part of his social rehabilitation but not an essential part and as a result its absence did not render the care and support effectively useless. Care and attention can be, and is, provided independently of SL's need for accommodation or its location.

The position after the Care Act 2014: restrictions compensated by innovative and strategic management

Now several years into its implementation, it is debatable whether the Care Act has delivered what it promised in practice. The new legal framework says little about provision for asylum seekers. In the wording of the Act, there is no mention of the word 'refugee' since no discrimination can be made against a refugee in respect of the provisions afforded to any citizen in respect of rights and privileges. Reference to asylum seekers *per se* is not made within the Act, or in the Statutory Guidance (DHSC, 2018a). Section 21 of the Act re-states the position applicable pre-Care Act, referring to the Immigration and Asylum Act 1999 and the Nationality, Immigration and Asylum Act 2002, and excluding from local authority care and support people who are subject to immigration control whose needs arise from destitution.

Local authorities do, however, hold key responsibilities in relation to asylum seekers. Support is available for asylum seekers with needs for care and support arising otherwise than through destitution as previously, and the appearance of care and support needs should trigger a proportionate assessment. Where there are particular communication needs the process should be adapted accordingly. Paragraph 6.23 of the Statutory Guidance (DHSC, 2018a) states that 'local authorities should consider whether the individual would have substantial difficulty in being involved in the assessment process and if so consider the need for independent advocacy', Consideration of whether a specialist or interpreter would be needed to support communication is also required. It would be valid criticism to note that the availability of this additional route to support is somewhat hidden, given there is no specific reference in the Statutory Guidance to the position of asylum seekers. In the UKVI leaflets providing advice and information to asylum seekers entering the country, this brief paragraph under the heading 'Disability Care Needs' appears in leaflet 4 'Your responsibilities and rights as an asylum applicant':

> *If you have a disability or special care need, you can contact your local social services to request a Community Care Assessment. The local authority may decide to offer you accommodation and support.*

Either the leaflet on 'Legal advice, additional help and assistance' or the leaflet on 'Asylum support' would be the more logical place for this information, but they remain silent.

Below a reported case is considered to demonstrate that the Act has not made significant progress in terms of care and support to asylum seekers. In fact, the care and support offered to asylum seekers through the Act seems to be more of a restriction than support. The Act provides the theory and much needed consolidated framework for care provision. However, practice under its provisions has taken its time to go through a process of trial and error while leaving much to the innovative and strategic management of professionals. Closing gaps in the provisions for vulnerable asylum seekers who are subject to immigration control has thus been subject to a 'hit and miss' approach.

Section 18 of the Care Act covers the duty to meet needs for care and support. The leading case of *R(SG) (a protected party by her litigation friend the Official Solicitor) v London Borough of Haringey* [2015], the first case to be heard on the accommodation provisions of the Care Act 2014, is illustrative of this innovative and strategic approach. SG, an Afghan national, was an asylum seeker woman; she was accommodated by the Home Office in the London Borough of Haringey while her asylum claim was pending. SG had physical health problems and significant mental health issues, described in the case at paragraph 7 as 'a victim of torture, rape and emotional and physical abuse. She suffers from severe mental health problems, including complex PTSD, insomnia, depression and anxiety. She speaks no English and is illiterate. She is in need of services to meet her needs for care and support.'

She had difficulty with basic self-care, food preparation and management of medication. It was argued that Haringey had a duty to accommodate her under Care Act 2014 due to her care needs. Haringey argued that the legal tests for this from case law prior to the Care Act 2014 were no longer applicable. The High Court quashed Haringey's assessment of SG's needs under the Care Act on the grounds that it was conducted without an independent advocate. At paragraph 40 the judge stated 'this appears to me the paradigm case where such an advocate was required, as in the absence of one the claimant was in no position to influence matters … I think the assessment was flawed as a result and must be redone'. It was argued that she was not assigned an advocate nor was she assessed by a suitably trained and competent agent, contrary to regulation 5 of the Care and Support (Independent Advocacy Support) Regulations 2014.

Also the case refers to the power of the local authority and the ramification of its discretion, which did not adequately consider the possibility of a duty to provide accommodation to meet SG's needs. The Court of Appeal in *SG v Haringey* [2017] dismissed the claimant's appeal against the High Court's decision. Subsequently SG was granted refugee status and then was accommodated by Haringey following termination of her asylum support as a result of her new immigration status.

The decision in *R (On the Application of GS) v London Borough of Camden (Rev 1)* [2016] raises a significant point – that a number of other avenues of redress can be explored in the event of refusal in relation to a need assessment under the Care Act; these may include raising issues under the Equality Act 2010, European Convention on Human Rights, and Localism Act 2011. Following an assessment under the Care Act, it was concluded that the claimant did not have a need for care and support, in particular a need for accommodation, and as a result they brought a judicial review. The local authority's position was that the need for accommodation was not a need for care and support within the Care Act 2014 and that it had no power under statute to provide for such a need; the claimant's situation was one that did not put her at risk of a breach of her rights under the European Convention on Human Rights. The authority had made the decision not to exercise its power to provide care and support under section 18 or 19 of the Care Act 2014 and section 1 of the Localism Act 2011.[3] The court decided that the defendant's decision not to exercise the power available to it under section 1 of the Localism Act was unlawful.

This case demonstrates the utilisation of the Localism Act as a means of meeting the needs of people who were short of meeting the threshold of the Care Act in order to avoid human rights violation. This point once again illustrates innovation as a means of closing the gaps that the Care Act leaves behind. In other words attempts are made to reach a fair, just and equitable outcome in cases where the Care Act does not meet the needs of the most vulnerable.

The restrictive and exclusionary measures enforced by legal rules reinforce the need for innovative and strategic approaches in providing accommodation and support in respect of asylum seekers and failed asylum seekers. Reference must also be made to other exclusionary legislation. Section 55, 'Late claim for asylum: refusal of support', contained in the Nationality, Immigration and Asylum Act 2002, authorises withdrawal of support from asylum seekers. Section 55(1) broadly states that the Secretary of State may not provide or arrange for the provision of support to a person if her claim was not made as soon as reasonably practicable after her arrival in the United Kingdom. Equally section 9 'Failed asylum seekers: withdrawal of support' of Asylum and Immigration (Treatment of Claimants, etc.) Act 2004 and section 115 of the Immigration and Asylum Act 1999 are further evidence of restrictive measures arguably for deterrent purposes (Da Lomba, 2005). A hostile environment designed to make it uncomfortable to remain in the UK and the threat of destitution are incentives to leave (Randall, 2015).

Local authority social services may be able to provide accommodation under section 18 of the Care Act 2014, or under the Localism Act 2011. The Localism Act should be considered and used for those who are likely to be solely destitute, without any appearance of care and support needs, pending enquiries. For people prohibited from receiving Care Act support under section 54/schedule 3 of the Nationality, Immigration and Asylum Act, the human rights/EU treaty rights exceptions justify use of section 19 of the Care Act to avoid an imminent breach of human rights or EU treaty rights.

Conclusion

UKVI, a part of the Home Office, is responsible for the provision of accommodation and support for the vast majority of asylum seekers in the UK (previously this role fell to the UK Border Agency and before that to the National Asylum Support Service). Local authority social services also play a parallel role in providing accommodation and support to asylum seekers, failed asylum seekers or those with accommodation, care and support needs. The chapter has drawn on wide-ranging materials to highlight the inherent vulnerability of asylum seekers in general. Many asylum seekers may have known and unknown underlying issues including mental health and anxiety concerns and educational deficiencies.

Asylum seekers face a system in which at each step of the way they need to prove their eligibility for legal, social and educational support. Similar challenges and complexity are also shared and experienced by frontline practitioners. Social workers need to have a workable knowledge of a number of fields in association with the provision and support they may need to offer to asylum seekers and their potential paucity of knowledge may

(Continued)

(Continued)

cost human beings their lives. One way to tackle these challenges would be to bring the law, policy and practice in respect of asylum seekers under the umbrella of one legal regime. However, in the context of the legislative restrictions that asylum seekers are currently subject to, the potential safeguards and exceptions depend upon the innovative and strategic management of individual cases by practitioners and rely heavily on their legal and cultural capital.

Case study: Arya and Beata

Arya and Beata were a married couple and environmentalists who lived in Iran with their daughter Bahar and Beata's elderly mother Azar. Caught up in a political power struggle in the midst of persecution and prosecution of environmentalists, the couple were accused of spying and were imprisoned. Beata died in prison under suspicious circumstances. Having feared for their lives, Azar and her grandchild Bahar fled to the UK. Azar speaks no English, and has severe arthritis and impaired sight due to several cataracts. Bahar is 15 and has a learning disability. Bahar and her grandmother are currently staying with Iranian acquaintances on a temporary basis and have claimed asylum. Both have had the screening but not as yet the Asylum Interview.

While on bail for the death of his wife in prison and fearing for his life, Arya travels with a trafficker and manages to escape on arrival in the UK but is extremely traumatised and has no documents. He finds his family but there is no room for them to remain with the friends. Arya intends to seek asylum in the UK too. They have very few clothes, possessions or money. The friends contact the Home Office Visas and Immigration and local authority.

Commentary

A health and social care assessment of needs should be carried out by social services in respect of Azar, Arya and Bahar. It must be noted that even through an interpreter these three asylum seekers (Arya is to seek asylum) may not be able to articulate their needs. Therefore 'needs assessment' ought to be carried out with language, knowledge and cultural sensitivity. As a child, Bahar's immigration status is irrelevant as she is subject to the Children Act 1989 and the associated guidelines and regulations.

Home office staff and relevant commercial partners should refer for needs assessment any adult asylum seeker who appears to have a care need. (For a more comprehensive coverage please see *Asylum seekers with care needs. Version 2.* Published for Home Office staff on 03 August 2018:

→

https://assets.publishing.service.gov.uk/government/uploads/system/uploads/
attachment_data/file/731907/Asylum-Seekers-With-Care-Needs-v2.0ext.pdf)

Non-urgent needs

Where a newly arrived asylum seeker has potential care needs that do not appear to be urgent, or otherwise to require assessment prior to dispersal, assessment of those needs may await the person being dispersed. A person dispersed to a local authority's area should be considered ordinarily resident in that area, and any needs or carer's assessment will be requested from that local authority.

Urgent needs

Where a person presents with urgent needs that may require any of the following:

- residential care;
- specific accommodation;
- day-to-day assistance with basic personal care

a needs assessment should be requested from the local authority in whose area the adult is present at the earliest practicable point in the process. For example, where a person claiming asylum at a port of entry presents with urgent care needs, the local authority in whose area the port is situated should be requested to do an urgent assessment. If in immediate need of medical care, it will be necessary in the first instance to refer the individual to the nearest hospital.

Urgent needs where the person has already been accommodated by the Home Office

Where, exceptionally, a person has already been accommodated by the Home Office before an urgent care need is revealed and therefore no request for assessment has been made, an urgent assessment must be requested from the authority in whose area the accommodation is situated. Such an assessment should be requested by the First Responder (for instance the accommodation provider, the caseworker or other person, using specialist safeguarding staff where appropriate) when made aware of the care need. Where a local authority is requested to do a needs assessment, either because the asylum seeker is ordinarily resident in its area or is present in its area but of no settled residence, that local authority is obliged to do so in accordance with the terms of the Care Act 2014.

Priority actions required after the needs assessment has been carried out are:

- GP registration for all three;
- school enrolment for Bahar;
- English classes for all.

Further Reading

Aspinall, P. and Watters, C. (2010) *Refugees and Asylum Seekers: A Review from an Equality and Human Rights Perspective.* London: Equality and Human Rights Commission.

Hayes, D. and Humphries, B. (2004) *Social Work, Immigration and Asylum: Debates, Dilemmas and Ethical Issues for Social Work and Social Care Practice.* London and New York: Jessica Kingsley.

SCIE (2015) *Good Practice in Social Care for Refugees and Asylum Seekers: SCIE Guide 37.* London: Social Care Institute for Excellence.

Williams, L. (2004) Refugees and asylum seekers as a group at risk of adult abuse, *Journal of Adult Protection,* 6 (4): 4–15.

Notes

1. The Community Legal Outreach Collaboration Keele (CLOCK) is an initiative launched on 24 October 2012 by the Law School at Keele University. By working with a number of partner organisations, CLOCK enables law students to provide vital help and support to disadvantaged communities through legal research, policy work and community legal education. CLOCK is part of the Litigant in Person Network (LIPN), a network committed to working in partnership to support each other to provide the best possible support to people seeking access to justice.

2. To be referred to the NRM, potential victims of trafficking or modern slavery must first be referred to one of the UK's two competent authorities (CAs). This initial referral will generally be handled by an authorised agency such as a police force, the NCA, the UK Border Force, Home Office Visas and Immigration, Social Services or certain NGOs. The referring authority is known as the 'first responder'. For further information please see the National Crime Agency site at www.nationalcrimeagency.gov.uk/about-us/what-we-do/specialist-capabilities/uk-human-trafficking-centre/national-referral-mechanism (accessed on 06/01/2019).

3. The general power of competence is a power available to local authorities in England to do 'anything that individuals generally may do' (S1(1) of the Act); even though this may be 'in nature, extent or otherwise... unlike anything that other public bodies may do', it accommodates for their functional creativity significantly. This was provided for in the Localism Act 2011 and replaces the wellbeing powers in the Local Government Act 2000. It was brought into force for local authorities on 18 February 2012.

12 Transitions to adult social care

Cath Holmström

Introduction

This chapter focuses on the impact of the Care Act upon the legal framework and social work practice in respect of young people making the transition to adult social care. The changes in legal duties, rights and powers are examined in respect of young people themselves and brief reference is also made to their parents and/or carers. Whilst the main areas of focus are upon transitions for disabled young people and care leavers, brief references are also made to other transitioning young people. Given the core areas of focus in this chapter, the interrelationship between the Care Act 2014 (CA 2014) and the Children and Families Act 2014 (CFA 2014) is examined along with the changes they, and their associated guidance, have brought about.

The term 'transition' refers here to the process of children and young adults transferring from children's to adult services for the provision of care or support. However, some young people will not have been known to children's services and yet may require support and/or care of varying degrees as an adult. This may be the case especially for those with degenerative conditions, acquired disabilities and those for whom their care and support needs were largely met within their educational setting, such as specialist residential schools.

Such transitions have generally occurred as young people reach the age of 18. Clearly, the years surrounding this age are times of significant change at many levels, with physical, psychological, emotional and practical changes being experienced. Even for young people with no additional needs or barriers to overcome, this can be a turbulent and unsettling time. For those young people with disabilities and for care leavers, this can be an even greater time of change as previous relationships with professionals come to an end and the unknown world of adult services is encountered. As Young-Southward et al. (2017) note, for young people with intellectual difficulties, as for many with disabilities, changes need to be planned carefully given the importance of routine for many disabled young people.

Care-leaving young people and those with disabilities are known to be amongst the groups in our society who are most vulnerable to poorer outcomes on a range of measures including educational attainment and employment or training prospects (Jackson and Cameron, 2012). In addition, the mental health of care leavers often declines in the first year after leaving care (Newton et al., 2017); this is amongst a group where mental health difficulties are four times as likely to affect young people than in the population as a whole. The need to plan for 'seamless' transitions for these young people is therefore all the more important in order to provide the best possible opportunities and outcomes, a core part of 'wellbeing' within the meaning of s1 of CA 2014. This is a significant and growing proportion of the population, given advances in medical treatment such that children with previously untreatable conditions now survive longer with around 45,000 under 19s living with long-term conditions (Carr and Goosey, 2017), and 14–15% of children in England are known to have at least one diagnosed long-term health condition (Public Health England, 2015). Similarly, with growing numbers of children and young people 'in care', support for care leavers will be increasingly important. Government statistics show that between 2016 and 2017, the 'in care' population grew by 3% to 72,600. These are young people who, unlike most living within their own families, have not historically been able to choose the right time to move out of or on from home, and cannot simply return when plans go awry or during college vacation times.

The 'wrongs' that the Care Act (2014) and the Children and Families Act (2014) were intended to put 'right'

Adult services have traditionally been designed around the needs of older people and those requiring end of life care. Young people remain a minority within adult social care services (Mitchell et al., 2017). Parents/carers and young people have experienced far from satisfactory contact with services where the approach and/or the environment (including mode of delivery) were not appropriate for younger people, causing further stress and anxiety at an already challenging, and sometimes overwhelming, time. In the aptly titled Care Quality Commission document 'From the pond into the sea' (CQC, 2014), we hear that 'Parents told us they felt "abandoned" by health and social care services at this most difficult time' (CQC, 2014:11). This is further compounded where multiple assessments and processes that are uncoordinated require navigation. In the same document, carers reported a lack of information about the likely nature and level of support once adult services were responsible for the provision of care and support, particularly important when it seems that there are few direct parallels with the kind of provision within children's services. Indeed, Broach et al., writing on behalf of the Council for Disabled Children, found that care packages for children generally changed significantly at the point of transition to adult services, with many experiencing a significant decline in the level of support provided (2016: 33). Indeed, accounts from families and service users (CQC, 2014) use phrases such as a 'cliff edge' and 'black hole' to refer to experiences of moving between services. For many, it has seemed that their experience was less about 'transition' and more about being caught between different systems and processes, and for others it was a case of experiencing a sudden withdrawal of pre-existing services at the age of 16 or 18 depending upon the service in question, with a gap in provision before being able to access adult services. The Research in Practice (RIP) strategic briefing (2018) on 'transitional safeguarding' also identifies the different cultures in respect of safeguarding approaches between children's and adult services, based upon different underpinning concepts such as risk aversion versus risk enablement and the impact of young people being caught between these approaches. This briefing also highlights the importance of providing services based upon a holistic approach for transitioning young people in which knowledge of the child, and especially cognitive development, the impact of adversity, is central to the services being provided.

Parents have made reference to the perception that only those most able and willing to 'push' for what was needed were able to secure appropriate services. As the researchers argue:

> It is completely unacceptable for parents and young people to become caught up in arguments … as to the most appropriate service to provide care during the transition phase. Or to find that a care service stops when the children's service ends but before the adult service commences. (CQC, 2014: 66)

However, perhaps even more concerning is the fact that many of those professionals responsible for providing care reported being unclear about relevant processes, and existing guidance and protocols were often not followed (CQC, 2014: 9). In addition, serious care reviews and safeguarding adult reviews, some of which are referred to below, indicate how serious the outcomes may be where transitions are poorly managed.

The main changes introduced by the Care Act 2014 and Children and Families Act 2014 affecting young people transitioning to adult services

For young people transitioning to adult services several parallel legal provisions have co-existed, albeit with a number of amendments over recent years. The range of these in relation to transitioning young people will be outlined in brief before examining in more depth the changes effected by the implementation of CA 2014 and CFA 2014 in particular.

The rights of children 'in need' of support (including disabled children) are detailed in s17, especially 17(10)(c) in the Children Act 1989 (CA 89). The CA 89 provisions have been amended in order to extend duties via the Children (Leaving Care) Act 2000 in which duties to 16- and 17-year-old care leavers ('relevant' young people) included the provision of personal advisers before leaving care, the introduction of pathway planning processes and an obligation to maintain contact until the age of 21. Support was further extended by s22 of the Children and Young Persons Act 2008, whereby assessments of need for support of previously looked after (former 'relevant') young people remaining in agreed education or training must take place until the age of 25, along with pathway plans. Additional measures to support care leavers are to be found in the more recent Children and Social Work Act 2017, wherein s2 places are requirements upon local authorities to publicise their local 'offer' for care leavers and s3 requires that personal advisers are provided until the age of 25.

With the enactment of CFA 2014 and associated guidance, 'staying put' arrangements were introduced, enabling those in foster care to remain rather than have to move on by their eighteenth birthday. Although not all will wish to remain in foster placements, and some may not be able to for carer-related reasons, government statistics based upon local authority returns for 2017 indicate that 25% of those aged 19 and 20 looked after by the local authority had remained in their foster placements. Additional statistics indicate that 53% of those who had reached 18 were still with their foster carers three months after their eighteenth birthday (https://assets. publishing.service.gov.uk/government/uploads/system/uploads/attachment_data/file/664995/ SFR50_2017-Children_looked_after_in_England.pdf).

The CFA 2014 introduced, for disabled young people, a requirement for a lead professional and a transition plan for health needs, and perhaps importantly on a practical level for many, a health 'passport' containing key information to avoid the need for the young person or their carer having to repeat the same information to seemingly endless numbers of professionals. The introduction of Education and Health Care Plans (EHCPs) via the CFA 2014 for those children with special/additional educational needs was also intended to provide the basis for more joined-up support for services with regular reviews.

Pre-implementation of the CA 2014, confusion about responsibilities and processes was no doubt further complicated by the fact that the previous adult social care law landscape was somewhat confusing and underpinned by a myriad different sections/pieces of legislation. However, this was even more the case in respect of children and young people, for whom some of this legislation was applicable in addition to CA 89, for example the Chronically Sick and Disabled Persons Act 1970, but who may also be supported and assessed via the CA 89.

The Law Commission, during the adult social care law reform process, had proposed that in order to create greater clarity and reduce confusion, local authorities should be granted the general power to assess and provide services to 16- and 17-year-olds under adult statute (Spencer-Lane, 2014). However, as will be clear below, whilst the government agreed that concerns relating to 'cliff edge' withdrawal of services upon transition to adult services, or upon reaching any particular age, required legal remedies, and certainly made assessment of transition needs a duty in certain circumstances under the Care Act, there was no parallel duty or power for adult services to provide specific services alongside this for those under 18.

Care Act assessments for transition purposes

The CA 2014's core principle of 'wellbeing' (s1) is as applicable to young people transitioning into adult services as it is to adults and holds the same meaning such that it incudes mental as well as physical health. Under the Act, planning and assessment processes must take needs, preferred outcomes and wishes into account, as well as identify strengths or 'assets'. Importantly, the possibility of combining assessments with others being completed (e.g. EHCPs under the CFA) was highlighted as a means of reducing the number of potentially complex processes within which young people and their carers are engaged.

The transition-specific sections of the Care Act 2014 are detailed in sections 58–66 and apply to all transitioning young people, rather than only the narrower examples referred to here. Section 58 identifies the duty of the local authority to assess transition needs where a young person is deemed likely to have care and support needs as an adult **and** where there is a 'significant benefit' for that particular young person, at the time in question, **and** the 'consent condition' is satisfied. The assessment must explore whether there are current care and support needs (s58(1) (a) and also whether the young person is likely to have needs as an adult and, if so, the nature of those needs (s58(1) b).

'Significant benefit' is a term that may be subject to future legal challenge, but it is clear from the wording of the Act and Statutory Guidance (DHSC, 2018a), wherein examples of indicators of significant benefit are listed at s16.10, that 'significant benefit' refers to the timing of the assessment and not the perceived level of need. The test therefore is whether it is appropriate to assess at any particular time or age for that individual rather than being convenient for professionals or service provision timescales. In considering this, we are guided to consider changes in educational stages, accommodation arrangements and employment status. An expectation is that the local authority will minimise disruption and combine assessments such as health assessments or ECHPs where possible. Whilst the CFA 2014 requires that ECHPs are commenced by age 14 and reviewed annually, transition assessments under the CA 2014 should be carried out at the *right time for the individual concerned*.

When considering whether a young person is 'likely to have care and support needs' as an adult, information must be provided by the assessing authority about identified needs, not merely eligible needs, that are likely to continue into adulthood. Whilst this assessment of future needs may be challenging, making the choice of timing especially important, it is clearly critical if young people and their carers are to be able to plan and to manage the uncertainty associated with this period. In addition, this is intended to manage expectations, as needs and likely eligibility for support will be assessed with reference to adult social care and not children's services criteria.

The 'consent condition' in respect of assessments is met when the child has capacity or is 'competent' to consent to the assessment and chooses to do so (58 (3a)). Where there is no capacity or competence, but the local authority judges it to be in the child's best interests to be assessed (58 (3b)), then the condition will also be satisfied. Whilst there may be a tendency in lay persons' thinking to conflate the terms 'capacity' and 'competence', within professional practice it is of course critical that the terms and their legal basis are understood and used appropriately. For young people, the Mental Capacity Act 2005 is of relevance for those aged 16 or over and in line with its principles there must be a presumption of capacity for this age group (s.1) unless proven to the contrary through the capacity assessment process (s.3). 'Competence' to consent, however, is assessed in the usual way, according to the Gillick Principles (*Gillick v West Norfolk and Wisbech Area Health Authority* [1986]): a child under 16 who is of sufficient age and understanding may consent without parental involvement. Whilst children may refuse this assessment, the local authority must still carry out the assessment if a child is experiencing or at risk of experiencing neglect or abuse (58 (4)) given the overriding Children Act 1989 duties in respect of children's safeguarding.

Requests for transition assessments under the CA 2014 may be made by children or their carers/ parents, and if refused, the local authority must give written reasons and signpost ways in which needs may be reduced in the future through the provision of information and advice. If the decision to decline to assess at the requested time is due to a perception that there is no significant benefit, and the assessment will be deferred, then it is the responsibility of the local authority to re-schedule and manage timings. Importantly, the child does not need to be in receipt of services in order to request an assessment, and therefore local authorities will need to establish mechanisms through which to increase awareness of children likely to have needs in adulthood, for example through enhanced liaison with schools, health services and other means, as well as publishing their support offers.

According to s59(1), the assessment must include consideration of the impact of care and support needs post-18, desired outcomes for the individual and if/how care and support could help achieving those, and also what else might help s59(3), including informal sources of support. Importantly in respect of transition planning, the local authority under s59(4) must provide an indicative account of whether any of the identified care and support needs are likely to be eligible for support under adult services. Once the assessment has been completed and the young person turns 18, the local authority has the power to decide that this constitutes a needs assessment in respect of needs assessment for an adult (s59(5)) or whether a new assessment is needed, taking into account issues such as the time gap between the assessment being completed and entering adult services, and any changes of circumstances.

In combination, the CA 2014 and CFA 2014 were intended to lead to more of a 'whole family' approach, despite the continued separation of service provision and, not insignificantly, the separation of oversight into different government departments. The power to include child carers and disabled children within a Care Act assessment of an adult and their needs is 'intended to enable practitioners to consider the effect of an individual's support needs on the rest of the family, and provide appropriate services that address the needs of the whole family' (Spencer Lane, 2014: 307). This may go some way to identifying those young people not already 'known' to the local authority but who may have needs for care and support upon reaching adulthood.

Perhaps the most significant changes that the CA 2014 introduced for transitioning young people and their carers make up the content of s66, which aims to prevent gaps in service provision through a right to 'continuity of care'. This should mean that nobody has their care and support suddenly removed upon reaching 18. Indeed, as Spencer-Lane notes, 'If a transition assessment has been requested, and the relevant assessment has not taken place or a conclusion has not been reached, then services must continue when the child reaches 18 until a conclusion has been reached' (2014: 309). Critically, until an appropriate assessment of needs has been completed and CA 2014 duties discharged, the local authority must continue to provide existing services. Indeed, if they continue to provide care and support beyond the age of 18, then children's services will need to mirror adult services provision in respect of care and support planning personal budgets (DHSC, 2018a, 16.61).

Sections 60 and 61 of the CA 2014 outline when there is a duty to assess carers of transitioning children and what those assessments must include. Whilst s60 includes reference to 'significant benefit', mirroring conditions for assessing young people, s61 draws together carers' rights under previous legislation and includes an assessment of their ability and willingness to continue to provide care once the young person reaches 18. By virtue of s62, local authorities have the power to provide any identified transitional support, mirroring that to be provided to young people.

Historically, responsibility for young people in secure facilities whilst serving custodial sentences has not rested with the local authority in respect of their needs for support upon turning 18. It is clear from the CA 2014 statutory guidance that the transfer from youth to adult criminal justice facilities and services, and from secure facilities to release, is recognised as a critical phase and local authorities will need to ensure that they are aware of the local services and transition arrangements, and have effective mechanisms for maintaining awareness of any young people in custodial settings for whom they may have responsibilities and who are likely to have care or support needs as adults. This applies too where a young person is intending to live in another area upon release, such that the authority in which they are resident must make contact with the future authority in order to plan and implement a smooth transition. Where young people are care leavers and entitled to support after care, their own local authority remains responsible for their care and support, either until 21or until 25 or longer if being supported with agreed education and training (DHSC, 2018a, 17.62).

Evaluation of early evidence about impact on services, practice/s and outcomes

Legislation and policy, most recently the Care Act (2014), all impact on personal experience, although policy makers and those at a distance from this may not fully grasp the impacts these changes bring about. When looking for support from professionals, and thinking about the new provisions within the Care Act (2014), I ponder on whether it will actually make a difference – to my daughter, to me, or to anyone? (Gant, 2017: 735)

As the above quotation from a parent of a disabled child illustrates, the actual impact of legislative and policy changes and those intended may differ. This may be especially true in the context of shrinking public sector services and reduced resourcing of most forms of care and support, as in the UK in recent years. The reduction of early intervention and other forms of preventative services that have occurred in recent years as part of cost saving measures runs counter to the good practice recommendations identified in the Research in Practice Strategic Briefing (2018), in which the longer-term costs of such approaches are recognised.

In one recently reported post-Care Act decision, the family of a young man with a complex range of needs was left unsupported once he reached 18. The previous care package had included holiday and regular respite care. Whilst the assessment of his needs identified 72 days per year of respite care being required, only 28 were funded with no reason for this failure to meet identified needs provided. Such situations are of great concern to the families involved and not only highlight worrying practices in terms of failure to meet identified needs in an appropriate manner, but also fail to provide a rationale where this is the case. The Local Government and Social Care Ombudsman (LGO), upon reviewing this case, stated that:

This family fell between the cracks as it moved from one council service to another. They were left without the essential support they needed for more than five months, and without any explanation as to why, when the council decided their previous level would be almost halved.

... There is a clear duty for councils to ensure there are no gaps in care and support by providing services until an adult social care package is in place. (LGSCO and Bromley LBC (2017))

Unfortunately, the case referred to above is far from an isolated one. Even a brief exploration of the LGO website illustrates that, several years after the implementation of the provisions referred to above in CA (2014) and CFA (2014), many local authorities struggle to meet their responsibilities in respect of transitioning children. For example, unreasonable delays in completing adult needs assessment left a young person and their family anxious about likely future provision, despite there being no gap in the case due to the ongoing support being provided by children's services (LGSCO and Trafford MBC (2018)). Similarly, in LGSCO and Wirral MBC (2018), an unreasonable delay in setting up direct payments had been acknowledged, but the *impact* of this, with the child's mother needing to chase the council for responses and the impact of this delay upon lack of choice of educational provision, was not acknowledged by the council. In this case the Ombudsman also reported a lack of information about the services available on their website, in contravention of CA 2014 responsibilities. In another case (LGSCO and Sefton MBC (2018)), the transition of a disabled young woman had rightly commenced prior to her eighteenth birthday, and the council had located a property suitable for her to move into, but they had failed to identify a care provider. Despite issuing her with notice to move out of her current children's home due to her age, the council ended up changing plans and timescales before and after a care provider was identified, greatly affecting the ability of the young woman to be prepared for her move, something that had been identified as key, given her specific needs.

Whilst case law directly relevant to the implementation of the CA 2014 in respect of transitions is limited, there are lessons from relevant judgments and also from safeguarding reviews. For example, in *R (JF) v London Borough of Merton* [2017], decisions about the nature of adult services to be provided upon transition from children's services were held not to be rational in the legal sense and therefore unlawful. Whilst no finding was made in respect of the planning for transition process *per se*, the proposal to place JF in a facility with no multi-disciplinary team onsite and without the communications approach deemed necessary for the last fifteen years received significant criticism. Whilst courts have been clear historically that they will be slow to interfere in areas of practice best left to professionals, the courts' role is to review decisions and processes rather than assess needs or stipulate how these should be met.

Lessons from reviews

Several pre- and post- CA 2014 reviews of serious cases, some statutory and some discretionary, have been examined in order to identify key themes in respect of transitions. One key theme is that of **information sharing**. Poor communication and inefficient processes were identified in 'Anne' (Southend SAB, 2016) where a referral from the local authority to continuing health care and communications back took too long. The review of Adult CA (Manchester SAB, 2018) also identified significant failings in the sharing of information. CA died at the age of 22, after being known to mental health services for six years. Although the police had routinely made safeguarding referrals after each contact with her, these were delayed whilst going through an internal process before being shared. In addition, on the final point of contact, there was no such referral made on the assumption that as they had handed her over to ambulance personnel, health staff would do this. The fact that no referral was made by any service that day illustrates the problems of such assumptions. In the Bristol Serious Case Review of 'Melissa' aged 18 (Bristol SAB, 2017), the pre-CA 2014 murder of a young woman living in an adult care home, evidence of good preparation and partnership at the early stages of transition planning was identified. However, formal record sharing was inadequate. Also identified was a failure to report to external agencies, such as the police, behaviour that was very risky on the part of another resident; the care home attempted to manage this in house and left Melissa vulnerable to the attack that killed her.

The **lack of stability and continuous relationships** for children in care is not a new concern, and both pre- and post- CA 2014 reviews demonstrate a recognition of these issues being significant in respect of stability for the young person concerned, but also for the knowledge that comes from longer-term relationships and can thus inform planning and support for transitions. The statistics included in the pre-CA 2014 Somerset review (Somerset SCB and SAB, 2014) are sobering in this context. Of the 13 young people who had died, all of whom had been in care, the number of moves of placement ranged from 6 to 47, with 16 to 21 changes in allocated worker. For 'Melissa' (Bristol SAB, 2017) the SAR found that she had had six allocated social workers in her final two years. The knowledge from children's services was 'lost' as a result and she did not have a leaving care or pathway plan or assessment, with the referral to the care home happening very late only a few months before her eighteenth birthday, at odds with CA 2014 expectations. The Somerset review (Somerset SAB, 2014) highlighted the very **strong 'pull' that a birth family exercises** over care leavers and the extent to which this can affect even those who appeared to have made 'successful' transitions to independence. One of the key issues identified was a lack of understanding on the part of the young people about why they are looked after and why they could not remain at home, and why other key decisions had been made, highlighting the importance of work around identity and decision-making as part of a child's transition plan.

Lack of suitable accommodation upon transition has been highlighted in several reviews. 'Anne' (Southend SAB, 2016) had been in a continuing health care placement as a child due to the severity of her epilepsy and her disabilities. Lack of appropriate accommodation led to her being placed in a children's home despite being 18 and is an indicator of a concerning lack of resources. In different circumstances, the same issue of lack of appropriate facilities and resources was highlighted in the Ealing management review (Ealing SAB, 2016) where a young man, aged 18, was stabbed by a fellow resident. The lesson identified for Ealing was the lack of strategic planning for those young people most at risk, and a lack of resources for those transitioning within mental health services in particular.

Poor coordination between CAMHS and adult mental health services was also highlighted as an issue for transitions in the South West SARs review (Preston-Shoot, 2017a) in which a lack of joint planning and coordination between services affected the experience of transition adversely. Even where adult services have been involved at an early stage, this has not always prevented failures to plan effectively having disastrous consequences. Anne (Southend SAB, 2016) had been known to adult services since the age of 16 and yet had no updated care plan and no record of how decisions to place in the residential facility she was referred to had been reached.

Whilst it is clear that for Melissa (Bristol SAB, 2017) the impact of ongoing 'cliff edge' and auto-withdrawal of services at this stage, when young people reach the age of 18, is especially significant – and is precisely what the CA 2014 was intended to prevent – additional barriers are experienced due to differing thresholds for access to services when moving to adult services.

Indeed, Anne (Southend SAB, 2016) was deemed to not have eligible needs for adult services despite having had respite care via children's services. Similarly, for Ms A (Havering SAB, 2017), her referral from children's services as a looked after child to adult services did not result in support being provided because of differing thresholds. Given the lack of formal provision for some young adults, the importance of engaging with families and also drawing upon their knowledge and expertise would seem especially critical. However, several reviews are critical of the failure to consider fully family expertise and thus demonstrate the 'think family' approach intended by the introduction of CA 2014 and CFA 2014. Indeed, as the review of Anne's death (Southend SAB, 2016: 12) identified, despite the legal and policy shifts, 'agency processes and staff learning could not always keep up with the pace that these changes required'. In the context of shrinking resources and a lack of appropriate accommodation it would appear that positive outcomes for transitions are, more than ever, dependent upon social workers being adept at managing relationships, information sharing, and confident in their knowledge of the law and ensuring lawful decision-making processes.

Conclusion

Key principles and good practice

As highlighted throughout this chapter, there has historically been a gulf between good practice recommendations and the lived experiences of those requiring care and support. Whilst the CA 2014 incorporates some admirable changes to the legal framework surrounding adult social care, the real impact of these and the extent to which the Act has indeed marked a watershed in terms of the experiences of transition from children's to adult services will not be fully known for some time. Early indications are that the legislation is as good as its application, so the duty to assess when there is 'significant benefit' could mark a positive change to provision. This is true also for the expectation of no gap in provision upon transition and the power for the local authority to provide adult services under the Children Act 1989. That said, there are still significant concerns reported by those using services and within safeguarding adult reviews about the lack of information sharing, joined-up processes and appropriate planning – all issues that the Care Act was intended to address – as well as other concerns about failures in following lawful decision-making processes.

A number of good practice points emerge from the evidence on transitions discussed in this chapter:

(Continued)

(Continued)

- Early and also proportionate planning for transition is key, including timely assessments that fulfil the statutory requirements enshrined in the relevant guidance as well as the legislation.
- Professional judgement, as in many areas of social work practice, must be fair and accompanied by lawful (i.e. rational) decision-making with any departures from guidance or assessed needs being explained.
- During assessments, the importance of expectation management is key, given the differences between children's services support and adult services support thresholds and resources.
- Adult services need to be designed appropriately with staff conversant with the developmental phases and stages and needs of young people as well as older adults, alongside a recognition that problems in childhood often continue or are exacerbated in adulthood (RIP, 2018).
- The importance of taking a more whole-family approach in line with policy intentions is vital. This is challenging when different government departments are involved as well as different approaches to organising and managing resources.
- Young people transitioning between services often identify the importance of meaningful and lasting relationships with those supporting them. How to develop this within a paid, often statutory relationship is a challenge no doubt, but a key consideration given what the state is aspiring to provide for these children.

Case study: Sam

Sam, aged 17, has been in foster care since the age of 5 as a result of safeguarding concerns arising from parental substance misuse and associated neglect of his needs. He has had sporadic contact with his father but his mother is known to have died from an overdose several years ago. He has been in the same foster placement for this whole time and has also had the same social worker for the last five years. Sam has a diagnosis of high functioning autism and epilepsy, managed by his GP and a specialist consultant, as well as more recently diagnosed depression, and has enjoyed regular weekend respite and holiday stays with a carer living on a small farm, as well as support from a specialist mentor. Sam has been educated within mainstream schools and has had an ECH plan that has been reviewed most years. Sam has thrived during his A-level studies and has indicated that he wishes to progress to university. He would like to study locally and stay with his foster carers but they will be selling their home and moving into supported retirement accommodation.

→

Commentary

In the scenario above, avoiding a 'cliff-edge' withdrawal of services (CA 2014 s66) is of course key, and it would have been good (and lawful) practice to have begun planning for the transitions that are now imminent over several years. Despite the fact that Sam has indicated a wish to remain with his current carers, and that this would be supported by the 'Staying Put' initiative within CFA 2014, this is not possible due to the foster carers' own needs, unless these can be met appropriately in any other way, and a careful assessment of their needs as part of this process would be appropriate (CA 2014 ss60–62).

Additional aspects of good (and lawful) practice in this scenario include the following:

- Ensuring that Sam is included in all reviews of his ECHP in the most appropriate way for him and that his wishes and preferred outcomes are known and considered (CA 2014 s1), as well as recognising the significance of relationships.
- Ensuring that those who know his strengths, abilities and likely needs are directly involved in planning with him for transitions (especially given the length of relationships involved here) and that a lead professional is identified (CFA 2014).
- Early sharing of information about the likely range and level of support once Sam has moved to adult health and/or care services would be important in order for any reduced levels of support to be planned for.
- Minimising the scale and impact of the process will be important given that, like many young people making this transition, routine and limited amounts of change are essential for 'wellbeing'. Perhaps here the transition to adult health services could be phased over several months with visits to new service providers accompanied by someone especially familiar to him, or even better that the existing and future specialists work together to manage this transition. In addition, consideration would need to be given to whether his transition from his foster placement could be phased, perhaps with him returning for weekends initially until settled in new accommodation that would need to be appropriate. Indeed, identifying suitable accommodation will be critical for Sam as it is for many young people.
- The assessment of whether Sam is likely to have care and support needs as an adult (CA 2014 s58, s59(1)) should ideally be incorporated into another relevant process, such as a review of his ECHP, thus minimising the need to repeat information. However, this assessment about future needs and wishes must take place at a time that is best for Sam, not simply for the convenience of others.
- If for whatever reason the assessment in relation to care and support needs as an adult is not complete or agreed when Sam reaches 18, then children's services will need to continue to provide the support assessed as being required.
- In addition, his status as a care leaver in these circumstances imposes duties upon the local authority to remain in contact and provide support to Sam up to the age of 25 via a personal adviser (CSWA 2017 s3); this may include financial support during his studies for example.

Further Reading

Holmes, D. and Smale, E. (2018) *Mind the Gap: Transitional Safeguarding – Adolescence to Adulthood*. Dartington: Research in Practice & Research in Practice for Adults. Available at: www.rip. org.uk/resources/publications/strategic-briefings/transitional-safeguarding--adolescence-to-adulthood-strategic-briefing-2018/

Newton, J. A., Harris, T., Hubbard, K. and Craig, T. (2017) Mentoring during the transition from care to prevent depression: care leavers' perspectives, *Practice: Social Work in Action*, 29 (5): 317–30.

The Children's Society (2016) *Barriers and Solutions to Implementing the New Duties in the Care Act 2014 and the Children and Families Act 2014*. London: The Children's Society.

13 Connecting people's lives with strategic planning, commissioning and market shaping

Margaret Flynn and Vic Citarella

Introduction

The Care Act 2014 introduced new provisions concerning prevention, integration, provision of information and advice, and working together strategically and operationally. Further, local authorities as commissioners have responsibility for 'market shaping' care and support provision. Just as in Serious Case Reviews prior to the Act, evidence[1] from subsequent Safeguarding Adults Reviews[2,3] questions the availability of services to meet people's complex needs. Typically, these criticise the inefficient disconnect between commissioning and contract monitoring, between health and social care, and between commissioners and providers. This chapter will explore the Act's impact on these aspects of strategic planning against a sample of reviews the authors have undertaken.

We begin with a story from our work in England, just prior to and since the implementation of the Care Act 2014. Given the magnitude and significance of '*strategic planning, commissioning and market shaping*' we share the interest of people with support needs and those of their families in how these processes work.

The first story concerns Keith. Having left his loving family home with a view to establishing his independence, he lived in 'supported living', that is, in rented accommodation with support from a commissioned provider. Keith had a learning disability, epilepsy and diabetes. Since these are not self-correcting conditions, he was assessed as requiring two visits a day for the specific purpose of ensuring that he took his prescribed, essential medication for epilepsy and diabetes. His family was assured that this assessed 'package of care' was adequate to maintain his health and provide light-touch oversight. For example, although Keith's was fundamentally a task-oriented contract, his family surmised that (i) the service providing the assistance would demonstrate delivery capability and ensure that Keith was in general good health, attending his day service and in cooperative contact with his family; and (ii) the commissioners would sustain and monitor the contract for as long as Keith required assistance in ensuring that he took his medication.

Keith's post-mortem noted *'some self-neglect with very elongated toe nails'*. It emerged that his death was unnoticed by the provider for several days until his family alerted them to his unaccustomed silence. His 'case' had been closed 12 months earlier by the Community Learning Disability Team. The daily visiting records barely acknowledged the purpose of their visits. It was unclear when Keith ceased to take his prescribed medication. Neither the provider service nor Keith had requested repeat medication from his GP. Since Keith's reading skills were limited, he was reliant on support workers to ensure that medical and all other appointments were kept. Because Keith was not alerted to correspondence concerning medical screening, he was not supported to attend and he was de-registered from the medical practice.

On paper, the local authority defined the type, conditions and intensity of services for Keith. It acted as his agent and as a steward of the public purse. Possibly due to the size of the contract – two visits a day – the local authority limited its oversight to an annual review and the contract was renewed without scrutiny. As Care Quality Commission (CQC) inspection of support at home tends to be limited to scrutiny of policies and procedures rather than the individual's care package, the unmerited confidence in Keith's contract effectively transferred quality control and accountability to the provider. Had attention been paid to the performance of the provider, the 'hard data' of daily records would have revealed that Keith's medication was infrequently mentioned, suggesting that the terms and requirement of the contract were not being met. Moreover, had the deployment of the provider's workforce been questioned, an inconsistent visiting pattern would have been revealed.

Although Keith's death pre-dated the introduction of the Care Act 2014, his circumstances underline a service provider attribute that exercises safeguarding reviews. CQC is responsible for the inspection of the whole service and in 'support at home' is limited to where the registered service indicates they are providing personal care[4] to an individual. It is the commissioner who maintains oversight of the contract for a specific service. In the absence of either detailed inspection or proactive case management then, care planning is provider led. However, there is nothing assured or contingent about a provider's attention to care plans, no matter how detrimental the consequences of setting these aside.

The assessment and obligations under the NHS and Community Care Act 1990[5] were underpinned by Fair Access to Care Services policy guidance on eligibility (Department of Health, 2002), which stated concerning reviews that these should:

- establish how far the services provided have achieved the outcomes set out in the care plan;
- reassess the needs and circumstances of individual service users;

- help determine individuals' continued eligibility for support;
- confirm or amend the current care plan or lead to closure.

It was not clear that Keith's local authority had a pre-determined review cycle or one concerning contract monitoring.

The Care Act 2014 requires the local authorities to: '*(a) keep under review generally care and support plans, and support plans, that it has prepared and (b) on a reasonable request by or on behalf of the adult to whom a care and support plan relates or the carer to whom a support plan relates, review the plan*' (S.27 (1)).

Keith would not have requested a review of his support plan. His family would not have challenged the decision-making of the local authority's Community Learning Disability Team since it trusted the professionals. The hurt, disorientation and frustration of families are further defining features of safeguarding reviews. Drawing on their experiential knowledge of supporting their relatives, they are confused and offended that commissioning decisions and actions, those of contract monitoring and those of providers, turn out to have been so deficient.

Achieving better lives for adults with assessed care and support needs

Although the context of facilitating and shaping commissioning and the 'market' must be grounded in learning from how care and support are provided to individuals, safeguarding adult reviews and their multi-agency 'action plans' are not the most suitable vehicles for achieving better lives for adults with assessed care and support needs. These reviews are partial and highly variable descriptions of a complex whole – regardless of whether they concern individuals or groups of individuals in residential and nursing settings. They are no substitute for effective commissioning, professional case management and assured service providers that are precisely registered and proportionately inspected. Certainly, it is possible for local procedures, practice, communications and training to be improved through a process of review, but it should not be necessary for harm and death to be the stimulants for learning. On a national level the cycle (Clough, 1999) of abuse, scandal and investment (whether this be for additional/alternative services, staffing or learning) remains prevalent.

It should not have required a review to pinpoint the shortcomings in the provision of Keith's care package. It was the service provider that failed Keith, but it was the service commissioner who failed to check that he was receiving the service contracted. Steven Hoskin (Cornwall APC, 2007) was similarly on the margins of social care eligibility criteria. Steven discontinued his weekly support from social care that had envisaged he would seek assistance when he needed to do so. He was murdered by people he believed to be his friends. Keith's death resulted from a negligent system. The support aspirations of the Care Act 2014 are unlikely to benefit individuals who are perceived as requiring modest support in terms of scale and intensity.

There are examples of safeguarding reviews reminding local authorities and Clinical Commissioning Groups of what the legislation requires of them.[6] For example, the following edited recommendations arose from the untimely deaths of two adults with learning disabilities from complications arising from constipation.

> *It is recommended that Suffolk's Safeguarding Adults Board[7]*
>
> i. *is assured by Suffolk CC and the CCGs that all 18+ adults with learning disabilities and complex support needs have a named care co-ordinator and that their health and social care needs are jointly reviewed on at least an annual basis. Such reviews should always consider whether an assessment for continuing health care is required;*
>
> ii. *is assured that named care coordinators work within structures that facilitate professional interdependence, recognise the value of complementary professional skills and encourage collaboration, most particularly with people's families or representatives;*
>
> iii. *is assured that care coordination is supported by record keeping and information sharing across professionals and services and that people's families or representatives are regularly consulted;*
>
> iv. *is assured that the CCGs commission a service that includes (i) the support of people with learning disabilities who have additional complex support needs, including health care needs and (ii) the provision of expert advice to generic services such as supported living, district nursing and primary care to address the disadvantaged health status of people with learning disabilities as compared with the general population and their significantly reduced lifespan which is associated with high rates of unmet health needs;*
>
> v. *is assured that its policies do not supersede the duty of care of health and social care professionals or their responsibility to assess and review the needs of individuals with complex support needs;*
>
> vi. *is assured by service providers that their training strategies on the Mental Capacity Act 2005 are credible and attentive to day to day decision making such as diet, as well as in relation to invasive treatments such as anal stretching, including how such decisions are recorded and collated and when these should be escalated for a clinical and professional assessment, for example;*
>
> vii. *is assured that health and social care commissioners have systems in place that ensure that contracts with providers address individual transfers i.e. if an adult moves*

between settings, or becomes the responsibility of a new provider, there is a formal transfer of documentation, explicitly describing their health care needs, and a verbal briefing to ensure that their support needs are fully understood;

viii. *engages with the Learning Disability Partnership Board and explains why it may wish to reconsider the promotion and use of Health Action Plans and instead explore how primary care might better fulfil their clinical responsibilities for supporting people with complex needs living in community settings;*

ix. *is assured that health and social care commissioners encourage support staff to (i) measure and record the waist and hip measurements of adults (most particularly those who are known to experience constipation and/or are prescribed phenothiazines) and (ii) to raise any changes or other concerns about weight or weight distribution during health checks and routine consultations.*

It appears that the purpose of safeguarding has been subverted to setting out (a) what it is that providers, service commissioners, contract monitors and inspectors should be doing anyway, in addition to (b) the remit, powers and enforcement resources of the organisations concerned.

This diagnosis accounts for the considerable reach of safeguarding activities and prompts the question: why is this not obvious enough to have been remedied? Perhaps the answer resides in a blend of answers to additional questions:

- Was the use of the term 'vulnerable adult' (which does not feature in the Care Act) needlessly distracting because it displaced the responsibility of others onto the individual?

- Was Fair Access to Care (Department of Health, 2002) the main culprit because it permitted services to be limited to people with 'critical' support needs whereas 'abuse and neglect' only constituted 'substantial needs'?

- Was it the 'No Secrets: Guidance on developing and implementing multi-agency policies and procedures to protect vulnerable adults from abuse' (Department of Health, 2000)? This only attended to adults who were in need of community care services who were also unable to protect themselves from significant harm and exploitation.

- Was it the complicated dovetailing with which process-driven adult protection arrangements had to 'fit' with law enforcement, inspection, professional regulation, clinical governance, complaints and internal disciplinary processes?

- Or was it the unwillingness of the Westminster government to give the regulator an investigatory role, in hand with its powers of entry and power to close failing homes and regulated social care services?

The prevailing review methodologies are designed to 'learn lessons' at multi-professional and agency levels. We detect an associated mood of fatigue, which is not new, because these 'lessons learned' are not in fact resolving anything in a permanent way. It seems to us that, despite hectoring recommendations, rarely are the systemic concerns around commissioning, the nature of the market and its regulation the subject of embedded change[8],[9]. What is achieved is often dependent on individual champions, soon eroded by an unreceptive climate, as well as fragile and short-lived organisational memories.

SARs may be launched with a positive mission to learn but encounter defensive attitudes and behaviours including unconstructive criticism and professional censure. The information that professionals and organisations are prepared to put in the public domain is incomplete or only extracted over extended and bureaucratic timescales. Reviews that hinge on 'learning lessons' are not the most effective ways of solving the problems of planning, commissioning and regulation that are associated with wretched and harmful events. Although we do not dismiss what it is that they reveal, neither can we ignore what it is that they overlook.

It is our opinion that the recommendations from SARs and the associated action planning are frequently unable to remedy the long-established inclination to express solutions to historical events in individualistic, partial and local organisational terms.

A tentative conclusion is that the answers lie in a better application of theory[10] around what is known, knowable, complex and sometimes chaotic in the systems where abuse and neglect occur: that is in families, communities, institutions and organisations. Legislation and regulations create the climate where this can happen but what reviews identify is a need to reassert the primacy of professional leadership, most particularly among social workers and nurses. In addition, such leadership is essential at the helm in social care in the guise of the registered manager. It is only here that lessons can be truly learned and handed on to future generations, with accountability to be readily demonstrated by people in the know rather than through reviewers. A lesson arising from children's services is that a 'serious' review is of national import and should be commissioned as such, whereas the process of practice reflection and review ought to be a routine, rapid and local matter (Department for Education, 2018).

Winterbourne View and Mendip House

What then have we learned about strategic planning from undertaking SARs since the Care Act 2014? We have ceased to include a 'lessons learned' section in reviews and now write of 'lessons identified'. Patently surveys of case reviews[11] – a process that continues – strongly suggest that lessons are not being learned since identical errors are repeated. We conclude that the process of reviewing, of itself, is not conducive to system learning since it focuses on *what* has gone wrong rather than *why*.[12]

Some clues to whether breakdown or recovery is to result from reviewing the circumstances in which adults with care and support needs are harmed are revealed by reviews on Winterbourne View Hospital in South Gloucestershire[13] and Mendip House in Somerset.[14]

For example, it is significant that the origin of Winterbourne View Hospital was not based on a local population needs assessment. Its owner, Castlebeck Ltd, spotted a business opportunity and was not discouraged by NHS commissioners. They had indicated their willingness to buy Castlebeck's services – for adults with learning disabilities, autism and mental health problems for whom placements were difficult to find – irrespective of national policy and guidance. The review endorsed the title of the *Panorama* TV broadcast 'Undercover Care: the Abuse Exposed' and the broadcast's assertion that it represented 'a huge failure at the heart of our system of care'. What was clear was that the apparatus of oversight across sectors was unequal to the task of uncovering the fact and extent of abuses and crimes at this hospital.

The NHS commissioners responsible for the placements believed that they were purchasing a bespoke service, yet there was no overall leadership among commissioners. They did not press for, or receive, detailed accounts of how Winterbourne View Hospital was spending the weekly fees (the average of which was £3,500 in 2011) on behalf of its patients, and neither did they request information concerning the outcomes or even destinations of former patients (for example, whether they returned to their pre-placement addresses or moved to other Castlebeck facilities). Even though the hospital was not meeting its contractual requirements in terms of the levels of supervision provided to individual patients, commissioners persisted in their 'place-hunting' by continuing to put people there. Neither self-advocates nor people's families, whose relatives were in crisis, could influence the placement decisions of commissioners. Although some commissioners funded advocacy services, Winterbourne View Hospital controlled patients' access to these. Castlebeck did not respond to evidence of the harmful restraints of patients. Winterbourne View Hospital strayed far from its stated purpose of assessment, treatment and rehabilitation. The hospital's management was discontinuous, its staff were unskilled, and staffing levels were inadequate. Absconding patients and escalating self-injurious behaviour were not perceived as evidence of a failing service, and the documented concerns of a whistleblower made no difference at this unnoticing environment.

Winterbourne View Hospital's patients were chronically under-protected. Among the recommendations (which were discussed with the Department of Health) was: 'Organisations providing NHS funded care should be required to demonstrate accountability for effective governance to commissioners and Council Adult Safeguarding' (Flynn and Citarella, 2012). It was *Private Eye's* forensic accountancy that revealed what Castlebeck had not shared with the review:

> The company that owns Winterbourne View, Castlebeck is itself part of a group called CB Care Ltd, which is itself owned, via Jersey, by Swiss-based private equity group, Lydian, backed by a group of Irish billionaires. The price of private equity is that all the money gets whipped out by the bankers and offshore owners and as soon as possible. So ... while CB Care makes healthy operating profits these disappear in interest payments, leaving the group hefty annual losses and, on latest figures, liabilities exceeding assets by £14m.

> *This could pose difficulties for anyone choosing to sue the company over the abuse, who might hope it has decent insurance …The Care Quality Commission … {confirmed} that for private providers, there is no provision to require insurance…So while private equity owners scoop the profits, it looks like taxpayers could end up having to pay for private care fiascos* (Private Eye, 2012: 31)

In turn, *Private Eye* confirmed our sense that pressures to meet impossible profit targets overwhelmed restraints against dishonesty.

The ambitions of values-based commissioning (Heginbotham, 2012) signalled part of the search for more efficient ways of closely connecting individual care and support needs with service commissioning – most particularly since there is too much distance between commissioning/ place-hunting and people's person- and relationship-centred plans. There are rarely tidy endings. The Department of Health's Transforming Care Programme (costing over £10m – end date March 2019) has not delivered the promised reduction in reliance on inpatient care following the Winterbourne View Hospital scandal.[15] There is no incentive for commercially provided, specialist inpatient care to discharge patients and retain empty beds.

The inspectorate, the Care Quality Commission, did deliver *Registering the Right Support* (CQC, 2017) as policy guidance on registration and variations to registration for providers supporting people with a learning disability and/or autism. It covers the new and changed registrations of care homes, specialist hospitals and supported living. It serves to regulate the types of services required in the community as a result of closing inpatient hospital beds. It is based on principles for commissioning good services which include 'quality of life, keeping people safe, and choice and control'. In the guidance the presumption of small services, 'usually accommodating six or less', appears to be the primary impact. It is leading some providers to switch to other, younger adult, provision such as mental health and physical disability. Significantly, there is no such consideration of the possible benefits of small group living for older adults who are typically required to seek accommodation and care in large institutions. So, however much strategic planners promote good design and positive values, these are trumped by economies of scale and the pull of cutting costs, making it harder for both practising commissioners and providers to keep people safe.

The case set out by Sir Roy Griffiths (and eventually enshrined in the NHS and Community Care Act 1990) for outsourcing services from the public sector was not an argument for either yielding all control to businesses or paying providers and businesses, irrespective of how they undertook to provide care and support. It intended to promote the 'mixed economy' as a challenge to quality across public, voluntary and private sectors. As a result, the public sector care provider has been decimated and the smaller enterprise (voluntary and business) sectors operate in an increasingly inimical environment.

As Hudson (2018) noted: '*Outsourcing public services, especially to the private sector, has been the model of choice in the UK for around 30 years. Nowhere has this been more the case than in adult social care, where private companies account for the vast majority of provision in both the care home and homecare market ... From the collapse of Southern Cross in 2011 to the handing back of contracts, the model is struggling. In addition, scandals such as Winterbourne View, the Morleigh Group in Cornwall and Mendip House are far from isolated incidents.'*

The intention of the Care Act 2014[16] in terms of strategic planning, commissioning and market shaping (section 5) creates a general duty for local authorities to promote diversity and quality in the market of care and support providers for people in their local area. Key messages are the requirements for variety, high quality and information on which to base choices. The section places a duty on local authorities to plan for the demand and supply of care provision, efficiently, effectively and sustainably fostering improvement and innovation. It recognises the importance of the workforce in this undertaking. Subsequent sections address provider failure (48–52) and market oversight (53–57).

Uncoordinated place-hunting clearly has no part in achieving effective services or promoting diversity and quality of provision; yet this gap between legislation, associated policy and practice has a long history. People with care and support needs, most particularly those with compromised communication, are neither consumers nor happy shoppers. The faith in the market and regulatory torpor is most evidently misplaced when considerations of value for money are raised.[17] There is no evidence that commissioners are ambitious and assertive on behalf of adults with autism for example.

The review in respect of Mendip House (part of a campus development) compelled commissioners and the regulator to take notice of particular forms of 'care and support':

Somerset Safeguarding Adults' Board[18] should recommend that

i.   *the Department of Health, NHS England and the Local Government Association are requested to:*

   o   *prepare consultations to regulate commissioning;*
   o   *include in those consultations the role of 'lead commissioner' who will assume responsibility for coordination when there are multiple commissioning bodies of a single service and assume responsibility for ensuring that individual resident reviews start with principles and make the uniqueness of each person the focus for designing and delivering credible and valued support;*
   o   *include in those consultations the expectation that commissioners must notify the host authority of prospective placements;*
   o   *set out in guidance the remit, powers, structure and enforcement resources of all agencies immersed in the task of achieving better lives for adults with autism;*
   o   *assert a new requirement to discontinue commissioning and registering "campus" models of service provision;*

o   *assert a new requirement for (a) formal consultation with Local Authorities with Social Services responsibilities and CCGs regarding all planning applications for building residential services that would require registration with the CQC to operate, and (b) to decline planning permission for types of service provision for which there is no local demand, and which fail to "think small" and "think community."*[19]

ii. *the Department of Health, NHS England and the Local Government Association be advised of the actions that Somerset County Council intends to take to address the detrimental persistence of "place hunting" by commissioners. That is, to require commissioners to:*

o   *fund essential monitoring and reviewing processes;*
o   *fund residents' access to local health services, most particularly community health services;*
o   *identify a lead commissioner.*

iii. *Since it is unlikely that CQC would register this model of service now, Somerset Safeguarding Adults' Board should write to the CQC requesting that it (a) makes this fact explicit in its inspection reports; (b) undertakes more searching inspections of such services; and (c) does not register "satellite" units which are functionally linked to "campus" models of service provision"* (Flynn, 2018).'

Thus, even after the enactment of the Care Act, the discredited culture of commissioning limps from scandal to scandal. There is little evidence of reinvigoration in planning or care management. Care management is at the sharp end of commissioning. This requires the tools to support service providers to deliver what they have been contracted to do and, if necessary, insist on this without resorting to safeguarding – unless a person is harmed frequently and/or intentionally. At the not so sharp end of commissioning are strategic planning, market development and procurement. These are failing to understand demand and collective need, and how the latter may be met cost effectively and in ways that people want. The question is, does the care represent the interests of the adult with support needs or the funder? If safeguarding is invoked, then this critical question is masked.[20]

Rarely have we undertaken a review where the terms of reference cannot be clustered under four headings: commissioning, care management, the role of the provider and quality assurance. Although the adult safeguarding system is a single aspect of quality assurance, the principles and practices do not permeate through the whole system. Other quality assurance activities are those of the provider, the contractor on behalf of the commissioner and service user, and of the Care Quality Commission on behalf of the public. Figure 13.1 seeks to show this in as simple a format as possible using a care home as an example.

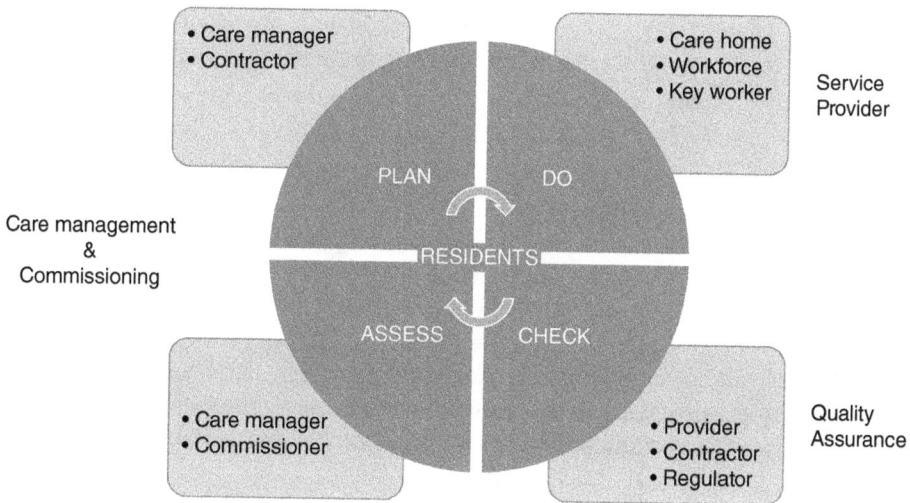

Figure 13.1

Adult safeguarding does not feature in this diagram because it is most commonly invoked when the assess, plan, do and check cycle has broken down for an individual or for all residents. Since tiers of quality assurance processes have been unequal to warning, predicting and preventing harmful practices, adult safeguarding processes cannot feasibly remedy the failings of strategic planning. Keith's family and the families of people with compromised health in South Gloucestershire, Suffolk and Somerset are disbelieving and angry that failures of accountability have not provided the trumpet call to revisiting the Nolan principles:[21] endorsing accredited and competent commissioning as an accountable profession; focusing on local commissioning; ensuring that providers are ethical employers, tax compliant and transparent, that is, with no recourse to 'commercial confidentiality' (Hudson, 2018). Quality assurance systems must be clear of duplication and mixed messages. The commissioner is responsible for checking the service to an individual and the inspector for regulating the whole service. The provider is responsible for supplying what is contracted for in the care plan within the law and regulations under which they are governed.

Great emphasis is given in reviews to setting out *what* was responsible rather than *who* was responsible, because the latter would weaken participation and lead to even more defensive practices. However, what is reasonably sought is accountability – the activity of explaining *why* something was done or not. If this elusive accountability is to be manifested in reviews arising from harm and deaths, then experience suggests that it must be integral to all parts of the system: in strategic planning where joint strategic needs assessments are co-produced with the public; in market development plans which demonstrably reference the contributions of individuals and businesses; in contracts that are understandable to the lay person and are enforceable; and in care plans that are led by people with care and support needs and their families, and are regularly reviewed. It means having service provision that is professionally led, characterised by a purposeful ethos where expectations are agreed and met, and where every adult has a named keyworker and/or advocate. Services should be regulated with greater stress placed on registration and its maintenance. The oversight of services between commissioners and regulators should be a single and coordinated inspection activity.

Conclusion

Adult safeguarding is not just about death and harm but also responses to the unexpected, the unexplained and unacceptable. All of these are the territory of effective case managers and registered managers backed by professional and clinical expertise. There can be no role for adult safeguarding in remedying the shortcomings of strategic planning, commissioning and inspection practices. The commissioning of health and social care services is of national strategic importance and requires regulation. Our experience of reviews confirms the absence of co-production and of case management when it is most needed to make sense of, and deal with, complexity. There is evidence of care providers and commissioners colluding to supply the impossible, using contracts that are unenforceable, and providers over-claiming and over-charging.

The Care Act 2014 is backed by statutory guidance (DHSC, 2018a) that is riddled with all the flaws – jargonistic, ambiguous and opaque in places – revealed about safeguarding policy, procedure and practice in reviews. It is a gargantuan product with countless pages, sections and annexes, reflecting multiple stakeholder interests. It would appear that every stakeholder, vested and special interest has crammed in their two penny-worth. It is not a formula for a straightforward system of accountability that adults and families known to social care, and indeed to safeguarding services, yearn for. Safeguarding cannot break the spell of the status quo.

In *Hope in the Dark*, Rebecca Solnit (2016: xiv) writes: *'Changing the story isn't enough in itself, but it has often been foundational to real changes. Making an injury visible and public is often the first step in remedying it, and political change often follows culture, as what was long tolerated is seen to be intolerable, or what was once overlooked becomes obvious ... '.*

The Care Act 2014 does change the safeguarding story and this reflection on our contributions through reviews glimpses the harm and neglect we have considered. Even though there is no statutory requirement, our reviews have been published in their entirety. Our fear is that the unacceptable is being accepted as the public becomes desensitised. Our hope is that by stubbornly demanding an answer to why such harms reoccur, we may cease to overlook the obvious.

Case study: a model for commissioning

Having continued to work with commissioning authorities that are emerging from the shadows of scandals, we propose a model of working that offers illuminating insights. These are:

- networks of purposeful leaders who want to provide concrete evidence that 'we can do better than this!'
- curiosity about how the barriers to better services are being lowered and removed in other places;
- fact-finding and learning about the aspirations of new parents and of the partners and families of people with new diagnoses, and about the aspirations of people who have not sampled many services and of those who have graduated from too many services;
- setting out the implications of fact-finding into principles and values;
- grounding authority-wide planning and assessments in quantitative data and in what is being learned from small-scale provision locally. For example, short-term funding plus specialist support is reaping successes in closing off the real possibility of individuals being transferred to 'more secure' provider services. Such 'micro lessons' are rooted in individual experience and a growing understanding of what it is that families are seeking over the life course;
- the toothless tigers of 'contract compliance monitoring' are re-aligned to aid case management. They start from 'ends' and are interested in a person's day-to-day experience of the 'means';
- a visceral feel for case management over time, and working knowledge of an individual's place in their relationships and community and of the opportunities and supports they value;
- advising the providers that a better 'fit' is required between what is required and what is provided. Disinvestment is painful, as the closure of long-stay hospitals has shown, but a new generation of provision is necessary.

Although the resource context is not promising, this is not an ideological tide which can be held back.

Further Reading

Citarella, V. (2017) *Developing Effective Commissioner and Service Provider Relationships. Strategic Briefing.* Dartington: Research in Practice for Adults.

Needham, C., Burn, E., Hall, K., McKay, S., Mangan, C., Allen, K. Henwood, M., Carr, S. and Glasby, J. (2018) *Shifting Shapes: Report of Work Package 1 – National Interviews, Local Authority Survey and Secondary Data Analysis.* Birmingham: University of Birmingham Health Services Management Centre.

Needham, C., Hall, K., Allen, K. Burn, E., Mangan, C. and Henwood, M. (2018) *Market Shaping and Personalisation in Social Care: A Realist Synthesis of the Literature*. Birmingham: University of Birmingham Health Services Management Centre.

Notes

1. See for example: What difference does legislation make? Adult safeguarding through the lens of Serious Case Reviews and Safeguarding Adult Reviews. A report for South West region Safeguarding Adults Boards, Michael Preston-Shoot, October 2017.

2. Section 44 of the Care Act 2014.

3. Safeguarding Adults Boards (SABs) must arrange a Safeguarding Adult Review when an adult in its area dies as a result of abuse or neglect, whether known or suspected, and there is concern that partner agencies could have worked more effectively to protect the adult (Care Act Guidance 14.162). SABs must also arrange a Safeguarding Adult Review if an adult in its area has not died, but the SAB knows or suspects that the adult has experienced serious abuse or neglect (14.163).

4. 'Personal care' means: (The Health and Social Care Act 2008 (Regulated Activities) Regulations 2014)

    (a) physical assistance given to a person in connection with:

    i. eating or drinking (including the maintenance of established parenteral nutrition),
    ii. toileting (including in relation to the process of menstruation),
    iii. washing or bathing,
    iv. dressing,
    v. oral care, or
    vi. the care of skin, hair and nails (with the exception of nail care provided by a person registered with the Health and Care Professions Council as a chiropodist or podiatrist pursuant to article 5 of the 2001 Order), or

    (b) the prompting, together with supervision, of a person, in relation to the performance of any of the activities listed in paragraph (a), where that person is unable to make a decision for themselves in relation to performing such an activity without such prompting and supervision.

5. Legislation that, among other things, made the state an enabler rather than a provider of care services and brought the roles of strategic planning and commissioning in the 'market' to the fore prior to the Care Act 2014.

6. Care Act 2014: http://www.legislation.gov.uk/ukpga/2014/23/part/1/crossheading/safeguarding-adults-at-risk-of-abuse-or-neglect/enacted (accessed 18/12/18).

7. The reports regarding 'Amy' and 'James' appear on the Suffolk Safeguarding Adults Board website along with notes about constipation and compromised health status. There is a response report and a strategic action plan. The latter includes a Policy Standards Matrix which poses the question, among others, *If the policy or procedure relates to commissioning, is it clear that adults at risk have been considered as part of the commissioning process?*

8. The practical implications of 'how to create sustainable change' are addressed in Preston-Shoot, M. (2018) 'Learning from safeguarding adult reviews on self-neglect: addressing the challenge of change', *Journal of Adult Protection,* 20 (2). Notable is the absence of a comprehensive national database of SARs.

9. Editor's footnote: SARs rarely make recommendations to the Department of Health and Social Care, despite the fact that shortcomings in commissioning and regulatory enforcement require national rather than local action.

10. See for example: Annabelle Mark and David Snowden, *Researching Practice or Practicing Research: Innovating Methods in Healthcare - The Contribution of Cynefin* (Palgrave, 2006).

11. See for example: Clay, S. (2014) *A decade of Serious Case Reviews, Hull Safeguarding Adults Partnership Board, and the continuing analysis of safeguarding reviews undertaken by Kings College.* London: Social Care Workforce Research Unit.

12. Michael Preston-Shoot reflects on this and adds to the growing thematic analysis of SARs in his articles for the *Journal of Adult Protection* in 2016, 2017 and 2018. See www.scie-socialcareonline.org.uk/search?q=author_name:%22preston-shoot%22 (accessed 19/12/18).

13. http://sites.southglos.gov.uk/safeguarding/adults/i-am-a-carerrelative/winterbourne-view/

14. https://ssab.safeguardingsomerset.org.uk/wp-content/uploads/20180206_Mendip-House_SAR_FOR_PUBLICATION.pdf

15. During October 2018, NHS Digital confirmed that there were 2,350 people with learning disabilities and/or autism in inpatient units; 250 of these people were under 18 years; there were 125 admissions during October 2018; and the average length of stay in these units is five years and four months.

16. See *Get in on the Act: The Care Act 2014* from the Local Government Association (2014) for a succinct summary.

17. The Public Services (Social Value) Act 2012 requires public sector commissioning to 'have regard to' economic, social and environmental wellbeing; see also www.inspiringimpact.org/ (accessed 24 November 2018); and Moore, M.H. (1995) *Creating Public Value: Strategic Management in Government.* Cambridge, MA: Harvard University Press.

18. It was suggested at the Safeguarding Adults' Board meeting of 7 December 2017 that other Adults' Boards in the South West and Healthwatch England may wish to be associated with this request.

19. This was suggested by the Safeguarding Adults' Board meeting on 7 December 2017.

20. Safeguarding processes are founded on the binary association of victim and perpetrator. By identifying the perpetrator as the 'system' it disperses and distorts accountability. Whilst it is the care provider (or their staff) that may have perpetrated harm and neglect it is in the interests of the purchaser of the sub-standard service to distribute responsibility for this around the system through the safeguarding processes. We have advocated, for some time now, the greater use of

consumer and contract legislation by commissioners as an appropriate response to harmful services. However, this necessitates intelligent commissioners and active case and/or contract management. See: 'In Search of Accountability; a review of the neglect of older people living in care homes investigated as Operation Jasmine', Margaret Flynn, Welsh Government (2016), as a study in blurred accountability.

21. Selflessness, integrity, objectivity, accountability, openness, honesty and leadership.

14 Social work and the Care Act 2014

Jill Manthorpe

Introduction

In this final chapter we explore some of the implications for social work of the implementation of the Care Act 2014. Implementation is an art and a science that has generally been overlooked in social work education but there is increasing interest in what helps or hinders getting good ideas into practice, why some policy goals turn out to have elements of ambiguity, and what conflicts arise in implementation of legal reforms. This chapter addresses some of the provisions of the Act's Guidance where social work is mentioned specifically and considers them in the light of implementation. Personalisation has moved beyond its own early implementation stages and the social work role here in regard to the Care Act is explored using work with homeless people as an example. Implementation evidence includes material from the courts and Local Government Ombudsman decisions and research on social work practice under the Act (excluding safeguarding and carers' support which are covered in earlier chapters) since there are as yet not many research findings. Emerging good practice is addressed; with the apology that all of this must by necessity be covered briefly – all probably merit a chapter or even a future book on their own. The chapter concludes with a plea for effectiveness to be mentioned more assertively in social work practice and commissioning, since, whatever the state of public expenditure and private contributions, social work needs to make the case for effectiveness and not leave such claims to others.

This chapter draws strongly on the Care Act Guidance edition published in October 2018 (DHSC, 2018a). Readers are reminded that other editions may be forthcoming and that future case law may affect some of the points discussed.

Social work uncertainties

In 2018 the James Lind Alliance Priority Setting Exercise for Adult Social Work produced its list of research priorities or uncertainties (James Lind Alliance, 2018). Top of the list were:

- How is availability of funding impacting on (a) adult social workers' practice and (b) the decisions made?

- What impact is the Care Act having on (a) adult social work practice and (b) the outcomes for people using services and their carers, particularly their wellbeing and safety?

- How is 'wellbeing' understood and incorporated into adult social work practice? How can we assess whether adult social workers impact on the wellbeing of people using services?

The James Lind Alliance approach combines the shared interests of service users, carers and practitioners (though traditionally it has had more of a healthcare focus). As a result, questions that these groups all consider important are discussed and prioritised, rather than what researchers like to research. The James Lind Alliance process of consultation has made a unique and important contribution to social work research in being co-produced and reflective of social work values. It is one of the building blocks of establishing more evidence for the effectiveness of adult social work (Manthorpe and Moriarty, 2016) and its focus on the Care Act shows that there is widespread interest in the potential of the Act and a strong desire to know what is happening and what needs to change.

The Care Act 2014 and social work

There are several mentions of social work and social workers in the Care Act 2014 and the Statutory Guidance (Department of Health and Social Care, 2018a), as noted in previous chapters. However, many practitioners are reporting that the radical changes promised are not turning out to be so transformative. They are not alone in this; for example, parliamentarians made many claims that the Act would be a major gain for family carers (as catalogued by Manthorpe et al., 2019), but some early evidence shows that the level of 'substantial change' predicted (Barnes et al., 2017) is not so profound. Whittington (2016a) had predicted that the level and substance of change might be over-claimed, asking if the anticipated 'liberations' of the Care Act were turning out to be a genuine prospect or false prospectus.

What often occurs is that discussion of the Care Act becomes swept up in the context of cuts in local authority resources (more generally termed 'austerity') and the implications of this for the lives of users and carers, social work practice, provision and decision-making. Indeed, the need to be mindful of money is explicit; the Statutory Guidance notes that:

> *In determining how to meet needs, the local authority may also take into reasonable consideration its own finances and budgetary position and must comply with its related public law duties.* (DHSC, 2018a: para 10.27)

The context of austerity is troubling to social workers at many levels and the James Lind Alliance priorities highlighted above were no surprise. They reflect a chorus of concern that it is hard to square the circle of demand and resources, still less to promote the aspirations of the Act to place wellbeing, not eligibility, at the heart of public support for individuals. As Allan (2015: 4) predicted, trying to maintain a 'sustainable, diverse, social care market in a time of austerity will be a careful balancing act'. Indeed, Slasberg and Beresford (2017a) have argued that there remain fundamental problems with eligibility following the Care Act, describing it as neither person-centred nor financially sustainable for local authorities.

At the time of writing, the funding gap in social care overall is well recognised and a Green Paper outlining possible options for reform is awaited. However, any changes are likely to take time and may affect future cohorts rather than current service users and carers. Meanwhile, in respect of the Care Act concerns have come from the highest levels about current pressures, with the Chief Social Worker for Adults declaring:

> Implementing the Care Act has been a significant challenge for local government and has taken place in the context of unprecedented financial and resource pressures. Understandably, however, there is growing concern that the lack of funding for adult social care is undermining councils' ability to meet their statutory responsibilities under the Act. (Romeo, 2017: 10)

While the National Audit Office (2018b: 12) found that between 2010–11 and 2016–17, local authority spending on adult social care services had reduced by 3.3% in real terms and social care expenditure has been relatively protected, for many social workers there is a feeling of being under enormous financial pressure and the realities of the funding gap in the context of austerity feature prominently in professional and employer debates. One particular pressure point seems to be the requirement to tell people that their needs are not eligible for publicly funded care and support (backed up with information and advice) – with Age UK (2017b) estimating that 1.2 million people over the age of 65 had some level of unmet care needs in 2016–17, up from 1 million in 2015–16. The other is the substantial pressure on enabling people 'stranded' in hospital to move to social care or back home, meaning that hospital social work is becoming a task for many working in community-based teams as well as traditional hospital social work (Moriarty et al., 2019).

Pressures can often be generalised and accounts of practice make them more fine-grained. In one of the few detailed accounts of practice in a local authority under the Care Act 2014 so far, the Social Care Institute for Excellence (SCIE, 2016: 15) presented a picture of frontline social work activity, including for example the observation that:

> There is a general recognition by operational managers that staffing levels are tight. Staff would welcome more time from managers to support them. Most members of staff felt too much valuable time was spent for example inputting on Care First and approval was needed for too many decisions.

Indeed some social workers may have internalised the language of 'cuts' so powerfully that it affects their communications with potential service users. Belinda Schwehr (2018), director of CASCAIDr, has summarised where in her opinion local authorities are going wrong in their implementation of the Care Act, top of her list being:

> *People's expectations being managed downwards by the front line being allowed (or instructed?) to be gloomy about the future*
>
> *This tendency presents as the message, before a decision has been taken under the Care Act, or before a review has been finished, to the effect that there have 'got to be cuts'.*
>
> *In legal terms, this loose language could indicate predetermination or a fetter of assessment or care planning discretion; it could indicate a disregard of the principle that resources are relevant to how needs must be met, but not to whether.*

This is supported by the Local Government and Social Care Ombudsman's (2018) overview report, which noted the ways in which efforts to restrain expenditure were affecting frontline staff as well as managers. It called upon local authorities to ensure frontline staff are suitably informed to advise service users effectively, drawing on its experience of upholding complaints that found:

> *Major changes in policies, thresholds and charging can be poorly communicated to frontline staff. We have found cases in fostering and adult social care where crucial changes to services, with significant financial implications for service users, have been made without involving frontline staff – leaving staff unable to guide people towards decisions in their best interests. Our investigations have found these failures to communicate involving managers as well as frontline staff. To address these issues, councils typically agree to improve handbooks, guidance notices and provide regular training for frontline staff.* (2018: 9)

While this may be hard in the context of funding gaps, this chapter now moves to a synthesis and commentary on a selection of areas of practice of substantial importance in the Care Act and its Statutory Guidance[1] where social workers may be involved. (In this section the social work/worker mentions made in the Guidance have been put in **bold**.) As noted above, some sections are not covered as they are addressed elsewhere in this volume.

Statutory Guidance – the search for social work

The first mentions of social work in the October 2018 edition of the *Care and Support Statutory Guidance* (DHSC, 2018a) relate not to Care Act activity *per se* but to the role of the Principal Social Worker (1.27–1.31). Such prominence highlights the value of this role within local authority organisational hierarchies and may be helpful in any attempts to possibly dilute it. In many ways it serves as a job description for the role and could also be used for such purposes as leadership coaching or inter-professional benchmarking. As Whittington (2016b) observed, the new addition of these sections to the 2016 second edition of the statutory Guidance was significant both as a symbolic position and as one having an operational remit. Indeed, he described its inclusion as making a 'potential contribution to social work's renaissance'.

Social work and others (is there a distinction?)

In several parts of the Act and its guidance **social work** is mentioned but so too are other professionals, almost interchangeably. Part of the challenge in locating specific social work roles or duties is the widespread use in the Guidance of the local authority as a 'being', for example, 'The local authority must support people to make informed, affordable and sustainable financial decisions about their care throughout all stages of their life' (DHSC, 2018a: 3.46).

In respect of prevention, mention of social work is made in the company of a large number of other groups:

> *Social workers, occupational therapists, other professionals, service providers and commissioners who are effective at preventing, reducing, or delaying needs for care and support are likely to have a holistic picture of the individuals and families receiving support. This will include consideration of a person's strengths and their informal support networks as well as their needs and the risks they face. This approach recognises the value in the resources of voluntary and community groups and the other resources of the local area.* (DHSC, 2018a: para 2.22)

However, the specialist role of social work does appear in the Guidance section on assessment (though the addition of 'registered' is a curious and possibly redundant addition):

> *To provide a comprehensive assessment, the assessor must be appropriately trained.* **Registered social workers** *and occupational therapists can provide important support and may be involved in complex assessments which indicate a wide range of needs, risks and strengths that may require a coordinated response from a variety of statutory and community services. Or they may be involved at the point of first contact to advise on whether preventative services would be more appropriate at that time.* (DHSC, 2018a: para 6.7)

Of note here is the term 'complex', meaning that there are many components to consider not that a problem is complicated (complicated meaning that something is difficult but not necessarily having several components). Health service professionals are increasingly using the term 'complexity' to refer to older people with multiple and interacting conditions, and it seems highly appropriate to many social work activities even if one is not a proponent of complexity theory (although a good case can be made for the relevance of this theory; see Fish and Hardy, 2015).

Moreover, staff who are often the first point of contact for individuals need to know how to access social workers:

> Staff who are involved in this first contact must have the appropriate training and should have the benefit of access to professional support from **social workers,** occupational therapists and other relevant experts as appropriate, to support the identification of any underlying conditions or to ensure that complex needs are identified early and that people are signposted appropriately. (DHSC, 2018a: para 6.27)

This back-up role for social workers is emphasised in respect of seriousness of needs – here with reference to people possibly lacking decision-making capacity:

> The more serious the needs, the more support people may need to identify their impact and the consequences. Professional qualified staff, such as **social workers,** can advise and support assessors when they are carrying out an assessment with a person who may lack capacity. (DHSC, 2018a: para 6.32)

Overall, and in a slightly disjointed section of the 2018 Guidance, the roles and responsibilities of social workers, occupational therapists and rehabilitation officers are stated thus:

> Assessments can be carried out by a range of professionals including **registered social workers,** occupational therapists and rehabilitation officers. **Registered social workers** and occupational therapists are considered to be 2 of the key professions in adult care and support. Local authorities should consider how adults who need care, carers, and assessors have access to registered social care practitioners, such as **social workers** or occupational therapists. (DHSC, 2018a: para 6.84)

Finally, in this section the role of social work in decision-making, support and review of personal budgets is mentioned but these activities are mentioned as being appropriate to others. The Guidance notes that under planned reviews these may be conducted with a social worker but equally that a social worker may not be necessary; indeed involving a social worker might be seen as rather exceptional:

> Local authorities should have regard to ensuring the planned review is proportionate to the circumstances, the value of the personal budget and any risks identified. In a similar way to care and support or support planning, there should be a range of review options available, which may include self-review, peer-led review, reviews conducted remotely, or face to face reviews with a social worker or other relevant professional. For example, where the person has a stable, longstanding support package with fixed or long-term outcomes,

they may wish to complete a self-review at the planned time which is then submitted to the local authority to sign-off, rather than have a face to face review with their social worker. (DHSC, 2018a: para 13.16)

Market shaping and commissioning of adult care and support (a social work service)

Here **social work** is listed as a service, not as a role facilitating information, assessment or planning. It is also differentiated from counselling, information, advocacy and advice (DHSC, 2018a: para 4.44).

Social workers as stakeholders

Of course, when describing the role of social work those holding this professional qualification are found at several positions within local authorities, from the frontline of first contacts and assessments to high-level managerial and leadership roles, including Principal Social Workers. Thus social workers are to be involved in the market-shaping duties of local authorities and in developing local strategies, while **social workers (and their representative organisations)** are also included in the long list of 'stakeholders' who should be consulted about local provision (alongside 'care and support managers') (DHSC, 2018a: para 4.54). This requires a form of policy or administrative literacy, for example in knowing what is the form and purpose of a Joint Strategic Needs Assessment (JSNA) and a Market Position Statement or equivalent document.

Social work – from 'being' advocates to arranging them

In one of the few case studies involving a social worker in the 2018 edition of the *Care Act Guidance* (DHSC, 2018a: para 7.16), that of Stephen, the social worker is described as recognising the need for advocacy during her assessment of Stephen:

> The **social worker** judges that because Stephen lacks insight into his personal relationships and future plans, he may well also have trouble estimating his true care and support needs. At this point the **social worker** decides that Stephen would have substantial difficulty in being fully involved in the rest of the assessment process and would therefore benefit from assistance … The **social worker** talks to Stephen about how an independent advocate could help him make sure his views, beliefs, wishes and aspirations are taken into account in the assessment and, with his agreement, arranges for an independent advocate with specialist brain injury training to support him.

This then seems the professional task: to consider people's right to an advocate, which as this case example conveys may well be associated with complex and possibly conflictual situations.

Implementation questions?

So, is there a problem with social work under the Care Act, and if so, is it one of basic design or implementation failure? Or has implementation been derailed by inherent conflicts between delivering its aspirations and working within a funding gap? As Hupe and Hill (2016) have commented, implementation often gets short shrift compared to policy formulation and it is only then that the conflicts and ambiguities emerge. As noted above, the Guidance gives substantial scope for local authorities to design and deploy their workforce how they want and need. The key role highlighted for social work appears to lie in contributing to assessments involving complexity. However, the local authority has many responsibilities and social workers appear to be the profession that is *de facto* carrying many of them out on its behalf.

There are several claims that implementation in the context of funding gaps is the obstacle to realising the ambitions of the Care Act; in other words two policy goals stand in conflict and social workers may be at the nexus of these. For example, details are beginning to emerge of the operationalisation of funding panels and their impact on social work practice. Community Care (2017) found that 75% of local authorities had a funding panel with one third of them having no financial threshold in place for a case to come to them for decision making (that is, they were not confined to complex or expensive care packages), although a quarter had a threshold of £500+. Later, a further Community Care (Carter, 2018) Freedom of Information request and survey (431 respondents) concluded that local authority funding panels are being used by managers beyond their intended purpose, as set out in the Care Act Statutory Guidance, and some were overriding social workers' recommendations (which of course would be the point of having them if they were set up to consider the quality of the decision).

Such panels pre-date the Care Act so it is only fair to try to disentangle what is directly attributable to the Act and what is contextual; even if they were not called panels they functioned in many localities under different labels, such as scrutiny, quality assurance, weekly resource, care authorisation and adult social care finance panels. What is emerging is a picture of them being used for routine decision-making or authorisation rather than offering an overview in complex cases and ensuring fairness and consistency when commissioning or funding expensive care packages. For example, Community Care found 60 local authorities with panels had terms of reference for them but these were sometimes poorly worded, e.g. 'needs not being met are critical', and some seemed to contradict statutory guidance, e.g. 'No more than 14 days respite per year'. Outwith the operation of panels the Ombudsman had earlier upheld a complaint that a local authority had placed a limit of four weeks to the respite it would fund (LGSCO and Knowsley MBC (2016)), while in another case it appeared that there was a blanket maximum local limit of two days respite provision (LGSCO and Bromley LBC (2017)).

Turning back to panels, an earlier example of their operation was provided in the Local Government and Social Care Ombudsman (2016) report which commented that local authorities should aim for panels to be used as an exception, 'if at all', and also noted that the then Care Act guidance had stated that local authorities should refrain from 'using panels that seek to amend planning decisions, micromanage the planning process or are in place purely for financial reasons'. As the Local Government and Social Care Ombudsman (LGSCO, 2018c: 13) commented in its overview thematic report on recent complaints:

> *Councils, like all large organisations, undergo frequent restructures. Pressures have increased the scale and pace of change with restructuring designed to reduce waste, overheads and improve ability to focus on service delivery.*

In terms of practice this description may ring true, but there are few comments on what social workers could and should do to act ethically within the workplace amid the conflicts and ambiguity of the legislation.[2] Comments then by trainers or practice-close observers are particularly welcome. Following one case that went to appeal, for example, trainer Pete Feldon (2017b) has described how a legally literate social worker could take on the task of working with a case such as *JF v The London Borough of Merton* following the judicial review in the High Court. Merton had been ordered to undertake a re-assessment of JF's needs in accordance with the provisions of the Care Act 2014. Feldon sets out how a social worker given such a re-assessment could ensure that it is undertaken legally:

> *'Although the requirement is to reassess JF's needs, I suggest that it would be better to undertake this reassessment in the context of a review of his care and support plan, in accordance with section 27 of the Care Act. This will help to ensure that there is a robust consideration of how JF's needs are best met ...'.*

Feldon suggests serious consideration of appointing an independent advocate and getting expert evidence about the impact of possible changes.

Other practice recommendations have been made by Symonds and colleagues whose early study of Care Act practice by social care assessors (two thirds of whom were social workers) asked whether the Care Act was meeting its aims of creating a more 'equal exchange' between assessor and assessed (Symonds et al., 2018). Overall the research team found that there were several continuities of pre- and post- Care Act practice, such as: managing tensions between what service users wanted and what could be supplied; dealing with administrative tasks; how to sort out claims and eligibility and what to do when decision-making seemed compromised. By the time of the study, most assessors were using Care Act phrases such as 'wellbeing' and 'outcomes'. Interestingly it was the sheer volume of work or demand that they reported to be the biggest challenge although budgetary constraints were prominent in their accounts.

Of particular relevance to this chapter is that some differences were found between the social workers participating in the study and those with other roles or professional backgrounds. While numbers were small (30 in all), social workers seemed more likely than other assessors to talk about holistic assessments, professional judgements, and how they might draw out relevant information in cases where there were multiple uncertainties. This helped them 'frame' the case for funding or to make decisions about eligibility. Their skills were not in simply advocating for service users' requests but in enquiry and applying criteria when undertaking assessments and making recommendations respectively. As the discussion above suggests about social work, they were acting very much in the persona of the local authority.

Making the most of the Care Act 2014

In contrast to the concerns expressed about the Care Act and its context covered above, there is a more optimistic view that for homeless people the Act offers a real opportunity for consideration of their needs. As Cornes and colleagues (Cornes et al., 2018) noted, the Act removed references to 'eligible' and 'ineligible' groups so that any adult with any level of need has a right to an assessment. They argue that many homeless people have been excluded from care and support in the past, but that the Act offers a fresh way for homeless organisations to work with local authorities to ensure fairer and more consistent access for people who often have needs for care and support that significantly affect their wellbeing.

This is because determining Care Act eligibility hinges on identifying how a person's needs affect their ability to achieve relevant outcomes, and how this impacts on their wellbeing. Indeed, it is difficult to think of a situation in which being homeless would not have a significantly negative impact on a person's wellbeing. However, what counts is not the fact of being 'homeless' *per se*, but the associated consequences which might give rise to physical and/or mental impairments. To access publicly-funded care and support (such as a personal or managed budget), the Act is potentially relevant to people who are homeless who are experiencing 'complex trauma' or 'personality disorder'. In addition, experiences of homelessness (e.g. the failure to maintain a habitable home environment and the associated difficulties of maintaining personal hygiene, nutrition and the ability to engage in work, training, and so on), impact or risk impacting significantly on wellbeing. In summary, homelessness is typically characterised by 'tri-morbidity' (linked to physical, mental ill-health and drug and alcohol problems) and other risk factors including poor nutrition, exposure to communicable diseases, harsh living environments, high rates of victimisation and unintentional injuries. The potential for homeless people to access care and support, with assistance from advocacy groups and social workers, may make a major change to their lives. For social workers, with a remit to work with people whose situations are complex, homelessness may be a growing and impactful area of practice.

Such analysis fits with Wittington's (2016b) analysis of the contents of the second edition of the Statutory Guidance for 'manifest' or surface meanings and the 'latent' or underlying meanings. He noted that strengths-based or assets-based approaches, variously also described as community-oriented social work or asset-based community development, while not well articulated in the guidance, were becoming evident within it, moving from latent to manifest.

For homelessness agencies, and to wider communities and service users, these may be particularly welcome initiatives. He described the approach (strengths-based) as an 'emblematic strategy' – another potential future milestone on the road to professional renaissance. Of course, taking a strengths-based approach might be liberating and transformative but Whittington warned that compromises might need to be made. He referred back to the Care Act's endorsement of social work roles as primarily being around adult safeguarding rather than holistic or community orientated practice. This he presented as the 'operational reality' – to which might also be added the 'operational reality' of working with or being allocated complex cases as mentioned above. Despite these conclusions, Whittington was positive about the stated support for social work with adults from government as represented in the Statutory Guidance; this is echoed in this present chapter, which concurs with his observation that the road to social work 'liberation' (Whittington, 2016b) is not straightforward but long and winding.

Conclusion

There is a much used (and possibly mythical) quote that Chinese leader Zhou Enlai, on being asked (in 1972) about the impact of the French Revolution, declared it was too early to tell (Wikipedia, n/d: https://en.wikiquote.org/wiki/Zhou_Enlai). At the time of writing there have been early observations on the implementation of the Act and several cases have featured in reports of complaints or legal proceedings, many of which are noted in earlier chapters. The nature of these is that good practice is not their focus; as is often the case with social work, its good practice is left under-reported and under-claimed by the profession. This contributes to a perception that social work is not effective and operates amid the uncertainties identified by the James Lind Alliance work that was highlighted at the start of this chapter. Nonetheless, this chapter has emphasised how the Care Act's implementation might not have provided the opportunity to show what social work can offer and that a more nuanced view of it as containing inherent ambiguities is needed.

A further difficulty is that social work is largely referred to in the Care Act guidance amid other professionals or indistinctly in the persona of the 'local authority'. This provides opportunities for social workers to embrace the ethical challenges of their work (not simply the financial context) and to exercise their creativity, but again their activities may be in the shadows and seemingly confined to assessments. Effectiveness should be mentioned more assertively in social work practice and commissioning, since, whatever the state of public expenditure and private contributions, social work needs to make the case that its legal literacy, skills and use of research are maximising the potential of the Care Act 2014 and will be at the forefront of any revisions.

Further Reading

Brammer, A. (2015) *Social Work Law* (4th edn). London: Pearson.

Cooper, A. and White, E. (eds) *Safeguarding Adults under the Care Act 2014*. London: Jessica Kingsley.

Simcock, P. and Castle, R. (2016) *Social Work and Disability*. London: Sage.

Acknowledgements and disclaimer

This chapter draws on research undertaken as background material for studies commissioned by the NIHR Health and Social Care Workforce Research Unit at King's College London. The views expressed are those of the author alone and should not be interpreted as being shared by the National Institute for Health Research, the NHS or the Department of Health and Social Care.

Notes

1. Editors' note: Statutory guidance is issued under section 7, Local Authority Social Services Act 1970. This requires those organisations to which the guidance is issued, including local authorities, to follow ministerial directions. Authorities may only depart from the guidance with good reason; otherwise it must be followed.

2. Editors' note: Social workers must follow the statutory guidance and refuse to follow local procedures that place their registration in potential jeopardy. That they often do not betrays either a lack of legal and ethical literacy or demonstrates the impact of being an employee. For further analysis see Preston-Shoot, M. (2000) 'What if? Using the law to uphold practice values and standards', *Practice*, 12 (4): 49–63; Kline, R. and Preston-Shoot, M. (2012) *Professional Accountability in Social Care and Health: Challenging Unacceptable Practice and its Management*. London: Sage/Learning Matters.

Appendix 1

The 9 Domains

1. PROFESSIONALISM – Identify and behave as a professional social worker, committed to professional development.

2. VALUES AND ETHICS – Apply social work ethical principles and value to guide professional practices.

3. DIVERSITY AND EQUALITY – Recognise diversity and apply anti-discriminatory and anti-oppressive principles in practice.

4. RIGHTS, JUSTICE AND ECONOMIC WELLBEING – Advance human rights and promote social justice and economic wellbeing.

5. KNOWLEDGE – Develop and apply relevant knowledge from social work practice and research, social sciences, law, other professional and relevant fields, and from the experience of people who use services.

6. CRITICAL REFLECTION AND ANALYSIS – Apply critical reflection and analysis to inform and provide a rationale for professional decision-making.

7. SKILLS AND INTERVENTIONS – Use judgement, knowledge and authority to intervene with individuals, families and communities to promote independence, provide support, prevent harm and enable progress.

8. CONTEXTS AND ORGANISATIONS – Engage with, inform, and adapt to changing organisational contexts, and the social and policy environments that shape practice. Operate effectively within and contribute to the development of organisations and services, including multi-agency and inter-professional settings.

9. PROFESSIONAL LEADERSHIP – Promote the profession and good social work practice. Take responsibility for the professional learning and development of others. Develop personal influence and be part of the collective leadership and impact of the profession.

Published with kind permission of BASW – www.basw.co.uk

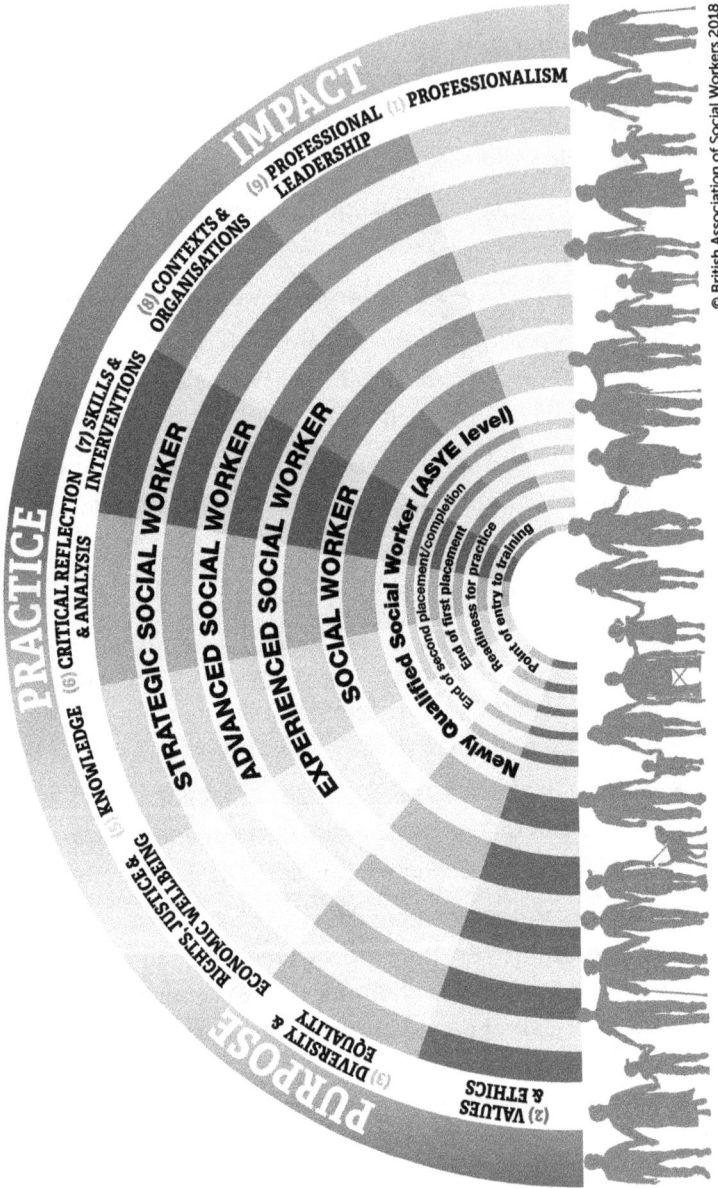

© British Association of Social Workers 2018

IMPACT

(9) PROFESSIONAL LEADERSHIP (1) PROFESSIONALISM

(8) CONTEXTS & ORGANISATIONS

PRACTICE

(7) SKILLS & INTERVENTIONS

(6) CRITICAL REFLECTION & ANALYSIS

(5) KNOWLEDGE

STRATEGIC SOCIAL WORKER

ADVANCED SOCIAL WORKER

EXPERIENCED SOCIAL WORKER

SOCIAL WORKER

Newly Qualified Social Worker (ASYE level)

End of second placement/completion

End of first placement

Readiness for practice

Point of entry to training

RIGHTS, JUSTICE & ECONOMIC WELLBEING

(3) DIVERSITY & EQUALITY

PURPOSE

(2) VALUES & ETHICS

Appendix 2
Subject benchmark for social work

5 Knowledge, understanding and skills
Subject knowledge and understanding

5.1 During their qualifying degree studies in Social Work, students acquire, critically evaluate, apply and integrate knowledge and understanding in the following five core areas of study.

5.2 Social Work theory, which includes:

  i. critical explanations from Social Work theory and other subjects which contribute to the knowledge base of Social Work

  ii. an understanding of Social Work's rich and contested history from both a UK and comparative perspective

  iii. the relevance of sociological and applied psychological perspectives to understanding societal and structural influences on human behaviour at individual, group and community levels, and the relevance of sociological theorisation to a deeper understanding of adaptation and change

  iv. the relevance of psychological, physical and physiological perspectives to understanding human, personal and social development, well-being and risk

  v. social science theories explaining and exploring group and organisational behaviour

  vi. the range of theories and research informed evidence that informs understanding of the child, adult, family or community and of the range of assessment and interventions which can be used

  vii. the theory, models and methods of assessment, factors underpinning the selection and testing of relevant information, knowledge and critical appraisal of relevant social science and other research and evaluation methodologies, and the evidence base for Social Work

  viii. the nature of analysis and professional judgement and the processes of risk assessment and decision making, including the theory of risk informed decisions and the balance of choice and control, rights and protection in decision making

  ix. approaches, methods and theories of intervention in working with a diverse population within a wide range of settings, including factors

5.3   Values and ethics, which include:

    i.   the nature, historical evolution, political context and application of professional Social Work values, informed by national and international definitions and ethical statements, and their relation to personal values, identities, influences and ideologies

    ii.   the ethical concepts of rights, responsibility, freedom, authority and power inherent in the practice of social workers as agents with statutory powers in different situations

    iii.   aspects of philosophical ethics relevant to the understanding and resolution of value dilemmas and conflicts in both interpersonal and professional contexts

    iv.   understanding of, and adherence to, the ethical foundations of empirical and conceptual research, as both consumers and producers of social science research

    v.   the relationship between human rights enshrined in law and the moral and ethical rights determined theoretically, philosophically and by contemporary society

    vi.   the complex relationships between justice, care and control in social welfare and the practical and ethical implications of these, including their expression in roles as statutory agents in diverse practice settings and in upholding the law in respect of challenging discrimination and inequalities

    vii.   the conceptual links between codes defining ethical practice and the regulation of professional conduct

    viii.   the professional and ethical management of potential conflicts generated by codes of practice held by different professional groups

    ix.   the ethical management of professional dilemmas and conflicts in balancing the perspectives of individuals who need care and support and professional decision making at points of risk, care and protection

    x.   the constructive challenging of individuals and organisations where there may be conflicts with Social Work values, ethics and codes of practice

    xi.   the professional responsibility to be open and honest if things go wrong (the duty of candour about own practice) and to act on concerns about poor or unlawful practice by any person or organisation

    xii.   continuous professional development as a reflective, informed and skilled practitioner, including the constructive use of professional supervision.

5.4   Service users and carers, which include:

    i.   the factors which contribute to the health and well-being of individuals, families and communities, including promoting dignity, choice and independence for people who need care and support

    ii.   the underpinning perspectives that determine explanations of the characteristics and circumstances of people who need care and support, with critical evaluation drawing on research, practice experience and the experience and expertise of people who use services

iii. the social and psychological processes associated with, for example, poverty, migration, unemployment, trauma, poor health, disability, lack of education and other sources of disadvantage and how they affect well-being, how they interact and may lead to marginalisation, isolation and exclusion, and demand for Social Work services

iv. explanations of the links between the factors contributing to social differences and identities (for example, social class, gender, ethnic differences, age, sexuality and religious belief) and the structural consequences of inequality and differential need faced by service users

v. the nature and function of Social Work in a diverse and increasingly global society (with particular reference to prejudice, interpersonal relations, discrimination, empowerment and anti-discriminatory practices).

5.5 The nature of Social Work practice, in the UK and more widely, which includes:

i. the place of theoretical perspectives and evidence from European and international research in assessment and decision-making processes

ii. the integration of theoretical perspectives and evidence from European and international research into the design and implementation of effective Social Work intervention with a wide range of service users, carers and communities

iii. the knowledge and skills which underpin effective practice, with a range of service-users and in a variety of settings

iv. the processes that facilitate and support service user and citizen rights, choice, co-production, self-governance, well-being and independence

v. the importance of interventions that promote social justice, human rights, social cohesion, collective responsibility and respect for diversity and tackle inequalities

vi. its delivery in a range of community-based and organisational settings spanning the statutory, voluntary and private sectors, and the changing nature of these service contexts

vii. the factors and processes that facilitate effective interdisciplinary, interprofessional and interagency collaboration and partnership across a plurality of settings and disciplines

viii. the importance of Social Work's contribution to intervention across service user groups, settings and levels in terms of the profession's focus on social justice, human rights, social cohesion, collective responsibility and respect for diversities

ix. the processes of reflection and reflexivity as well as approaches for evaluating service and welfare outcomes for vulnerable people,

5.6 The leadership, organisation and delivery of Social Work services, which includes:

i. the location of contemporary Social Work within historical, comparative and global perspectives, including in the devolved nations of the UK and wider European and international contexts

ii.   how the service delivery context is portrayed to service users, carers, families and communities

iii. the changing demography and cultures of communities, including European and international contexts, in which social workers practise

iv.   the complex relationships between public, private, social and political philosophies, policies and priorities and the organisation and practice of social work, including the contested nature of these

v.   the issues and trends in modern public and social policy and their relationship to contemporary practice, service delivery and leadership in Social Work

vi.   the significance of legislative and legal frameworks and service delivery standards, including on core social work values and ethics in the delivery of services which support, enable and empower

vii. the current range and appropriateness of statutory, voluntary and private agencies providing services and the organisational systems inherent within these

viii. development of new ways of working and delivery, for example the development of social enterprises, integrated multi-professional teams and independent Social Work provision

ix.   the significance of professional and organisational relationships with other related services, including housing, health, education, police, employment, fire, income maintenance and criminal justice

x.   the importance and complexities of the way agencies work together to provide care, the relationships between agency policies, legal requirements and professional boundaries in shaping the nature of services provided in integrated and interdisciplinary contexts

xi.   the contribution of different approaches to management and leadership within different settings, and the impact on professional practice and on quality of care management and leadership in public and human services

xii. the development of person-centred services, personalised care, individual budgets and direct payments all focusing upon the human and legal rights of the service user for control, power and self determination

xiii. the implications of modern information and communications technology for both the provision and receipt of services, use of technologically enabled support and the use of social media as a process and forum for vulnerable people, families and communities, and communities of professional practice.

Subject-specific skills and other skills

5.7   The range of skills required by a qualified social worker reflect the complex and demanding context in which they work. Many of these skills may be of value in many situations, for example, analytical thinking, building relationships, working as a member of an organisation, intervention, evaluation, and reflection. What defines the specific nature of these skills as developed by Social Work students is:

  i. the context in which they are applied and assessed (for example communication skills in practice with people with sensory impairments or assessment skills in an interprofessional setting)

  ii. the relative weighting given to such skills within Social Work practice (for example the central importance of problem-solving skills within complex human situations)

  iii. the specific purpose of skill development (for example the acquisition of research skills in order to build a repertoire of research-based practice)

  iv. a requirement to integrate a range of skills (that is, not simply to demonstrate these in an isolated and incremental manner).

5.8 All Social Work graduates demonstrate the ability to reflect on and learn from the exercise of their skills, in order to build their professional identity. They understand the significance of the concepts of continuing professional development and lifelong learning, and accept responsibility for their own continuing development.

5.9 Social Work students acquire and integrate skills in the following five core areas.

Problem-solving skills

5.10 These are sub-divided into four areas.

5.11 Managing problem-solving activities: graduates in Social Work are able to:

  i. think logically, systematically, creatively, critically and reflectively, in order to carry out a holistic assessment

  ii. apply ethical principles and practices critically in planning problem-solving activities

  iii. plan a sequence of actions to achieve specified objectives, making use of research, theory and other forms of evidence

  iv. manage processes of change, drawing on research, theory and other forms of evidence.

5.12 Gathering information: graduates in Social Work are able to:

  i. demonstrate persistence in gathering information from a wide range of sources and using a variety of methods, for a range of purposes. These methods include electronic searches, reviews of relevant literature, policy and procedures, face-to-face interviews, and written and telephone contact with individuals and groups

  ii. take into account differences of viewpoint in gathering information and critically assess the reliability and relevance of the information gathered

  iii. assimilate and disseminate relevant information in reports and case records.

5.13 Analysis and synthesis: graduates in Social Work are able to analyse and synthesise knowledge gathered for problem-solving purposes, in order to:

  i. assess human situations, taking into account a variety of factors (including the views of participants, theoretical concepts, research evidence, legislation and organisational policies and procedures)

  ii. analyse and synthesise information gathered, weighing competing evidence and modifying their viewpoint in the light of new information, then relate this information to a particular task, situation or problem

  iii. balance specific factors relevant to Social Work practice (such as risk, rights, cultural differences and language needs and preferences, responsibilities to protect vulnerable individuals and legal obligations)

  iv. assess the merits of contrasting theories, explanations, research, policies and procedures and use the information to develop and sustain reasoned arguments

  v. employ a critical understanding of factors that support or inhibit problem solving including societal, organisational and community issues as well as individual relationships

  vi. critically analyse and take account of the impact of inequality and discrimination in working with people who use Social Work services.

5.14 Intervention and evaluation: graduates in Social Work are able to use their knowledge of a range of interventions and evaluation processes creatively and selectively to:

  i. build and sustain purposeful relationships with people and organisations in communities and interprofessional contexts

  ii. make decisions based on evidence, set goals and construct specific plans to achieve outcomes, taking into account relevant information including ethical guidelines

  iii. negotiate goals and plans with others, analysing and addressing in a creative and flexible manner individual, cultural and structural impediments to change

  iv. implement plans through a variety of systematic processes that include working in partnership

  v. practice in a manner that promotes well-being, protects safety and resolves conflict

  vi. act as a navigator, advocate and support to assist people who need care and support to take decisions and access services

  vii. manage the complex dynamics of dependency and, in some settings, provide direct care and personal support to assist people in their everyday lives

  viii. meet deadlines and comply with external requirements of a task

  ix. plan, implement and critically monitor and review processes and outcomes

  x. bring work to an effective conclusion, taking into account the implications for all involved

  xi. use and evaluate methods of intervention critically and reflectively.

Communication skills

5.15   Graduates in Social Work are able to communicate clearly, sensitively and effectively (using appropriate methods which may include working with interpreters) with individuals and groups of different ages and abilities in a range of formal and informal situations, in order to:

   i.   engage individuals and organisations, who may be unwilling, by verbal, paper-based and electronic means to achieve a range of objectives, including changing behaviour
   ii. use verbal and non-verbal cues to guide and inform conversations and interpretation of information
   iii. negotiate and where necessary redefine the purpose of interactions with individuals and organisations and the boundaries of their involvement
   iv. listen actively and empathetically to others, taking into account their specific needs and life experiences
   v.   engage appropriately with the life experiences of service users, to understand accurately their viewpoint, overcome personal prejudices and respond appropriately to a range of complex personal and interpersonal situations
   vi. make evidence informed arguments drawing from theory, research and practice wisdom including the viewpoints of service users and/or others
   vii. write accurately and clearly in styles adapted to the audience, purpose and context of the communication
   viii. use advocacy skills to promote others' rights, interests and needs
   ix. present conclusions verbally and on paper, in a structured form, appropriate to the audience for which these have been prepared
   x.   make effective preparation for, and lead, meetings in a productive way.

Skills in working with others

5.16   Graduates in Social Work are able to build relationships and work effectively with others, in order to:

   i.   involve users of Social Work services in ways that increase their resources, capacity and power to influence factors affecting their lives
   ii. engage service users and carers and wider community networks in active consultation
   iii. respect and manage differences such as organisational and professional boundaries and differences of identity and/or language
   iv. develop effective helping relationships and partnerships that facilitate change for individuals, groups and organisations while maintaining appropriate personal and professional boundaries

    v. demonstrate interpersonal skills and emotional intelligence that creates and develops relationships based on openness, transparency and empathy

    vi. increase social justice by identifying and responding to prejudice, institutional discrimination and structural inequality

    vii. operate within a framework of multiple accountability (for example, to agencies, the public, service users, carers and others)

    viii. observe the limits of professional and organisational responsibility, using supervision appropriately and referring to others when required

    ix. provide reasoned, informed arguments to challenge others as necessary, in ways that are most likely to produce positive outcomes.

Skills in personal and professional development

5.17   Graduates in Social Work are able to:

    i. work at all times in accordance with codes of professional conduct and ethics

    ii. advance their own learning and understanding with a degree of independence and use supervision as a tool to aid professional development

    iii. develop their professional identity, recognise their own professional limitations and accountability, and know how and when to seek advice from a range of sources including professional supervision

    iv. use support networks and professional supervision to manage uncertainty, change and stress in work situations while maintaining resilience in self and others

    v. handle conflict between others and internally when personal views may conflict with a course of action necessitated by the Social Work role

    vi. provide reasoned, informed arguments to challenge unacceptable practices in a responsible manner and raise concerns about wrongdoing in the workplace

    vii. be open and honest with people if things go wrong

    viii. understand the difference between theory, research, evidence and expertise and the role of professional judgement.

Use of technology and numerical skills

5.18   Graduates in Social Work are able to use information and communication technology effectively and appropriately for:

    i. professional communication, data storage and retrieval and information searching

    ii. accessing and assimilating information to inform working with people who use services

    iii. data analysis to enable effective use of research in practice

    iv. enhancing skills in problem-solving

    v. applying numerical skills to financial and budgetary responsibilities

    vi. understanding the social impact of technology, including the constraints of confidentiality and an awareness of the impact of the 'digital divide'.

References

Abbott, S. N. (2018) 'Using the Law in Social Work: Approved Mental Health Professional Practice'. Doctoral thesis, University of Sussex.

Acquired Brain Injury and Mental Capacity Act Interest Group (2014) *Acquired Brain Injury and Mental Capacity: Recommendations for Action following the House of Lords Select Committee Post-Legislative Scrutiny Report into the Mental Capacity Act. Making the Abstract Real.* Acquired Brain Injury and Mental Capacity Act Interest Group. Available at: www.biswg.co.uk/blog/acquired-brain-injury-and-mental-capacity-making-abstract-re/ (accessed 21 July 2019).

Action on Elder Abuse (2013) *Operation Jasmine: An Example of Why We Need a New Law on Ill-treatment or Neglecting Adults.* London: Action on Elder Abuse.

Adam, S. K. and Osborne, S. (2016) *Oxford Handbook of Critical Care Nursing.* Oxford: Oxford University Press.

Adams, R. (2008) *Empowerment, Participation, and Social Work.* Basingstoke: Palgrave Macmillan.

ADASS (2017) *ADASS Budget Survey 2017.* London: Association of Directors of Adult Social Services.

ADASS (2018a) *ADASS Budget Survey 2018.* London: Association of Directors of Adult Social Services. Available at: www.adass.org.uk/media/6434/adass-budget-survey-report-2018.pdf (accessed 21 July 2019).

ADASS (2018b) *Guidance and Principles for Aftercare Services Under s117.* London: Association of Directors of Adult Social Services.

Age UK (2017a) *Social Care Parliamentary Briefing.* London: Age UK. Available at: www.ageuk.org.uk/globalassets/age-uk/documents/reports-and-publications/reports-and-briefings/care--support/rb_dec17_social_care.pdf (accessed 21 July 2019).

Age UK (2017b) *Health and Care of Older People in England 2017.* London: Age UK.

Allan, S. (2015) *Implications of the Care Act 2014 on Social Care Markets for Older People. Guest Editorial: Unit Costs of Health and Social Care 2015.* Canterbury, University of Kent: PSSRU.

Alston, P. (2019) *Report of the Special Rapporteur on Extreme Poverty and Human Rights on his Visit to the United Kingdom of Great Britain and Northern Ireland.* Geneva: UN Human Rights Council. Available at: https://undocs.org/A/HRC/41/39/Add.1

Anderson, M. I., Simpson, G. K. and Morey, P. J. (2012) The impact of neurobehavioral impairment on family functioning and the psychological well-being of male versus female caregivers of relatives with severe traumatic brain injury: multigroup analysis, *Journal of Head Trauma Rehabilitation*, 28 (6):453–63.

Anderson, V., Brown, S., Newitt, H. and Hoile, H. (2011) Long-term outcome from childhood traumatic brain injury: intellectual ability, personality and quality of life, *Neuropsychology*, 25: 176–84.

Anka, A., Sorensen, P., Brandon, M. and Bailey, S. (2017) Social work intervention with adults who self-neglect in England: responding to the Care Act 2014, *Journal of Adult Protection*, 19 (2): 67–77.

Audit Commission (2008) *The Effect of Fair Access to Care Services Bands on Expenditure and Service Provision*. London: Commission for Social Care Inspection.

BABICM (2019) *About Us*. Manchester: British Association of Brain Injury and Complex Case Management. Available at: www.babicm.org/about-us/

Bach, L. and David, A. (2006) Self-awareness after acquired and traumatic brain injury, *Neuropsychological Rehabilitation*, 16: 397–414.

Baginsky, M. and Manthorpe, J. (2016) The views and experiences of step-up to social work graduates: two and a half years following qualification, *British Journal of Social Work*, 46 (7): 2016–32.

Bajo, A. and Fleminger, S. (2002) Brain injury rehabilitation: what works for whom and when?, *Brain Injury*, 16: 385–95.

Barnes, D., Boland, B., Linhart, K. and Wilson, K. (2017) Personalisation and social care assessment: The Care Act 2014, *British Journal of Psychiatry Bulletin*, 41 (3): 176–80.

BASW (2018a) *Professional Capabilities Framework for Social Work in England: The 2018 Refreshed PCF*. Birmingham: British Association of Social Workers.

BASW (2018b) *Professional Capabilities Framework for Social Work in England: Guidance on Using the 2018 Refreshed PCF*. Birmingham: British Association of Social Workers.

BASW (2019) *Open letter from BASW to the Local Government Association (LGA), 7th January 2019*. Birmingham: British Association of Social Workers. Available at: www.basw.co.uk/media/news/2019/jan/basw-england-response-lives-we-want-lead-local-government-association-lga-green (accessed 21 July 2019).

BBC (2014) 'Planned Cap on Social Care Costs "Will help few people"', 12 May. Available at: www.bbc.co.uk/news/uk-27363896 (accessed 21 July 2019).

Bee, M. (2015) 'How to learn the Care Act 2014 while juggling your caseload', *Community Care*. Available at: www.communitycare.co.uk/2015/2004/2028/learn-care-act-2014-juggling-caseload/

Beresford, P. (2014) *Personalisation*. Bristol: Policy.

Beresford, P. (2016) *All Our Welfare*. Bristol: Policy.

Bishop, M. D., Degeneffe, C. E. and Mast, M. (2006) Family needs after traumatic brain injury: implications for rehabilitation counselling, *Australian Journal of Rehabilitation Counselling*, 12: 73–87.

BISWG and BASW (2016) *Practice Guidance for Social Workers Working With People with an Acquired Brain Injury*. Birmingham: British Association of Social Workers Brain Injury Social Work Group.

Black, K. (2005) Advance directive communication practices: social workers' contributions to the interdisciplinary health care team, *Social Work in Health Care*, 40: 39–55.

Blake, H. (2014) Caregiver stress in traumatic brain injury, *International Journal of Therapy and Rehabilitation*, 15: 263–71.

Blake, M., Bowes, A., Gill, V., Husain, F. and Mir, G. (2017) A collaborative exploration of the reasons for lower satisfaction with services among Bangladeshi and Pakistani social care users, *Health and Social Care in the Community*, 25: 1090–99.

Blake, M., Lambert, C. and Signaporla, Z. (2017b) *Unmet Need for Care*. London: Ipsos MORI.

Boss, P. (2006) *Loss, Trauma, and Resilience: Therapeutic Work with Ambiguous Loss*. New York: Norton.

Bourdieu, P. (1987) The force of law: toward a sociology of the juridical field, *Hastings Law Journal*, 38: 805–53.

Bourdieu, P. (1990) *The Logic of Practice*. Stanford, CA: Stanford University Press.

Bows, H. and Penhale, B. (2018) Editorial: Elder abuse and social work: research, theory and practice, *British Journal of Social Work*, 48: 873–86.

Boyle, G. (2008) The Mental Capacity Act 2005: promoting the citizenship of people with dementia?, *Health and Social Care in the Community*, 16 (5): 529–37.

Braye, S., Orr, D. and Preston-Shoot, M. (2011) *The Governance of Adult Safeguarding: Findings from Research into Safeguarding Adults Boards. SCIE Report 45*. London: Social Care Institute for Excellence.

Braye, S., Orr, D. and Preston-Shoot, M. (2012) The governance of adult safeguarding: findings from research, *Journal of Adult Protection*, 14 (2): 55–72.

Braye, S., Orr, D and Preston-Shoot, M. (2014) *Self-Neglect Policy and Practice: Building an Evidence Base for Adult Social Care*. London: SCIE.

Braye, S., Orr, D. and Preston-Shoot, M. (2015a) Learning lessons about self-neglect? An analysis of serious case reviews, *Journal of Adult Protection*, 17 (1): 3–18.

Braye, S., Orr, D. and Preston-Shoot, M. (2015b) Serious case review findings on the challenge of self-neglect: indicators for good practice, *Journal of Adult Protection*, 17 (2): 75–87.

Braye, S., Orr, D. and Preston-Shoot, M. (2017) Autonomy and protection in self-neglect work: the ethical complexity of decision-making, *Ethics and Social Welfare*, 11 (4): 320–35.

Braye, S. and Preston-Shoot, M. (1990) On teaching and applying the law in social work: it is not that simple, *British Journal of Social Work*, 20 (4): 333–353.

Braye, S. and Preston-Shoot, M. (2005) *Learning, Teaching and Assessment of Law in Social Work Education*, London: Social Care Institute for Excellence.

Braye, S. and Preston-Shoot, M. (2006) The role of welfare reform: critical perspectives on the relationship between law and social work practice, *International Journal of Social Welfare*, 15: 19–26.

Braye, S. and Preston-Shoot, M. (2016) *Practising Social Work Law* (4th edn). London: Palgrave.

Braye, S. and Preston-Shoot, M. (2017a) *Learning from Safeguarding Adult Reviews: A Report for the London Safeguarding Adults Board*. London: London Safeguarding Adults Board.

Braye, S. and Preston-Shoot, M. (2017b) *Safeguarding Adults Review: Adult A*. Lewes: East Sussex Safeguarding Adults Board.

Braye, S., Preston-Shoot, M. and Wigley, V. (2011) Deciding to use the law in social work practice, *Journal of Social Work*, 13 (1): 75–95.

Briggs, M. and Cooper, A. (2018) Making safeguarding personal: progress of English local authorities, *Journal of Adult Protection*, 20 (1): 59–68.

Brimblecombe, N., Pickard, L., King, D. and Knapp, M. (2017) Barriers to receipt of social care services for working carers and the people they care for in times of austerity, *Journal of Social Policy*, 1–19. Available at: http://dx.doi.org/10.1017/S0047279417000277 (accessed 19 July 2019).

Brindle, D. (2014) 'What Are the Most Important Changes to the Care Act?', *The Guardian*, 5 June. Available at: www.theguardian.com/social-care-network/2014/jun/05/care-act-most-important-amendments (accessed 19 July 2019).

Bristol SAB (2017) *A Safeguarding Adult Review in Respect of Melissa*. Bristol: Bristol Safeguarding Adults Board. Available at: https://bristolsafeguarding.org/adults/safeguarding-adult-reviews/bristol-sars/melissa-serious-case-review/ (accessed 21 July 2019).

Broach, S., Clements, L. and Read, J. (2016) 'Chapter 10: Transition to Adulthood', in *Disabled Children: A Legal Handbook* (4th edn). London: Legal Action Group. Available at: https://councilfordisabledchildren.org.uk/sites/default/files/field/attachemnt/chapter-10.pdf (accessed 18 July 2019).

Bronstein, L. R. (2003) A model for interdisciplinary collaboration, *Social Work*, 48: 297–306.

Brophy, L. and McDermott, F. (2013) Using social work theory and values to investigate the implementation of community treatment orders, *Australian Social Work*, 66 (1): 72–85.

Butler, L. and Manthorpe, J. (2016) Putting people at the centre: facilitating Making Safeguarding Personal approaches in the context of the Care Act 2014, *Journal of Adult Protection*, 18 (4): 204–13.

Cameron, D. (2013) *Lord Mayor's Banquet: Prime Minister's Speech*. London: Cabinet Office. Available at: www.gov.uk/government/speeches/lord-mayors-banquet-2013-prime-ministers-speech (accessed 21 July 2019).

Campbell, J. (2010) Deciding to detain: the use of compulsory mental health law by UK social workers, *British Journal of Social Work*, 40 (1): 328–34.

Campbell, J. and Davidson, G. (2009) Coercion in the community: a situated approach to the examination of ethical challenges for mental health social workers, *Ethics and Social Welfare*, 3 (3): 249–63.

CareKnowledge (2018) *The Three Conversations: Special Report*. Hove: Pavilion.

Carers Trust (2016a) *Care Act for Carers: One Year On*. London: Carers' Trust. Available at: https://carers.org/sites/default/files/care_act_one_year_on.pdf (accessed 21 July 2019).

Carers Trust (2016b) *Care Act for Carers One Year On: Good Practice Box*. London: Carers UK. Available at: https://carers.org/sites/default/files/related_documents/good_practice_box.pdf (accessed 21 July 2019).

Carers UK (2018a) *State of Caring Report 2018*. London: Carers UK. Available at: www.carersuk.org/images/Downloads/SoC2018/State-of-Caring-report-2018.pdf (accessed 21 July 2019).

Carers UK (2018b) *Caring for your Future: The Long-term Financial Impact of Caring*, London: Carers UK. Available at: www.carersuk.org/images/News_and_campaigns/Carers_Rights_Day/CUK-Carers-Rights-Day-Research-Report-2018-WEB.PDF (accessed 21 July 2019).

Carey, M. (2014) The fragmentation of social work and social care: some ramifications and a critique, *British Journal of Social Work*, 45: 2406–22.

Carr, H. and Goosey, D. (2017) *Law for Social Workers*. Oxford: Oxford University Press.

Carter, R. (2018) The funding panel policies testing the limits of the Care Act, *Community Care*. Available at: www.communitycare.co.uk/2018/09/26/funding-panel-policies-testing-limits-care-act/ (accessed 21 July 2019).

Challenging Behaviour Foundation (2018) *The Impact of Caring on Families*. Canterbury: Challenging Behaviour Foundation. Available at: www.challengingbehaviour.org.uk/learning-disability-assets/12impactofcaringonfamiliesweb2018.pdf (accessed 21 July 2019).

City & Hackney SAB (2016) *Safeguarding Adults Review of the Circumstances Concerning Mrs Y*. London: CHSAB.

Clark, T. and Heath, A. (2014) *Hard Times*. London: HUP.

Clark-Wilson, J., Giles, G. M. and Baxter, D. M. (2014) Revisiting the neurofunctional approach: conceptualizing the core components for the rehabilitation of everyday living skills, *Brain Injury*, 28: 1646–56.

Clark-Wilson, J., Giles, G. M., Seymour, S., Tasker, R., Baxter, D. M. and Holloway, M. (2016) Factors influencing community case management and care hours for clients with traumatic brain injury living in the UK, *Brain Injury*, 30: 872–82.

Clark-Wilson, J. and Holloway, M. (2015) Life care planning and long-term care for individuals with brain injury in the UK, *NeuroRehabilitation*, 36: 289–300.

Clough, R. (1999) Scandalous care: interpreting public enquiry reports of scandals in residential care, *Journal of Elder Abuse and Neglect*, 10: 1–2, 13–27.

Cohen, S. (1984) *Visions of Social Control: Crime, Punishment and Classification*. Cambridge: Polity.

Commission for Social Care Inspection (2008a) *Cutting the Cake Fairly*. London: CSCI.

Commission for Social Care Inspection (2008b) *Raising Voices: Views on Safeguarding Adults*. London: CSCI.

Commission on Funding of Care and Support (2011) *Fairer Care Funding: The Report of the Commission on Funding of Care and Support: Volume I*. London: Commission on Funding of Care and Support.

Commission on the Future of Health and Social Care in England (2014) *A New Settlement for Health and Social Care: Interim Report*. London: King's Fund.

Communities and Local Government Committee (2017) *9th Report. Adult Social Care*. London: HMSO.

Community Care (2017) Councils 'misusing funding panels for decisions on care packages', *Community Care*. Available at: www.communitycare.co.uk/2017/02/14/councils-misusing-funding-panels-decisions-care-packages/ (accessed 21 July 2019).

Cooper, A. and Bruin, C. (2017) Adult safeguarding and the Care Act (2014): the impacts on partnerships and practice, *Journal of Adult Protection*, 19 (4): 209–19.

Cooper, A., Cocker, C. and Briggs, M. (2018) Making safeguarding personal and social work practice with older adults: findings from local-authority survey data in England, *British Journal of Social Work*, 48 (4): 1014–32.

Cornes, M., Ornelas, B., Bennett, B., Meakin, A., Mason, K., Fuller, J. and Manthorpe, J. (2018) Increasing access to Care Act 2014 assessments and personal budgets among people with experiences of homelessness and multiple exclusion: a theoretically informed case study, *Housing Care and Support*, 21 (1): 1–12.

Cornwall APC (2007) *The Murder of Stephen Hoskin: A Serious Case Review*. Cornwall: Cornwall Adult Protection Committee.

Courtney, M. and Moulding, N. T. (2014) Beyond balancing competing needs: embedding involuntary treatment within a recovery approach to mental health social work, *Australian Social Work*, 67 (2): 214–26.

Cox, S. (2015) Decision-making and dementia: how well does the Mental Capacity Act serve people living with the condition?, *Elder Law Journal*, 5 (1): 74–83.

CQC (2014) *From the Pond into the Sea*. London: Care Quality Commission. Available at: www.cqc.org.uk/sites/default/files/CQC_Transition%20Report.pdf (accessed 18 July 2019).

CQC (2017) *Registering the Right Support*. London: Care Quality Commission.

CQC (2018a) *Monitoring the Mental Health Act in 2016/17*. Newcastle: Care Quality Commission.

CQC (2018b) *The State of Health Care and Adult Social Care in England 2016/17*. Newcastle: Care Quality Commission.

CQC (2018c) *The State of Health Care and Adult Social Care in England 2017/18*. Newcastle: Care Quality Commission.

CQC (2018d) *Mental Health Act: The Rise in the Use of the MHA to Detain People in England*. London: Care Quality Commission.

Crawley, C. (2015) A view from the Department of Health, *Journal of Adult Protection*, 17 (3): 151–52.

Crossland, J. (2016) Exploring the Care Act's potential for anti-discriminatory practice with lesbian, gay, bisexual and trans older people, *Quality in Ageing and Older Adults*, 17 (2): 97–106. doi: 10.1108/QAOA-05-2015-0026

Da Lomba, S. (2005) The threat of destitution as a deterrent against asylum seeking in the European Union, *Refuge*, 23 (2): 81–93.

Dalley, G. (1988) *Ideologies of Caring: Rethinking Community and Collectivism*. London: Macmillan.

Dalley, G., Gilhooly, M. L., Gilhooly, K., Levi, M. and Harries, P. (2017) Researching the financial abuse of individuals lacking mental capacity, *Journal of Adult Protection*, 19 (6): 394–405.

Dalrymple, J. and Burke, B. (2006) *Anti Oppressive Practice, Social Care and the Law*. Milton Keynes: Open University Press.

Davidson, G., Brophy, L. and Campbell, J. (2016) Risk, recovery and capacity: competing or complementary approaches to mental health social work, *Australian Social Work*, 69 (2): 158–68.

Davidson, G. and Campbell, J. (2007) An examination of the use of coercion by assertive outreach and community mental health teams in Northern Ireland, *British Journal of Social Work*, 37 (3): 537–55.

Davies, B. and Challis, D. (1986) *Matching Resources to Needs in Community Care*. Aldershot: Gower.

DCA (2007) *Mental Capacity Act 2005: Code of Practice*. London: Department for Constitutional Affairs.

Degeneffe, C. E. (2001) Family caregiving and traumatic brain injury, *Health and Social Work*, 26 (4): 257–68.

Department for Education (2017) *Children Looked after in England*. London: DfE. Available at: https://assets.publishing.service.gov.uk/government/uploads/system/uploads/attachment_data/file/664995/SFR50_2017-Children_looked_after_in_England.pdf (accessed 18 July 2019).

Department for Education (2018) *Working Together to Safeguard Children: A Guide to Interagency Working to Safeguard and Promote the Welfare of Children*. London: DfE.

Department of Health (1991) *Care Management and Assessment: Practitioners' Guide*. London: HMSO.

Department of Health (1996) *A Hidden Disability: Report of the SSI Traumatic Brain Injury Rehabilitation Project*. London: DoH.

Department of Health (1999) *Caring about Carers: A National Strategy*. London: DoH.

Department of Health (2000) *No Secrets: Guidance on Developing and Implementing Multi-Agency Policies and Procedures to Protect Vulnerable Adults from Abuse*. London: HMSO.

Department of Health (2002) *Fair Access to Care Services*. London: DoH.

Department of Health (2008) *Carers at the Heart of 21st Century Families and Communities: A Caring System on Your Side, A Life of Your Own*. London: DoH.

Department of Health (2010) *Recognised, Valued and Supported: Next Steps for the Carers' Strategy*. London: DoH.

Department of Health (2012a) *Caring for our Future: Progress Report on Funding Reform*. London: HMSO, Cm.8381.

Department of Health (2012b) *Draft Care and Support Bill*. London: HMSO, Cm.8386.

Department of Health (2012c) *Reforming the Law for Adult Care and Support: The Government's Response to Law Commission Report 326 on Adult Social Care*. London: HMSO, Cm.8379.

Department of Health (2013a) *Caring for Our Future: Consultation on Reforming What and How People Pay for their Care and Support*. London: DoH.

Department of Health (2013b) *The Care Bill: The Law for Carers, Factsheet Number 8*. London: DoH. Available at: https://assets.publishing.service.gov.uk/government/uploads/system/uploads/attachment_data/file/268684/Factsheet_8_update__tweak_.pdf (accessed 21 July 2019).

Department of Health (2014a) *Care Bill Becomes Care Act 2014*. Available at: www.gov.uk/government/speeches/care-bill-becomes-care-act-2014 (accessed 21 July 2019).

Department of Health (2014b) *Regulations and Guidance for Implementation of Part 1 of the Act Impact Assessment*. London: HMSO.

Department of Health (2015a) *Winterbourne View: Transforming Care Two Years On*. London: HMSO.

Department of Health (2015b) *The Care and Support (Eligibility Criteria) Regulations 2015*. London: HMSO.

Department of Health (2015c) *Mental Health Act 1983: Code of Practice*. London: HMSO.

Department of Health (2015d) *Knowledge and Skills Statement for Social Workers in Adult Services*. London: DoH.

Department of Health (2017) *Strengths-Based Social Work Practice with Adults: Roundtable Report*. London: DoH.

DHSC (2018a) *Care and Support Statutory Guidance: Issued under the Care Act 2014. (February 2018 update)*. London: Department of Health & Social Care. Available at: www.gov.uk/government/

publications/care-act-statutory-guidance/care-and-support-statutory-guidance (accessed 21 July 2019).

DHSC (2018b) *Carers Action Plan, 2018–2020*. London: Department of Health and Social Care. Available at: www.gov.uk/government/publications/carers-action-plan-2018-to-2020 (accessed 21 July 2019).

DHSC (2018c) *National Framework for NHS Continuing Healthcare and NHS-funded Nursing Care*. London: Department of Health and Social Care.

Diaper, A. and Yeomans, P. (2016) Contribution to society: a footnote for the Care Act 2014, *Practice*, 28 (5): 321–39.

Dikmen, S. S., Corrigan, J. D., Levin, H. S., Machamer, J., Stiers, W. and Weisskopf, M. G. (2009) Cognitive outcome following traumatic brain injury, *Journal of Head Trauma Rehabilitation*, 24 (6): 430–38.

Dixon, J., Laing, J. and Valentine, C. (2018) A human rights approach to advocacy for people with dementia: a review of current provision in England and Wales, *Dementia: The International Journal of Social Research and Practice*. DOI: 10.1177/1471301218770478.

Donnelly, M. (2009a) Best interests, patient participation and the Mental Capacity Act 2005, *Medical Law Review*, 17 (1): 1–29.

Donnelly, M. (2009b) Capacity assessment under the Mental Capacity Act 2005: delivering on the functional approach?, *Legal Studies*, 29 (3): 464–91.

Drennan, V., Norrie, C., Cole, L. and Donovan, S. (2013) Addressing incontinence for people with dementia living at home: a documentary analysis of local English community nursing service continence policies and clinical guidance, *Journal of Clinical Nursing*, 22 (3–4): 339–46.

Duffy, J., Davidson, G. and Kavanagh, D. (2016) Applying the recovery approach to the interface between mental health and child protection services, *Child Care in Practice*, 22 (1): 35–49.

Dunér, A. (2017) Equal or individual treatment: contesting storylines in needs assessment conversations within Swedish eldercare, *European Journal of Social Work*, 1–13.

Dunn, M., Clare, I. and Holland, A. (2008) To empower or to protect? Constructing the 'vulnerable adult' in English law and public policy, *Legal Studies*, 28 (2): 234–53.

Dustin, D. (2007) *The McDonaldization of Social Work*. Aldershot: Ashgate.

Dyke, C. (2016) *Writing Analytical Assessments in Social Work*. Northwich: Critical Publishing.

Ealing SAB (2016) *A Management Review in respect of IH*. Ealing: Ealing Safeguarding Adults Board. Available at: https://search3.openobjects.com/mediamanager/ealing/directory/files/executive_summary_report_ih_2016.pdf (accessed 21 July 2019).

Ellis, K. (2011) 'Street-level bureaucracy' revisited: the changing face of frontline discretion in adult social care in England, *Social Policy & Administration*, 45 (3): 221–44.

Emmett, C., Poole, M., Bond, J. and Hughes, J. C. (2013) Homeward bound or bound for a home? Assessing the capacity of dementia patients to make decisions about hospital discharge: comparing practice with legal standards, *International Journal of Law and Psychiatry*, 36 (1): 73–82.

Emmett, C., Poole, M., Bond, J. and Hughes, J. C. (2014) A relative safeguard? The informal roles that families and carers play when patients with dementia are discharged from hospital into care in England and Wales , *International Journal of Law, Policy and the Family*, 28 (3): 302–20.

Engel, G. (1977) The need for a new medical model: a challenge for biomedicine, *Science*, 196 (4286): 129–36.

Engel, G. (1980) The clinical application of the biopsychosocial model, *American Journal of Psychiatry*, 137 (5): 535–44.

Evans, J. (2003) *The Independent Living Movement in the UK*, The Independent Living Institute. Available at: www.independentliving.org/docs6/evans2003.html - 1 (accessed 21 July 2019).

Evans, T. and Harris, J. (2004) Street-level bureaucracy, social work and the (exaggerated) death of discretion, *British Journal of Social Work*, 34 (6): 871–95.

Ewick, P. and Sibley, S. S. (1998) *The Common Place of Law: Stories from Everyday Life*. Chicago, IL: University of Chicago Press.

Exworthy, M., Powell, M. and Glasby, J. (2017) The governance of integrated health and social care in England since 2010: great expectations not met once again?, *Health Policy*, 121 (11): 1124–30.

Farmer, N. J. (2017) 'No recourse to public funds', insecure immigration status and destitution: the role of social work?, *Critical and Radical Social Work*, 5 (3): 357–67.

Feldon, P. (2017a) *The Social Worker's Guide to the Care Act 2014*. St Albans: Critical Publishing.

Feldon, P. (2017b) How can you ensure care and support reviews comply with the Care Act's duties?, *Community Care*, 1 August. Available at: www.communitycare.co.uk/2017/08/01/can-ensure-care-support-reviews-comply-care-acts-duties/ (accessed 19 July 2019).

Fenge, L-A. and Lee, S. (2018) Understanding the risks of financial scams as part of elder abuse prevention, *British Journal of Social Work*, 48 (4): 906–23.

Fennell, P. (2010) 'Institutionalising the Community: The Codification of Clinical Authority and the Limits of Rights-based Approaches'. In B. McSherry and P. Weller (eds), *Rethinking Rights-Based Mental Health Laws*. Oxford: Hart.

Fernandez, L. and Snell, T. (2012) *A Survey of Fair Access to Care Services Assessment Criteria among Local Authorities in England*. London: Personal Social Services Unit.

Finch, J. and Groves, D. (eds) (1983) *A Labour of Love: Women, Work and Caring*. London: Routledge and Kegan Paul.

Fins, J. (2015) *Rights Come to Mind: Brain Injury, Ethics, and the Struggle for Consciousness*. New York: Cambridge University Press.

Fish, S. and Hardy, M. (2015) Complex issues, complex solutions: applying complexity theory in social work practice, *Nordic Social Work Research*, 5: sup1, 98–114. DOI: 10.1080/2156857X.2015.1065902

Fisher, M. (1994) Man-made care: community care and older male carers, *British Journal of Social Work*, 24 (6): 659–80.

FitzGerald, G. and Ruck Keene, A. (2014) *Briefing Paper on the Need for a New Power of Access in Defined Circumstances: Analysis of Current Powers of Entry*. London: Action on Elder Abuse.

Fleminger, S. (2012) Why do some patients after head injury deteriorate over the long term?, *Journal of Neurology, Neurosurgery and Psychiatry*, 83: 1036.

Fleminger, S., Oliver, D. L., Williams, W. H. and Evans, J. (2003) The neuropsychiatry of depression after brain injury, *Neuropsychological Rehabilitation*, 13: 65–87.

Fleminger, S. and Ponsford, J. (2005) Long term outcome after traumatic brain injury, *British Medical Journal*, 331: 1419–20.

Flynn, M. (2015) *In Search of Accountability: A Review of the Neglect of Older People Living in Care Homes Investigated as Operation Jasmine*. Cardiff: Welsh Government.

Flynn, M. (2016) *The death of 'Tom': A Serious Case Review*. Somerset: Somerset Safeguarding Adults Board.

Flynn, M. (2017) *Safeguarding Adult Review – Mendip House*. Taunton: Somerset Safeguarding Adults Board.

Flynn, M. (2018) *Mendip House: Safeguarding Adults Review*. Somerset: Somerset Safeguarding Adults Board.

Flynn, M. and Citarella, V. (2012) *Winterbourne View Hospital: A Serious Case Review*. Bristol: South Gloucestershire Safeguarding Adults Board.

Forbat, L. (2005) *Talking About Care: Two Sides to the Story*. Bristol: Policy.

Francis, R. (2013) *Report of the Mid Staffordshire NHS Foundation Trust Public Inquiry:Executive Summary*, HC 898. London: HMSO.

Gajwani, R., Parsons, H., Birchwood, M. and Singh SP (2016) Ethnicity and detention: are Black and minority ethnic (BME) groups disproportionately detained under the Mental Health Act 2007?, *Social Psychiatry & Psychiatric Epidemiology*, 51 (5): 703–11.

Gant, V. (2017) 'Reflections on a birthday': an auto ethnographic account of caring for a child with a learning disability, *Qualitative Social Work*, 16 (5): 734–74.

Garland, E. L. and Howard, M. O. (2009) Neuroplasticity, psychosocial genomics, and the biopsychosocial paradigm in the 21st century, *Health & Social Work*, 34 (3): 191–99.

George, M. S. and Gilbert, S. (2018) Mental Capacity Act (2005) assessments: why everyone needs to know about the frontal lobe paradox, *The Neuropsychologist*: 59–66.

Giacino, J. T., Fins, J. J., Laureys, S. and Schiff, N. D. (2014) Disorders of consciousness after acquired brain injury: the state of the science, *Nature Reviews Neurology*, 10 (2): 99–114.

Giles, G. M. (2001) 'The Effectiveness of Neurorehabilitation'. In R. L. Wood and T. M. McMillan (eds), *Neurobehavioural Disability and Social Handicap Following Traumatic Brain Injury*. Hove: Psychology.

Giles, G. M., Clark-Wilson, J., Baxter, D. M., Tasker, R., Holloway, M. and Seymour, S. (2018) The interrelationship of functional skills in individuals living in the community, following moderate to severe traumatic brain injury, *Brain Injury* (Early online). Available at: https://doi.org/10.1080/02699052.2018.1539762 (accessed 22 July 2019).

Glasby, J. (2005) Direct payments and the social model of disability, *Social Work and Social Sciences Review*, 12: 48–58.

Glasby, J. (2018) Health and social care: what's in a name?, *British Medical Journal*, 360: k201.

Glover, B. (2018) *A New Settlement Between Carers and the State: The Carers' Covenant*. London: Demos.

Golisz, K. (2015) *Traumatic Brain Injury: Interventions to Support Occupational Performance*. Bethesda: AOTA.

Graham, K., Norrie, C., Stevens, M., Moriarty, J., Manthorpe, J. and Hussein, S. (2016) Models of adult safeguarding in England: a review of the literature, *Journal of Social Work*, 16 (1): 22–46.

Graham, K., Stevens, M., Norrie, C., Manthorpe, J., Moriarty, J., and Hussein, S. (2017) Models of safeguarding in England: identifying important models and variables influencing the operation of adult safeguarding, *Journal of Social Work*, 17 (3): 255–76.

Greenwood, N., Habibi, R., Smith, R. and Manthorpe, J. (2015) Barriers to access and minority ethnic carers' satisfaction with social care services in the community: a systematic review of qualitative and quantitative literature, *Health and Social Care in the Community*, 23 (1): 64–78.

Gridley, K. (2013) *Good Support for People with Complex Needs: What Does It Look Like and Where Is The Evidence?* London: National Institute for Health Research School for Social Care Research.

Hamilton, S., Tew, J., Szymczynska, P., Clewett, N., Manthorpe, J., Larsen, J. and Pinfold, V. (2016) Power, choice and control: how do personal budgets affect the experiences of people with mental health problems and their relationships with social workers and other practitioners?, *British Journal of Social Work*, 46 (3): 719–36.

Hammond, F. M., Gassaway, J., Abeyta, N., Freeman, E. S., Primack, D., Kreifer, S. E. D. and Whiteneck, G. (2012) Outcomes of social work and case management services during inpatient spinal cord injury rehabilitation: the SCIRehab project, *Journal of Spinal Cord Medicine*, 35 (6): 611–23.

Hancock, R., Pickard, L., Wittenberg, R., Comas-Herrera, A., Juarez-Garcia, A., King, D. and Malley, J. (2006) *Paying for Long-Term Care for Older People in the UK: Modelling and Distributional Effects of a Range of Options*. London: PSSRU.

Hansard (HC) (2013a) Public Bill Committee, 23 January 2014 (AM): Ninth Sitting, col.351 (Meg Munn MP).

Hansard (HC) (2013b) 16 December 2013, Vol.572, col.530 (Nick Smith MP).

Hansard (HC) (2014a) March 10 2014, Vol.577, col.85 (Norman Lamb MP).

Hansard (HC) (2014b) March 10, 2014, Vol.577, col.83 (Grahame M. Morris MP).

Hansard (HL) (2013a) 21 May 2013, Vol.745, col.769 (Baroness Bakewell).

Hansard (HL) (2013b) 22 July 2013, Vol.747, col.1101 (Lord Touhig).

Hansard (HL) Deb., Vol. 793 cols. 732–6, 22 October 2018. Available at: https://hansard. parliament.uk/Lords/2018-10-22/debates/9C079B0F-817E-444B-9E9E-0B09D848EC15/ MentalCapacity(Amendment)Bill(HL) (accessed 22 July 2019).

Harding, R. and Tascioglu, W. (2017) *Supporting Legal Capacity Through Care, Support and Empowerment: Everyday Decisions Project Report*. Birmingham: Birmingham Law School, University of Birmingham.

Harris, N. (1987) Defensive social work, *British Journal of Social Work*, 17 (1): 61–69.

Hatfield, B. (2008) Powers to detain under mental health legislation in England and the role of the Approved Social Worker: an analysis of patterns and trends under the 1983 Mental Health Act in six local authorities, *British Journal of Social Work*, 38 (8): 1553–71.

Havering SAB (2017) *A Safeguarding Adult Review in Respect of Ms A*. Havering: Havering Safeguarding Adults Board. Available at: www.havering.gov.uk/download/downloads/id/1408/ ms_a_safeguarding_adult_review.pdf (accessed 22 July 2019).

Haynes, L. (2019) Minister moves to dampen expectations of social care green paper after two-year delay, *Community Care*, 10 May. Available at: www.communitycare.co.uk/2019/05/03/ minister-moves-dampen-expectations-social-care-green-paper-two-year-delay/ (accessed 22 July 2019).

Headway (2015) *Brain Injury Statistics* [Online]. Nottingham: Headway. Available at: www. headway.org.uk/brain-injury-statistics.aspx (accessed 22 July 2019).

HCPC (2017) *Standards of Proficiency for Social Workers in England*. London: Health & Care Professions Council.

Healthwatch (2018) *What's It Like To Be A Carer? Healthwatch England Policy Briefing*. Available at: www.healthwatch.co.uk/sites/healthwatch.co.uk/files/20181001_being_a_carer_0.pdf (accessed 22 July 2019).

Healy, K. (2015) After the biomedical technology revolution: where to now for a bio-psycho-social approach to social work?, *British Journal of Social Work*, 46: 1446–62.

Heginbotham, C. (2012) *Values-Based Commissioning of Health and Social Care*. Cambridge: Cambridge University Press.

HM Government (2008) *The Case for Change: Why England Needs a New Care and Support System.* London: HM Government.

HM Government (2012) *Caring for Our Future: Reforming Care and Support.* London: HMSO, Cmd 8378.

HM Government (2018) *National Mental Capacity Forum: Chair's Annual Report 2017.* London: HMSO.

Holloway, M. (2014) How is ABI assessed and responded to in non-specialist settings? Is specialist education required for all social care professionals?, *Social Care and Neurodisability*, 5 (4): 201–13.

Holloway, M. (2017) Acquired Brain Injury: The Lived Experience of Family Members. DSW thesis, University of Sussex.

Holloway, M. and Fyson, R. (2016) Acquired brain injury, social work and the challenges of personalisation, *British Journal of Social Work*, 46 (5): 1301–17.

Holloway, M. and Tyrrell, L. (2016) Acquired brain injury, parenting, social work, and rehabilitation: supporting parents to support their children, *Journal of Social Work in Disability and Rehabilitation*, 15 (3–4): 234–59.

Hollway, W. and Jefferson, T. (2013) *Doing Qualitative Research Differently: A Psychosocial Approach* (2nd edn). London: Sage.

Hood, R., Brent, M., Abbott, S. and Sartori, D. (2019) A study of practitioner–service user relationships in social work, *British Journal of Social Work*, 49 (3): 787–805. Available at: https://doi.org/10.1093/bjsw/bcy082 (accessed 18 July 2019).

House of Lords House of Commons Joint Committee on the Draft Care and Support Bill (2013) *Draft Care and Support Bill Report, Session 2012–13.* HL paper 143, HC 822. London: HMSO.

House of Lords Select Committee on the Mental Capacity Act 2005 Report of Session 2013–14 (2014) *Mental Capacity Act 2005 Post-Legislative Scrutiny.* London: HMSO.

Howe, D. (1991) Knowledge, Power and the Shape of Social Work Practice. In M. Davies (ed.), *The Sociology of Social Work.* London: Routledge.

Hristova, T., Apostolova, R., Deneva, N. and Fiedler, M. (2014) *Trapped in Europe's Quagmire: The Situation of Asylum Seekers and Refugees in Bulgaria*, bordermonitoring.eu. Available at: http://bordermonitoring.eu/wp-content/uploads/reports/bm.eu-2014-bulgaria.en.pdf (accessed 22 July 2019).

Hudson, B. (2018) The Only Way is Ethics: A New Approach to Outsourcing Social Care, *The Guardian*, 20 August.

Hull Safeguarding Adults Partnership Board (2014) *A Decade of Serious Case Reviews.* Hull: Hull Safeguarding Adults Partnership Board.

Humphries, B. (2004) An unacceptable role for social work: implementing immigration policy, *British Journal of Social Work*, 34 (1): 93–107.

Humphries, R., Thorlby, R., Holder, H., Hall, P. and Charles, A. (2016) *Social Care for Older People: Home Truths*. London: King's Fund/Nuffield Trust.

Hupe, P. L. and Hill, M. J. (2016) 'And the rest is implementation': comparing approaches to what happens in policy processes beyond Great Expectations, *Public Policy and Administration*, 31 (2): 103–21.

In Control (2016) *Independent Living Survey 2016*. Birmingham: In Control. Available at: www.in-control.org.uk/media/243039/independent%20living%20survey%202016%20v2.pdf (accessed 22 July 2019).

Independent Age (2016) *Year One of Care Act: Taking its First Steps*. London: Independent Age. Available at: https://independent-age-assets.s3.eu-west-1.amazonaws.com/s3fs-public/2016-05/Care%20Act%20Report%20-%20Final_spreads.pdf (accessed 22 July 2019).

Ingram, R. and Smith, M. (2018) *Relationship-based Practice: Emergent Themes in Social Work Literature*. Glasgow: IRISS. Available at: www.iriss.org.uk/resources/insights/relationship-based-practice-emergent-themes-social-work-literature (accessed 22 July 2019).

Institute of Fiscal Studies (IFS) (2019) *English Council Funding: What's Happened and What's Next?* Available at: www.ifs.org.uk/uploads/publications/bns/BN250.pdf (accessed 22 July 2019).

International Federation of Social Workers (2014) *Global Definition of Social Work*. Available at: http://ifsw.org/policies/definition-of-social-work/ (accessed 22 July 2019).

Ismail, L. and Mackenzie, J. (2003) Convening and facilitating support groups for South Asian family carers of people with dementia: experiences and challenges, *Dementia*, 2 (3): 433–38.

Iverson, G. L. (2005) Outcome from mild traumatic brain injury, *Current Opinion in Psychiatry*, 18 (3): 301–17.

Jackson, H., Hague, G., Daniels, L., Aguilar, R. Jr., Carr, D. and Kenyon, W. (2014) Structure to self-structuring: infrastructures and processes in neurobehavioural rehabilitation, *NeuroRehabilitation*, 34: 681–94.

Jackson, H. and Manchester, D. (2001) Towards the development of brain injury specialists, *NeuroRehabilitation*, 16 (1): 27–40.

Jackson, S. and Cameron, C. (2012) Leaving care: looking ahead and aiming higher, *Children and Youth Services Review*, 34 (6): 1107–14.

James Lind Alliance (2018) *Adult Social Work Top 10*. Available at: www.jla.nihr.ac.uk/priority-setting-partnerships/adult-social-work/top-10-priorities.htm (accessed 22 July 2019).

Jarrett, T. (2019) *Social Care: Forthcoming Green Paper (England)*, House of Commons Library, 13 May. Available at: https://researchbriefings.parliament.uk/ResearchBriefing/Summary/CBP-8002 (accessed 22 July 2019).

Jenness, V. and Grattet, R. (2005) The law-in-between: the effects of organizational perviousness on the policing of hate crime, *Social Problems*, 52 (3): 337–59.

Johns, R. (2017) *Using the Law in Social Work*. London: Sage.

Karban, K. (2017) Developing a health inequalities approach for mental health social work, *British Journal of Social Work*, 47 (3): 885–992.

Kent and Medway SAB (2018) *Safeguarding Adult Review – Beryl Simpson*. Swanley: Kent County Council Adult Social Care & Health.

Keywood, K. (2010) Vulnerable adults, mental capacity and social care refusal, *Medical Law Review*, 18 (1): 103–10.

Keywood, K. and Flynn, M. (2010) Healthcare decision-making by adults with learning disabilities: ongoing agendas, future challenges, *Psychiatry*, 5 (1): 360–62.

Kidd, J. and Manthorpe, J. (2017) Modern slavery – the adult safeguarding interface, *Journal of Adult Protection*, 19 (3): 158–66.

Kieffer-Kristensen, R. and Johansen, K. L. G. (2013) Hidden loss: a qualitative explorative study of children living with a parent with acquired brain injury, *Brain Injury*, 27 (13–14): 1562–69.

Kitzinger, C. and Kitzinger, J. (2014) Grief, anger and despair in relatives of severely brain injured patients: responding without pathologising, *Clinical Rehabilitation*, 28 (7): 627–31.

Kitzinger, C. and Kitzinger, J. (2015) Withdrawing artificial nutrition and hydration from minimally conscious and vegetative patients: family perspectives, *Journal of Medical Ethics*, 41 (2): 157–60.

Klemen, P. and Grmec, Š. (2006) Effect of pre-hospital advanced life support with rapid sequence intubation on outcome of severe traumatic brain injury, *Acta Anaesthesiologica Scandinavica*, 50 (10): 1250–54.

Knox, L., Douglas, J. M. and Bigby, C. (2015) 'The biggest thing is trying to live for two people': spousal experiences of supporting decision-making participation for partners with TBI, *Brain Injury*, 29 (6): 745–57.

Kreutzer, J. S., Mills, A. and Marwitz, J. H. (2016) Ambiguous loss and emotional recovery after traumatic brain injury, *Journal of Family Theory & Review*, 8 (3): 386–97.

Lamb, N (2014) *Care Bill Becomes Care Act 2014*. London: Department of Health. Available at: www.gov.uk/government/speeches/care-bill-becomes-care-act-2014 (accessed 22 July 2019).

Law Commission (2008) *Adult Social Care: Scoping Report*. London: Law Commission.

Law Commission (2010) *Adult Social Care: A Consultation Paper, Law Commission Consultation Paper No.192*. London: Law Commission.

Law Commission (2011) *Adult Social Care, Law Com No.326*. London: Law Commission.

Lawson, J., Lewis, S. and Williams, C. (2014) *Making Safeguarding Personal 2013/14: Report of Findings*. London: Local Government Association and Association of Directors of Adult Social Services. Available at: www.adass.org.uk/media/4653/making-safeguarding-personal-report-findings.pdf (accessed 22 July 2019).

Leece, D. and Leece, J. (2006) Direct payments: creating a two-tiered system in social care?, *British Journal of Social Work*, 36 (8): 1379–93.

Leece, J. and Leece, D. (2011) Personalisation: perceptions of the role of social work in a world of brokers and budgets, *British Journal of Social Work*, 41 (2): 204–23.

Leece, J. and Peace, S. (2010) Developing new understandings of independence and autonomy in the personalised relationship, *British Journal of Social Work*, 40 (6): 1847–65.

Lennard, C. (2016) Fluctuating capacity and impulsiveness in acquired brain injury: the dilemma of 'unwise' decisions under the Mental Capacity Act, *Journal of Adult Protection*, 18 (4): 229–39.

LGA (2017) *Adult Social Care Funding: State of the Nation 2017*. London: Local Government Association.

LGA (2018a) *The Lives We Want To Lead: The LGA Green Paper for Adult Social Care And Wellbeing*. London: Local Government Association.

LGA (2018b) *The Lives We Want To Lead: Findings, Implications and Recommendations on the LGA Green Paper for Adult Social Care and Wellbeing: LGA Consultation Response*. London: Local Government Association.

LGSCO (2018a) *Review of Adult Social Care Complaints 2017–2018*. Coventry: Local Government and Social Care Ombudsman.

LGSCO (2018b) *Review of Local Government Complaints 2017–2018*. Coventry: Local Government and Social Care Ombudsman.

LGSCO (2018c) *Under Pressure: The Impact of the Changing Environment on Local Government Complaints*. London: Local Government and Social Care Ombudsman.

Linden, M. A. and Boylan, A. M. (2010) 'To be accepted as normal': public understanding and misconceptions concerning survivors of brain injury, *Brain Injury*, 24 (4): 642–50.

Lipsky, M. (1980) *Street Level Bureaucracy: Dilemmas of the Individual in Public Service*. London: Sage.

Litwin, H. and Shiovitz-Ezra, S. (2010) Social network type and subjective well-being in a national sample of older Americans, *The Gerontologist*, 51 (3): 379–88.

Lively, P. (2013) *Ammonites & Leaping Fish: A Life in Time*. London: Penguin.

Local Government Lawyer (2017) Council to review policy on transition to adult care after Ombudsman criticisms, *Local Government Lawyer*. Available at: www.localgovernmentlawyer. co.uk/index.php?option=com_content&view=article&id=30276%3Acouncil-to-review-policy-on-transition-to-adult-care-after-ombudsman-criticisms&catid=52%3Aadult-social-services-articles&Itemid=20 (accessed 18 July 2019).

Lonbay, S. (2018) 'These are vulnerable people who don't have a voice': exploring constructions of vulnerability and ageing in the context of safeguarding older people, *British Journal of Social Work*, 48 (4): 1033–51.

Lonbay, S. and Brandon, T. (2017) Renegotiating power in adult safeguarding: the role of advocacy, *Journal of Adult Protection*, 19 (2): 78–91.

Lövdén, M., Wenger, E., Mårtensson, J., Lindenberger, U. and Bäckman, L. (2013) Structural brain plasticity in adult learning and development, *Neuroscience and Biobehavioral Reviews*, 37 (9): 2296–2310.

Lukersmith, S., Millington, M. and Salvador-Carulla, L. (2016) What is case management? A scoping and mapping review, *International Journal of Integrated Care*, 16 (4).

Lymbery, M. (1998) Care management and professional autonomy: the impact of community care legislation on social work with older people, *British Journal of Social Work*, 28 (6): 863–78.

Lymbery, M. (2012) Social work and personalisation, *British Journal of Social Work*, 42 (4): 783–92.

Lymbery, M. (2014) Understanding personalisation: implications for social work, *Journal of Social Work*, 14 (3): 295–312.

Manchester, D., Priestley, N. and Jackson, H. (2004) The assessment of executive functions: coming out of the office, *Brain Injury*, 18: 1067–81.

Manchester SAB (2018) *A Safeguarding Adult Review in respect of Adult CA*. Manchester: Manchester Safeguarding Adults Board. Available at: www.manchestersafeguardingboards.co.uk/wp-content/uploads/2018/03/2018-03-02-MSAB-SAR-Adult-CA-FINAL-PUBLISHED.pdf (accessed 21 July 2019).

Manson, S. (2017) *Report from a Thematic Review of Safeguarding Adult Reviews within the East Midlands*, East Midlands ADASS.

Mantell, A. (2010) Traumatic brain injury and potential safeguarding concerns, *Journal of Adult Protection*, 12 (4): 31–42.

Mantell, A., Simpson, G., Jones, K., Strandberg, T., Simonson, P. and Vungkhanching, M. (2012) Social work practice with traumatic brain injury: the results of a structured review, *Brain Injury*, 26 (9): 459–60.

Mantell, A., Simpson, G., Vungkhanching, M., Jones, K., Strandberg, T. and Simonson, P. (2017) Social work-generated evidence in traumatic brain injury from 1975 to 2014: a systematic scoping review, *Health & Social Care in the Community*, 26 (4): 433–48.

Manthorpe, J., Fernandez, J. L., Brimblecombe, N., Knapp, M., Snell, T. and Moriarty, J. (2019) Great expectations – ambitions for family carers in UK Parliamentary debates on the Care Bill, *International Journal of Care and Caring*, in press.

Manthorpe, J. and Martineau, S. (2011) Serious case reviews in adult safeguarding in England: an analysis of a sample of reports, *British Journal of Social Work*, 41 (2): 224–41.

Manthorpe, J. and Martineau, S. (2016) Serious case reviews into dementia care: an analysis of context and content, *British Journal of Social Work*, 46 (2): 514–53.

Manthorpe. J. and Martineau, S. (2017) Engaging with the new system of safeguarding adults reviews concerning care homes for older people, *British Journal of Social Work*, 47 (7): 2086–99.

Manthorpe, J. and Moriarty, J. (2016) *The Effectiveness of Social Work with Adults: A Systematic Scoping Review*. London: King's College. Available at: https://kclpure.kcl.ac.uk/portal/files/49460119/Moriarty_Manthorpe_2016_Effectiveness_of_social_work_with_adults.pdf

Manthorpe, J., Rapaport, J. and Stanley, N. (2008) The Mental Capacity Act 2005 and its influences on social work practice: debate and synthesis, *Practice: Social Work in Action*, 20 (3): 151–62.

Manthorpe, J., Samsi, K. and Rapaport, J. (2012) When the profession becomes personal: dementia care practitioners as family caregivers, *International Psychogeriatrics*, 24 (6): 902–10.

Manthorpe, J., Samsi, K. and Rapaport, J. (2013) 'Capacity is key': investigating new legal provisions in England and Wales for adult safeguarding, *Journal of Elder Abuse & Neglect*, 25 (4): 355–73.

Manthorpe, J., Samsi, K. and Rapaport, J. (2014) Dementia nurses' experience of the mental Capacity Act 2005: a follow up study, *Dementia*, 13 (1): 131–43.

Manthorpe, J., Stevens, M., Martineau, S. and Norrie, C. (2017) Safeguarding practice in England where access to an adult at risk is obstructed by a third party: findings from a survey, *Journal of Adult Protection*, 19 (6): 323–32.

Marshall, S., Bayley, M., McCullagh, S., Velikonja, D., Berrigan, L., Ouchterlony, D. and Weegar, K. (2015) Updated clinical practice guidelines for concussion/mild traumatic brain injury and persistent symptoms, *Brain Injury*, 29 (6): 688–700.

Masel, B. E. and Dewitt, D. S. (2010) Traumatic brain injury: a disease process, not an event, *Journal of Neurotrauma*, 27 (8): 1529–40.

McKinlay, A., Corrigan, J., Horwood, L. and Fergusson, D. (2014) Substance abuse and criminal activities following traumatic brain injury in childhood, adolescence, and early adulthood, *Journal of Head Trauma Rehabilitation*, 29 (6): 498–506.

McMillan, T. M., Laurie, M., Oddy, M., Menzies, M., Stewart, E. and Wainman-Lefley, J. (2015) Head injury and mortality in the homeless, *Journal of Neurotrauma*, 32 (2): 116–19.

McMillan, T. M., Teasdale, G. M. and Stewart, E. (2012) Disability in young people and adults after head injury: 12–14 year follow-up of a prospective cohort, *Journal of Neurology, Neurosurgery and Psychiatry*, 83 (11): 1086–91.

McSherry, B. and Freckelton, P. I. (eds) (2015) *Coercive Care: Rights, Law and Policy.* Abingdon: Routledge.

Milne, A., Cambridge, P., Beadle-Brown, J., Mansell, J. and Whelton, B. (2013) The characteristics and management of elder abuse: evidence and lessons from a UK case study, *European Journal of Social Work*, 16 (4): 489–505.

Milner, J., Myers, S. and O'Byrne, P. (2015) *Assessment in Social Work* (4th edn). London: Palgrave.

Minsky, R. (1998) *Psychoanalysis and Culture: Contemporary States of Mind.* Cambridge: Polity.

Mitchell, W. and Beresford, B., Brooks, J., Moran, N. and Glendinning, C. (2017) Taking on choice and control in personal care and support: the experiences of physically disabled young adults, *Journal of Social Work*, 17 (4): 413–33.

Mitter, N., Ali, A. and Scior, K. (2018) Stigma experienced by family members of people with intellectual and developmental disabilities: multidimensional construct, *British Journal of*

Psychiatry Open, 4 (5): 332–38. doi:10.1192/bjo.2018.39. Available at: www.ncbi.nlm.nih.gov/pmc/articles/PMC6094883/ (accessed 21 July 2019).

Morgan, P. (2017) A response to a preventable death? A family's perspective on an adult safeguarding review regarding an adult with traumatic brain injury, *Journal of Adult Protection*, 19 (1): 4–9.

Moriarty, J. and Butt, J. (2004) Inequalities in quality of life among older people from different ethnic groups, *Ageing & Society*, 24 (5): 729–53.

Moriarty, J., Sharif, N. and Robinson, J. (2011) *Black and Minority Ethnic People with Dementia and Their Access to Support and Services*. London: Social Care Institute for Excellence.

Moriarty, J., Steils, N. and Manthorpe J. (2019) *Hospital Social Work: A Review and Research Agenda*. London: King's College (forthcoming).

Moxley, D. P. (1996) Teaching case management: essential content for the preservice preparation of effective personnel, *Journal of Teaching in Social Work*, 13 (1/2): 111–40.

Mukadam, N., Cooper, C. and Livingston, G. (2011) A systematic review of ethnicity and pathways to care in dementia, *International Journal of Geriatric Psychiatry*, 26 (1):12–20.

Murphy, D., Duggan, M. and Joseph, S. (2013) Relationship-based social work and its compatibility with the person-centred approach: principled versus instrumental perspectives, *British Journal of Social Work*, 43 (4): 703–19.

Murrell, A. and McCalla, L. (2016) Assessing decision-making capacity: the interpretation and implementation of the Mental Capacity Act 2005 amongst social care professionals, *Practice: Social Work in Action*, 28 (1): 21–36.

Nabors, N. A., Seacat, J. and Rosenthal, M. (2002) Predictors of caregiver burden following traumatic brain injury, *Brain Injury*, 16: 1039–50.

National Audit Office (2016) *Personalised Commissioning in Social Care*. London: HMSO.

National Audit Office (2018a) *Financial Sustainability of Local Authorities 2018*. London: HMSO.

National Audit Office (2018b) *Adult Social Care at a Glance*. London: National Audit Office. Available at: www.nao.org.uk/wp-content/uploads/2018/07/Adult-social-care-at-a-glance.pdf (accessed 21 July 2019).

Needham, C., Hall, K., Allen, K., Burn, E., Mangan, C. and Henwood, M. (2018) *Market Shaping and Personalisation in Social Care: A Realist Synthesis of the Literature*. Birmingham: University of Birmingham Health Services Management Centre.

Newbigging, K., Ridley, J., McKeown, M., Machin, K. and Poursanidou, K. (2015) 'When you haven't got much of a voice': an evaluation of the quality of Independent Mental Health Advocate (IMHA) services in England, *Health & Social Care in the Community*, 23 (3): 313–24.

Newbigging, K., Ridley, J. and Sadd, J. (2016) *Commissioning Care Act Advocacy: A Work In Progress*. Birmingham: University of Birmingham.

Newcastle Safeguarding Adults Board (2014) *Review – Adult D*. Newcastle: Newcastle Safeguarding Adults Board.

Newcastle Safeguarding Adults Board (2017) *The Death of Lee Irving: Safeguarding Adults Review*. Available at: www.newcastle.gov.uk/sites/default/files/wwwfileroot/adult_g_sar_overview_report_-_final.pdf (accessed 18 July 2019).

Newton, J. A., Harris, T., Hubbard, K. and Craig, T. (2017) Mentoring during the transition from care to prevent depression: care leavers' perspectives, *Practice: Social Work in Action*, 29 (5): 317–30.

NHS Digital (2016) *Inpatients Formally Detained in Hospitals Under the Mental Health Act 1983 and Patients Subject to Supervised Community Treatment: 2015/16*. London: NHS Digital.

NHS Digital (2017a) *Personal Social Services Survey of Adult Carers in England (SACE)*. London: NHS Digital. Available at: https://files.digital.nhs.uk/publication/a/o/sace_report_2016-17.pdf (accessed 21 July 2019).

NHS Digital (2017b) *Safeguarding Adults Collection (SAC) England 2016–17 Experimental Statistics*. Available at: https://digital.nhs.uk/data-and-information/publications/statistical/safeguarding-adults/2016-17 (accessed 18 July 2019).

NHS Digital (2018) *Safeguarding Adults Collection (SAC) England 2017–18 Experimental Statistics*. Available at: https://digital.nhs.uk/data-and-information/publications/statistical/safeguarding-adults/2017-18 (accessed 10 July 2019).

NICE (2014) *Head Injury: Triage, Assessment, Investigation and Early Management of Head Injury in Children, Young People and Adults. NICE guideline {CG176}*. London: National Institute for Health and Care Excellence. Available at: www.nice.org.uk/guidance/CG176

NICE (2018) *Decision-making and Mental Capacity. NICE guideline {NG108}*. London: National Institute for Health and Care Excellence. Available at: www.nice.org.uk/guidance/ng108 (accessed 21 July 2019).

Norman, A. (2016) A preventable death? A family's perspective on an adult safeguarding review regarding an adult with traumatic brain injury, *Journal of Adult Protection*, 18 (6): 341–52.

Norrie, C., Stevens, M., Graham, K., Moriarty, J., Hussein, S. and Manthorpe, J. (2017) The advantages and disadvantages of different models of organising adult safeguarding, *British Journal of Social Work*, 47 (4): 1205–23.

Norrie, C., Stevens, M., Martineau, S. and Manthorpe, J. (2018) Gaining access to possibly abused or neglected adults in England: practice perspectives from social workers and service-user representatives, *British Journal of Social Work*, 48 (4): 1071–89.

Nosowska, G. (2014) *Good Assessment: Practitioners' Handbook*. Dartington: Research in Practice for Adults.

Nuffield Trust (2018) *Unpaid Carers: Informal Yet Integral*. London: Nuffield Trust. Available at: www.nuffieldtrust.org.uk/news-item/unpaid-carers-informal-yet-integral#drop-in-satisfaction (accessed 21 July 2019).

O'Connor, D. (2007) Self-identifying as a caregiver: exploring the positioning process, *Journal of Aging Studies*, 21 (2): 165–74.

Oddy, M. and Da Silva Ramos, S. (2013) The clinical and cost-benefits of investing in neurobehavioural rehabilitation: a multi-centre study, *Brain Injury*, 27: 1500–07.

Oddy, M., Moir, J. F., Fortescue, D. and Chadwick, S. (2012) The prevalence of traumatic brain injury in the homeless community in a UK city, *Brain Injury*, 26: 1058–64.

Oliver, M. F. (1990) *The Politics of Disablement*. Basingstoke: Macmillan.

Olivier, S., Burls, T., Fenge, L-A. and Brown, K. (2016) Safeguarding adults and mass marketing fraud: perspectives from the police, trading standards and the voluntary sector, *Journal of Social Welfare and Family Law*, 38 (2): 140–51.

Olver, J. H., Ponsford, J. L. and Curran, C. A. (1996) Outcome following traumatic brain injury: a comparison between 2 and 5 years after injury, *Brain Injury*, 10 (11): 841–48.

ONS (2011) *National Population Projections, 2010-Based Statistical Bulletin* (26 October). London: Office for National Statistics.

Osborne, G. (2010) *Comprehensive Spending Review, HC Deb* 20 October. Available at: https://hansard.parliament.uk/Commons/2010-10-20/debates/10102049000003/ComprehensiveSpendingReview (accessed 22 July 2019).

Owen, G. S., Freyenhagen, F., Martin, W. and David, A. S. (2017) Clinical assessment of decision-making capacity in acquired brain injury with personality change, *Neuropsychological Rehabilitation*, 27 (1): 133–48.

Ownsworth, T., Clare, l. and Morris, R. (2006) An integrated biopsychosocial approach to understanding awareness deficits in Alzheimer's disease and brain injury, *Neuropsychological Rehabilitation*, 16 (4): 415–38.

Ownsworth, T. L., McFarland, K. and Young, R. M. (2010) Self-awareness and psychosocial functioning following acquired brain injury: an evaluation of a group support programme, *Neuropsychological Rehabilitation*, 10 (5): 465–84.

PAC (2016) *Personal Budgets in Social Care*. London: Public Accounts Committee. Available at: https://publications.parliament.uk/pa/cm201617/cmselect/cmpubacc/74/7403.htm#_idTextAnchor004

Parker, J. (2006) *Good Practice in Brain Injury Case Management*. London, Philadelphia: Jessica Kingsley.

Parkinson, K., Pollock, S. and Edwards, D. (2018) Family group conferences: an opportunity to re-frame responses to the abuse of older people?, *British Journal of Social Work*, 48 (4): 1109–26.

Parry, I. (2014) Adult serious case reviews: lessons for housing providers, *Journal of Social Welfare & Family Law*, 6 (2): 168–89.

Penhale, B., Brammer, A., Morgan, P., Kingston, P. and Preston-Shoot, M. (2017) The Care Act 2014: a new legal framework for safeguarding adults in civil society, *Journal of Adult Protection*, 19 (4): 169–74.

Perkins, N., Penhale, B., Reid, D., Pinkney, L., Hussein, S. and Manthorpe, J. (2007) Partnership means protection? Perceptions of the effectiveness of multi-agency working and the regulatory framework within adult protection in England and Wales, *Journal of Adult Protection*, 9 (3): 9–23.

Petersen, H. and Sanders, S. (2015) Caregiving and traumatic brain injury: coping with grief and loss. *Health and Social Work*, 40 (4): 325–28.

Phillips, D. and Simpson, P. (2017) *National Standards, Local Risks: The Geography of Local Authority Funded Social Care, 2009–10 to 2015–16*. London: Institute of Fiscal Studies.

Pike, L. and Walsh, J. (2015) *Making Safeguarding Personal 2014/15: Evaluation Report*. London: Local Government Association. Available at: www.adass.org.uk/media/5144/making-safeguarding-personal-2014-15-evaluation-report.pdf (accessed 21 July 2019).

Pilgrim, D. (2002) The biopsychosocial model in Anglo-American psychiatry: past, present and future?, *Journal of Mental Health*, 11 (6): 585–94.

Pinkney, L., Penhale, B., Manthorpe, J., Perkins, N., Reid, D. and Hussein, S. (2008) Voices from the frontline: social work practitioners' perceptions of multi-agency working in adult protection in England and Wales, *Journal of Adult Protection*, 10 (4): 12–24.

Ponsford, J. (2013) Factors contributing to outcome following traumatic brain injury, *NeuroRehabilitation*, 32 (4): 803–15.

Postle, K. (2001) 'The social work side is disappearing. I guess it started with us being called care managers', *Practice*, 13 (1): 13–26.

Powell, T. (1997) *Head Injury: A Practical Guide*. London: Speechmark.

Preston-Shoot, M. (2000) What if? Using the law to uphold practice values and standards, *Practice*, 12 (4): 49–63.

Preston-Shoot, M. (2016) Towards explanations for the findings of serious case reviews: understanding what happens in self-neglect work, *Journal of Adult Protection*, 18 (3): 131–48.

Preston-Shoot, M. (2017a) *What Difference Does Legislation Make? Adult Safeguarding through the Lens of Serious Case Reviews and Safeguarding Adult Reviews: A Report for South West Region Safeguarding Adults Boards*. Bristol: South West ADASS. Available at: http://ssab.safeguardingsomerset.org.uk/wp-content/uploads/SW-SCRs-SARs-Report-Final-Version-2017.pdf (accessed 21 July 2019).

Preston-Shoot, M. (2017b) On self-neglect and safeguarding adult reviews: diminishing returns or adding value?, *Journal of Adult Protection*, 19 (2): 53–66.

Preston-Shoot, M. (2018) Learning from safeguarding adult reviews on self-neglect: addressing the challenge of change, *Journal of Adult Protection*, 20 (2): 78–92. doi: 10.1108/JAP-01-2018-0001

Preston-Shoot, M. (2019) *Making Good Decisions: Law for Social Work Practice* (2nd edn). Basingstoke: Palgrave Macmillan.

Preston-Shoot, M. and Cornish, S. (2014) Paternalism or proportionality? Experiences and outcomes of the Adult Support and Protection (Scotland) Act 2007, *Journal of Adult Protection*, 16 (1): 5–16.

Preston-Shoot, M. and McKimm, J. (2012) Perceptions of readiness for legally literate practice: a longitudinal study of social work student views, *Social Work Education*, 31 (8): 1071–89.

Preston-Shoot, M. and Pratt, M. (2014) On Local Safeguarding Children Boards: Their Contribution and Challenges. In M. Blyth (ed.), *Moving on from Munro: Improving Children's Services*. Bristol: Policy.

Priestley, M., Jolly, D., Pearson, C., Ridell, S., Barnes, C. and Mercer, G. (2006) Direct payments and disabled people in the UK: supply, demand and devolution, *British Journal of Social Work*, 37: 1189–1204.

Priestley, N., Manchester, D., and Aram, R. (2013) Presenting evidence of executive functions deficit in court: issues for the expert neuropsychologist, *Journal of Personal Injury Law*, 4: 240–47.

Prigatano, G. P. (2005) Disturbances of self-awareness and rehabilitation of patients with traumatic brain injury: a 20-year perspective, *Journal of Head Trauma Rehabilitation*, 20 (1): 19–29.

Pritchard-Jones, L. (2016a) The good, the bad, and the 'vulnerable older adult', *Journal of Social Welfare and Family Law*, 38 (1): 51–72.

Pritchard-Jones, L. (2016b) 'This man with dementia' – 'othering' the person with dementia in the Court of Protection, *Medical Law Review*, 24 (4): 518–43.

Pritchard-Jones, L. (2018) 'Adults at risk': 'vulnerability' by any other name?, *Journal of Adult Protection*, 20 (1): 47–58.

Private Eye (2012) Passing the 'beck', *Private Eye*, No.1327, 29 November.

Public Accounts Committee (2018) UK Parliament verbal evidence. Available at: www.parliamentlive.tv/Event/Index/ee3374a8-92f0-48f9-aaf7-d920168cf21b

Public Health England (2015) *Child and Maternal Health*. Available at: https://fingertips.phe.org.uk/profile/child-health-profiles/data#page/3/gid/1938133231/pat/6/par/E12000004/ati/102/are/E06000015/iid/91816/age/44/sex/4 (accessed 19 July 2019).

Public Health England (2016) *Improving the Physical Health of People with Mental Health Problems: Actions for Mental Health Nurses*. London: Department of Health.

QAA (2016) *Subject Benchmark Statement: Social Work*. London: Quality Assurance Agency for Higher Education.

Ramezankhah, F. (2013) Asylum Stories: A Socio-Legal Study of Iranian Claims for Asylum in the UK. PhD thesis, Keele University.

Ramezankhah, F. (2017) The tale of two men: testimonial styles in the presentation of asylum claims, *International Journal of Refugee Law*, 29 (1): 110–37.

Randall, A. (2015) *Challenging the Destitution Policy: Civil Society Organisations Supporting Destitute Migrants (Working Paper 131)*. Birmingham: University of Birmingham.

Ravalier, J. (2017) *UK Social Workers: Working Conditions and Wellbeing*. Bath: Bath Spa University.

Research in Practice and Research in Practice for Adults (2018) *Mind the Gap: Transitional Safeguarding – Adolescence to Adulthood*. Dartington: RIP. Available at: www.rip.org.uk/resources/publications/strategic-briefings/transitional-safeguarding--adolescence-to-adulthood-strategic-briefing-2018/ (accessed 18 July 2019).

Romano, M. D. (1974) Family response to traumatic head injury, *Scandinavian Journal of Rehabilitation Medicine*, 6: 1–4.

Romeo, L. (2015) Social work and safeguarding adults, *Journal of Adult Protection*, 17 (3): 205–7.

Romeo, L. (2017) *Annual Report by the Chief Social Worker for Adults 2016–17: Being the Bridge*. London: Department of Health. Available at: https://assets.publishing.service.gov.uk/government/uploads/system/uploads/attachment_data/file/601865/CSW_AR_2016_Accessible.pdf (accessed 21 July 2019).

Romeo, L. (2018) *Chief Social Worker for Adults Annual Report 2017–18: From Strength to Strength – Strengths-based Practice and Achieving Better Lives*. London: Department of Health and Social Care.

Romeo, L. and Hunter, T. (2017) *Strengths-based Social Work Practice with Adults: Roundtable Report*. London: Department of Health.

Roulstone, A. and Morgan, H. (2009) Neo-liberal individualism or self-directed support: are we all speaking the same language on modernising adult social care?, *Social Policy and Society*, 8: 333–45.

Ruck Keene, A., Stricklin-Coutinho, K. and Gilfillan, H. (2015) The role of the Court of Protection in safeguarding, *Journal of Adult Protection*, 17 (6): 380–90.

Samsi, K., Manthorpe, J., Nagendran, T. and Heath, H. (2012) Challenges and expectations of the Mental Capacity Act 2005: an interview-based study of community-based specialist nurses working in dementia care, *Journal of Clinical Nursing*, 21 (11-12): 1697–1705.

Sariaslan, A., Sharp, D. J., D'Onofrio, B., Larsson, H. and Fazel, S. (2016) Long-term outcomes associated with traumatic brain injury in childhood and adolescence: a nationwide Swedish cohort study of a wide range of medical and social outcomes, *PLoS Medicine*, 13 (8).

Schramm, J. (2016) *Advances and Technical Standards in Neurosurgery*. Cham: Springer.

Schwehr, B. (2018) Where councils are going wrong in their implementation of the Care Act, *Community Care*, 8 June. Available at: www.communitycare.co.uk/2018/06/08/councils-going-wrong-implementation-care-act/ (accessed 21 July 2019).

SCIE (2010) *Personalisation Briefing: Implications for Social Workers in Adult Services*. London: Social Care Institute for Excellence.

SCIE (2015a) *Eligibility Determination for the Care Act 2014*. London: Social Care Institute for Excellence.

SCIE (2015b) *Strengths-based Approaches for Assessment and Eligibility under the Care Act 2014*. London: Social Care Institute for Excellence.

SCIE (2016) *External Care Act Implementation Review in Norfolk County Council*. London: Social Care Institute for Excellence. Available at: file:///C:/Users/stra9316/Downloads/External%20 Care%20Act%20Implementation%20SCIE%20review%20in%20NCC.pdf

SCIE (2017) *Asset-based Places: A Model for Development*. London: Social Care Institute for Excellence.

Scottish Government (n.d.) *Care Support Planning Toolkit*. Edinburgh: Scottish Government. Available at: https://pilotlight.iriss.org.uk/sites/pilotlight.iriss.org.uk/files/materials/Carer%20 support%20plan%20toolkit_0.pdf (accessed 21 July 2019).

Scottish Government (2016) *Carers (Scotland) Act 2016*. Edinburgh: Scottish Government. Available at: https://www2.gov.scot/Topics/Health/Support-Social-Care/Unpaid-Carers/Implementation/Carers-scotland-act-2016 (accessed 21 July 2019).

Shakespeare, T. (2014) *Disability Rights and Wrongs Revisited*. London: Routledge.

Shapiro, M. (2008) The War Inside: Child Psychoanalysis and Remaking the Self in Britain, 1930–1960. Unpublished PhD Thesis (Abstract), Rutgers, State University of New Jersey.

Sherwood-Johnson, F. (2016) Independent advocacy in adult support and protection work, *Journal of Adult Protection*, 18 (2): 109–18.

Shiroma, E. J., Ferguson, P. L. and Pickelsimer, E. E. (2012) Prevalence of traumatic brain injury in an offender population: a meta-analysis, *Journal of Head Trauma Rehabilitation*, 27: E1–E10.

Siddique, H. (2015) System Failure of NHS Mental HealthDervices Puts Pressure on A&E Wards, *The Guardian*, 6 May. Available at: www.theguardian.com/society/2015/may/06/system-failure-nhs-mental-health-services-pressure-ae-wards-crisis-care-concordat (accessed 2 October 2018).

Sibley, S. S. (2005) After legal consciousness, *Annual Review of Law and Social Sciences*, 1 (1): 323–68.

Simpson, G. K. and Tate, R. L. (2007) Suicidality in people surviving a traumatic brain injury: prevalence, risk factors and implications for clinical management, *Brain Injury*, 21: 1335–51.

Skills for Care (2018) *The Size and Structure of the Adult Social Care Workforce*. London: Skills for Care. Available at: www.skillsforcare.org.uk/NMDS-SC-intelligence/Workforce-intelligence/documents/Size-of-the-adult-social-care-sector/Size-and-Structure.pdf (accessed 21 July 2019).

Skowron, P. (2018) The relationship between autonomy and adult mental capacity in the law of England and Wales, *Medical Law Review*, Online first. Available at: https://doi.org/10.1093/medlaw/fwy016 (accessed 21 July 2019).

Slade, M. (2009) The contribution of mental health services to recovery, *Journal of Mental Health*, 18 (5): 367–71.

Slasberg, C. (2017) A blueprint for a person-centred system of assessment and support planning, *Research, Policy and Planning*, 32 (3): 151–67.

Slasberg, C. and Beresford, P. (2016a) The false narrative about personal budgets in England: smoke and mirrors, *Disability and Society*, 31 (8): 1132–37.

Slasberg, C., and P. Beresford (2016b) The eligibility question – the real source of depersonalisation?, *Disability & Society*, 31 (7): 969–73.

Slasberg, C. and Beresford, P. (2017a) 'The need to bring an end to the era of eligibility policies for a person-centred, financially sustainable future', *Disability & Society*, 32 (8): 1263–68.

Slasberg, C. and Beresford, P. (2017b) Strengths-based practice: social care's latest elixir or the next false dawn?, *Disability & Society*, 32 (2): 269–73.

Slasberg, C., Beresford, P. and Schofield, P. (2015) Further lessons from the continuing failure of personal budgets, *Research Policy and Planning*, 31 (1): 43–53.

Solnit, R. (2016) *Hope in the Dark: Untold Histories, Wild Possibilities*. Edinburgh: Canongate.

Somerset SCB and SAB (2014) *Learning Review into Deaths of Vulnerable Adults*. Somerset: Somerset Safeguarding Children Board and Somerset Safeguarding Adults Board. Available at: https://ssab.safeguardingsomerset.org.uk/wp-content/uploads/2016/03/Somerset-Learning-Review-into-Deaths-of-Vulnerable-Young-Adults.pdf (accessed 21 July 2019).

Southend SAB (2016) *A Safeguarding Adult Review in respect of Anne*. Southend: Southend Safeguarding Adults Board. Available at: www.safeguardingsouthend.co.uk/adults/downloads_13_3357100109.pdf (accessed 22 July 2019).

Spencer-Lane, T. (2014) *Care Act Manual*. London: Sweet & Maxwell.

Spicker, P. (2013) Personalisation falls short, *British Journal of Social Work*, 43 (7): 1259–75.

Stanley, T. (2016) A practice framework to support the Care Act 2014, *Journal of Adult Protection*, 18 (1): 53–64.

Stevens, M., Martineau, S., Norrie, C. and Manthorpe, J. (2017a) *Helping or Hindering in Adult Safeguarding: An Investigation of Practice*. London: Social Care Workforce Research Unit, King's College London.

Stevens, M., Martineau, S., Manthorpe, J. and Norrie, C. (2017b) Social workers' power of entry in adult safeguarding concerns: debates over autonomy, privacy and protection, *Journal of Adult Protection*, 19 (6): 312–22.

Stevens, M., Woolham, J., Manthorpe, J., Aspinall, F., Hussein, S., Baxter, K., Samsi, K. and Ismail, M. (2018a) Implementing safeguarding and personalisation in social work: findings from research, *Journal of Social Work*, 18 (1): 3–22.

Stevens, M., Manthorpe, J., Martineau, S. and Norrie, C. (2018b) Practice perspectives and theoretical debates about social workers' legal powers to protect adults, *Journal of Social Work*. Available at: http://dx.doi.org/10.1177/1468017318794275 (accessed 21 July 2019).

Stevens, M., Moriarty, J., Harris, J., Manthorpe, J., Hussein, S. and Cornes, M. (2019) Social care managers and care workers' understandings of personalisation in older people's services, *Working with Older People*, 23 (1): 37–45.

Stuss, D. T. (1991) Disturbance of Self-awareness After Frontal System Damage. In G. P. Prigatono and D. L. Schacter (eds), *Awareness of Deficit after Brain Injury: Clinical and Theoretical Issues*. New York: Oxford University Press.

Sullivan, W. P. and Floyd, D. F. (2012) There's more than meets the eye: the nuances of case management, *Journal of Social Work in Disability and Rehabilitation*, 11 (3): 184–96.

Summerfield, P. (2011) *Serious Case Review Executive Summary in Respect of Child H*. North Tyneside: North Tyneside Local Safeguarding Children Board.

Symonds, J., Williams, V., Miles, C., Steel, M. and Porter, S. (2018) The social care practitioner as assessor: 'people, relationships and professional judgement', *British Journal of Social Work*, 48 (7): 1910–28.

Taherkhani, S., Negarandeh, R., Simbar, M. and Ahmadi, F. (2017) Barriers to seeking help among abused Iranian women, *Journal of Adult Protection*, 19 (5): 261–73. Available at: www.keele.ac.uk/law/legaloutreachcollaboration/ (accessed 21 July 2019).

Tanner, D., Ward, L., and Ray, M. (2018) 'Paying our own way': application of the capability approach to explore older people's experiences of self-funding social care, *Critical Social Policy*, 38 (2): 262–82.

Tate, R. L., Lulham, J. M., Broe, G. A., Strettles, B. and Pfaff, A. (1989) Psychosocial outcome for the survivors of severe blunt head injury: the results from a consecutive series of 100 patients, *Journal of Neurology Neurosurgery and Psychiatry*, 52 (10): 1128–34.

Taylor, I. (1991) For Better or For Worse: Caring and the Abused Wife. In C. Baines, P. Evans and S. Neysmith (eds), *Women's Caring: Feminist Perspectives on Social Welfare*. Toronto: McLelland and Stewart.

Taylor, I. (1999) 'She's There For Me': Caring in a Rural Community. In S. Watson and L. Doyal (eds), *Engendering Social Policy*. Buckingham: Open University Press.

TCSW (2014) *The College of Social Work Guide to the Social Work Practice Implications of the Care Act 2014*. London: The College of Social Work. Available at: www.basw.co.uk/system/files/resources/basw_110648-10_0.pdf (accessed 21 July 2019).

Teater, B. (ed.) (2010) *An Introduction to Applying Social Work Theories and Methods*. Maidenhead: Open University Press.

Templeton, R. (2017) *Safeguarding Adults Boards: Auditing the Impact of Becoming Statutory*. London: National Network for Chairs of Safeguarding Adult Boards/Local Government Association.

Tew, J. (2005) *Social Perspectives in Mental Health: Developing Social Models to Understand and Work with Mental Distress*. London: Jessica Kingsley.

Tew, J. (2011) *Social Approaches to Mental Distress*. Basingstoke: Palgrave Macmillan.

Tew, J., Larsen, J., Hamilton, S., Manthorpe, J., Clewett, N., Pinfold, V. and Szymczynska, P. (2015) 'And the stuff that I'm able to achieve now is really amazing': the potential of personal budgets as a mechanism for supporting recovery in mental health, *British Journal of Social Work*, 45 (1): 179–97.

Tew, J., Ramon, S., Slade, M., Bird, V., Melton, J. and Le Boutillier, C. (2012) Social factors and recovery from mental health difficulties: a review of the evidence, *British Journal of Social Work*, 42 (3): 443–60.

The Children's Society (2016) *Barriers and Solutions Implementing the New Duties in the Care Act 2014 and the Children and Families Act 2014*. London: The Children's Society.

The Economist (2017) Britain's Local Councils Face Financial Crisis, *The Economist*, 28 January. Available at: www.economist.com/britain/2017/2001/2028/britains-local-councils-face-financial-crisis

Thomas, E. J., Levack, W. M. M. and Taylor, W. J. (2014) Self-reflective meaning making in troubled times: change in self-identity after traumatic brain injury, *Qualitative Health Research*, 24 (8): 1033–47.

Thorlby, R., Starling, A., Broadbent, C. and Watt, T. (2018) *What's the Problem with Social Care, and Why Do We Need to Do Better?* London: Health Foundation.

Thornicroft, G. (2006) *Shunned: Discrimination Against People with Mental Illness*. Oxford: Oxford University Press.

TLAP (2017a) *Exploring the Impact of the Care Act on the Lives of People with Care and Support Needs*. London: Think Local Act Personal. Available at: www.thinklocalactpersonal.org.uk/_assets/Resources/TLAP/CareActSurveyResults-002.pdf (accessed 21 July 2019).

TLAP (2017b) *Developing a Wellbeing and Strengths-based Approach to Social Work Practice*. London: Think Local Act Personal.

TLAP (2017c) *The Care Act 2014 Survey Results: Exploring the Impact of the Care Act on the Lives of People with Care and Support Needs*. London: Think Local Act Personal. Available at: www.thinklocalactpersonal.org.uk/_assets/Resources/TLAP/CareActSurveyResults-002.pdf (accessed 21 July 2019).

Tronto, J.C. (1993) *Moral Boundaries: A Political Argument for an Ethic of Care*. New York: Routledge.

Tucker, S., Hargreaves, C., Roberts, A., Anderson, I., Shaw, J. and Challis, D. (2018) Social care in prison: emerging practice arrangements consequent upon the introduction of the 2014 Care Act, *British Journal of Social Work*, 48 (6): 1627–44.

Turner-Stokes, L. (2008) Evidence for the effectiveness of multi-disciplinary rehabilitation following acquired brain injury: a synthesis of two systematic approaches, *Journal of Rehabilitation Medicine*, 40 (9): 691–701.

UN (2007) *Convention on the Rights of Persons with Disabilities: Resolution 61/106*. New York: United Nations.

UN High Commissioner for Refugees (2011) *Handbook and Guidelines on Procedures and Criteria for Determining Refugee Status under the 1951 Convention and the 1967 Protocol Relating to the Status of Refugees.* Geneva: UNHCR.

Van Velzen, J. M., Van Bennekom, C. A. M., Edelaar, M. J. A., Sluiter, J. K. and Frings-Dresen, M. H. W. (2009) How many people return to work after acquired brain injury? A systematic review, *Brain Injury*, 23 (6): 473–88.

Walsh, K. W. (1985) *Understanding Brain Damage: A Primer of Neuropsychological Evaluation.* Edinburgh: Churchill Livingstone.

Webber, M., Reidy, A., Stevens, M. and Holosko, M. J. (2016) Developing and modelling complex social interventions: introducing the connecting people intervention, *Research on Social Work Practice*, 26 (1): 14–19.

Wenger, G. C. (1991) A network typology: from theory to practice, *Journal of Aging Studies*, 5 (2): 147–62.

Wenger, G. C. (1997) Social networks and the prediction of elderly people at risk, *Aging & Mental Health*, 1 (4): 311–20.

West Midlands Adult Safeguarding Editorial Group (2016) *Multiagency Policy and Procedures for the Protection of Adults with Care and Support Needs in West Midlands.* West Midlands: West Midlands Adult Safeguarding Editorial Group.

White, C., Marsland, D. and Manthorpe, J. (2016) Relocation, portability and social care practice: a scoping review, *Journal of Social Work*, 16 (5): 521–40.

Whitnall, L., McMillan, T. M., Murray, G. D. and Teasdale, G. M. (2006) Disability in young people and adults after head injury: 5–7 year follow up of a prospective cohort study, *Journal of Neurology, Neurosurgery and Psychiatry*, 77 (5): 640–45.

Whittington, C. (2016a) The promised liberation of adult social work under England's 2014 Care Act: genuine prospect or false prospectus?, *British Journal of Social Work*, 46: 1942–61.

Whittington, C. (2016b) Another step towards the promised liberation of adult social work under England's 2014 Care Act? The implications of revised statutory guidance and the politics of liberation, *British Journal of Social Work*, 46 (7): 1962–80.

Wikipedia (n.d.) https://en.wikiquote.org/wiki/Zhou_Enlai

Wilkinson, R. and Pickett, K. (2009) *The Spirit Level: Why More Equal Societies Almost Always Do Better.* London: Allen Lane.

Williams, V., Boyle, G., Jepson, M., Swift, P., Williamson, T. and Heslop, P. (2012) *Making Best Interests Decisions: People and Processes.* London: Mental Health Foundation.

Williams, W. H. and Evans, J. J. (2003) Brain injury and emotion: an overview to a special issue on biopsychosocial approaches in neurorehabilitation, *Neuropsychological Rehabilitation*, 13 (1–2): 1–11.

Williams, W. H., Mewse, A. J., Tonks, J., Mills, S., Burgess, C. N. W. and Cordan, G. (2010) Traumatic brain injury in a prison population: prevalence and risk for re-offending, *Brain Injury*, 24 (10): 1184–88.

Williamson, T., Boyle, G., Heslop, P., Jepson, M. J., Swift, P. and Williams, V. J. (2012) Listening to the lady in the bed: the Mental Capacity Act 2005 in practice for older people, *Elder Law Journal*, 2 (2): 185–92.

Wilson, B. A., Robertson, C. and Mole, J. (2015) *Identity Unknown: How Acute Brain Disease Can Destroy Knowledge of Oneself and Others*. Hove: Psychology Press.

Wilson, B. A., Winegardner, J. and Ashworth, F. (2014) *Life after Brain Injury: Survivors' Stories*. Hove: Psychology Press.

Wilson, J. T. L., Pettigrew, L. E. L. and Teasdale, G. M. (1998) Structured interviews for the Glasgow outcome scale and the extended Glasgow outcome scale: guidelines for their use, *Journal of Neurotrauma*, 15 (8): 573–80.

Woolham, J., Steils, N., Daly, G. and Ritters, K. (2018) The impact of personal budgets on unpaid carers of older people, *Journal of Social Work*, 18 (2): 119–41.

World Health Organisation (2014) *Social Determinants of Mental Health*. Geneva: World Health Organisation.

Wydall, S., Clarke, A., Williams, J. and Zerk, R. (2018) Domestic abuse and elder abuse in Wales: a tale of two initiatives, *British Journal of Social Work*, 48 (4): 962–81.

Yeates, G. N., Gracey, F. and McGrath, J. C. (2008) A biopsychosocial deconstruction of 'personality change' following acquired brain injury, *Neuropsychological Rehabilitation*, 18 (5–6): 566–89.

Young-Southward, G., Cooper, S. A. and Philo, C. (2017) Health and wellbeing during transition to adulthood for young people with intellectual disabilities: a qualitative study, *Research in Development Disabilities*, 70: 94–103.

Zittel, K. M., Lawrence, S. and Wodarski, J. S. (2002) Biopsychosocial model of health and healing: implications for health social work practice, *Journal of Human Behavior in the Social Environment*, 5 (15): 19–33.

Index

Added to a page number 'f' denotes a figure, 't' denotes a table and 'n' denotes a note.

www.ingramcontent.com/pod-product-compliance
Lightning Source LLC
Chambersburg PA
CBHW080619030426
42336CB00018B/3017